Innovation:
applying knowledge
in development

Lead authors
Calestous Juma, Coordinator
Lee Yee-Cheong, Coordinator

UN Millennium Project
Task Force on Science, Technology, and Innovation
2005

EARTHSCAN

London • Sterling, Va.

MillenniumProject

First published by Earthscan in the UK and USA in 2005

ISBN: 1-84407-218-5 paperback

For a full list of publications please contact:

Earthscan
8–12 Camden High Street
London, NW1 0JH, UK
Tel: +44 (0)20 7387 8558
Fax: +44 (0)20 7387 8998
Email: earthinfo@earthscan.co.uk
Web: www.earthscan.co.uk
22883 Quicksilver Drive, Sterling, VA 20166-2012, USA

Earthscan is an imprint of James and James (Science Publishers) Ltd and publishes in association with the International Institute for Environment and Development

A catalogue record for this book is available from the British Library

Library of Congress Cataloging-in-Publication Data

A catalog record has been requested

This publication should be cited as: UN Millennium Project 2005. *Innovation: Applying Knowledge in Development*. Task Force on Science, Technology, and Innovation.

Photos: Front cover Pete Turner/Getty Images; back cover, top to bottom, Christopher Dowswell, Pedro Cote/ UNDP, Giacomo Pirozzi/Panos Pictures, Liba Taylor/Panos Pictures, Jørgen Schytte/UNDP, UN Photo Library, Giacomo Pirozzi/UNICEF, Curt Carnemark/World Bank, Pedro Cote/UNDP, Franck Charton/UNICEF, Paul Chesley/Getty Images, Ray Witlin/World Bank, Pete Turner/Getty Images.

This book was edited, designed, and produced by Communications Development Inc., Washington, D.C., and its UK design partner, Grundy & Northedge.

The Millennium Project was commissioned by the UN Secretary-General and sponsored by the United Nations Development Programme on behalf of the UN Development Group. The report is an independent publication that reflects the views of the members of the Task Force on Science, Technology, and Innovation, who contributed in their personal capacity. This publication does not necessarily reflect the views of the United Nations, the United Nations Development Programme, or their Member States.

Printed on elemental chlorine-free paper

Foreword

The world has an unprecedented opportunity to improve the lives of billions of people by adopting practical approaches to meeting the Millennium Development Goals. At the request of UN Secretary-General Kofi Annan, the UN Millennium Project has identified practical strategies to eradicate poverty by scaling up investments in infrastructure and human capital while promoting gender equality and environmental sustainability. These strategies are described in the UN Millennium Project's report *Investing in Development: A Practical Plan to Achieve the Millennium Development Goals*, which was coauthored by the coordinators of the UN Millennium Project task forces.

The task forces have identified the interventions and policy measures needed to achieve each of the Goals. In *Innovation: Applying Knowledge in Development*, the Task Force on Science, Technology, and Innovation underscores the critical importance of knowledge and innovation for development in every country—an emphasis that is echoed in *Investing in Development*. Responding to challenges in areas such as economic productivity, agriculture, education, gender inequity, health, water, sanitation, environment, and participation in the global economy will require increased use of scientific and technical knowledge. Technological innovation and the associated institutional adjustments underpin long-term growth and must be at the center of any strategy to strengthen the private sector.

Innovation proposes concrete and practical steps that governments and international agencies can undertake to bring science, technology, and innovation to bear on development.

This report was prepared by a group of leading experts who contributed in their personal capacity and volunteered their time to this important task.

I am very grateful for their thorough and skilled efforts, and I am sure that the practical options for action in this report will make an important contribution to achieving the Millennium Development Goals. I strongly recommend it to anyone interested in how to mobilize science and technology for development.

Jeffrey D. Sachs
New York
January 17, 2005

Contents

Figure

Tables

Task force members

Task force coordinators

Calestous Juma, Kennedy School of Government, Harvard University, Cambridge, Mass.

Lee Yee-Cheong, World Federation of Engineering Organizations, Paris, and Academy of Sciences of Malaysia, Kuala Lumpur

Task force executive secretary

James Bradfield Moody, International Young Professionals Foundation, Queensland, Australia

Task force members

Kamel Ayadi, Ministry of Infrastructure, Housing, and Land Planning, Tunis

Susan Brandwayn, United Nations Conference on Trade and Development, New York

Norman Clark, Kabarak University, Nakuru, Kenya

Sakiko Fukuda-Parr, United Nations Development Programme, New York

Denis Gilhooly, United Nations Development Programme, New York

Vijaya Kumar, University of Peradeniya, Sri Lanka and United Nations Commission on Science and Technology for Development

Sanjaya Lall, Green College, University of Oxford, United Kingdom

Tony Marjoram, United Nations Educational, Scientific and Cultural Organization, Paris

Kenneth Nwabueze, SageMetrics Corporation, United States

Teresa Poon, The Open University of Hong Kong

Hu Qiheng, Institute of Automation, Chinese Academy of Sciences, Beijing

Tony Ridley, Imperial College, University of London

Francisco Sercovich, United Nations Industrial Development
Organization, Vienna
Judith Sutz, Universidad de la República, Montevideo
Brendan Tuohy, Department of Communications, Marine and Natural
Resources, Dublin
Caroline Wagner, RAND Europe and University of Amsterdam

Genomics and Nanotechnology Working Group

Tara Acharya, University of Toronto, Canada
Erin Court, University of Toronto, Canada
Abdallah S. Daar, University of Toronto, Canada
Elizabeth Dowdeswell, University of Toronto, Canada
Deepa Persad, University of Toronto, Canada
Peter A. Singer, University of Toronto, Canada
Fabio Salamanca-Buentello, University of Toronto, Canada
Halla Thorsteinsdóttir, University of Toronto, Canada

Task force staff

Smita Srinivas, Research Fellow
Brian Torpy, Task Force Administrator

Task force researchers

Hezekiah Agwara
Allison Archambault
Josphat Ayamunda
Leah Aylward
Muriel Calo
Jeremy Carl
Beatriz de Castro Fialho
Derya Honça
Fareeha Iqbal
Laura Ledwith
Emi Mizuno
Adithya Raghunathan
Apiwat Ratanawaraha
Victoria Salinas
Megan White
Elizabeth Willmott
Jarunee Wonglimpiyarat

Preface

The aim of this report is to share lessons learned from the past five decades of development practices. It is not a collection of recommendations of what countries should do but a source of ideas on how to approach development challenges. It emphasizes the need to create space for policy experimentation and learning in developing countries. Development is largely an expression of local initiative and international partnership; it cannot be sustained without local ownership and champions.

The Task Force on Science, Technology, and Innovation is part of the UN Millennium Project commissioned by the UN Secretary-General to advise on the implementation of the Millennium Development Goals arising from the United Nations Millennium Summit in 2000. It is one of 10 task forces charged with addressing sectoral and thematic areas.

The task force's work focused on Goal 8, target 18, which charges the international community "in cooperation with the private sector, [to] make available the benefits of new technologies, especially information and communication." The task force interpreted its mandate broadly to include all forms of technological innovation and the associated institutional adjustments.

The report outlines the significant role that science, technology, and innovation can play in implementing the Goals. It questions the conventional view that holds that countries that belong to the same income group should share the same policy strategies. Instead, it suggests that policymakers draw from the global pool of lessons and avoid artificial classifications of countries, which tend to reduce the scope for policy learning. Policymakers do not mechanically adopt and implement recommendations, they are engaged in a process that involves continuous learning. The report stresses the need to create international partnerships that allow for mutual learning.

The task force members believe that development is a learning process that involves considerable experimentation. The report therefore presents experiences and ideas that can help communities, countries, and regions pursue their development strategies. While the focus is on new technologies, the report synthesizes many lessons learned in applying science, technology, and innovation to development over the past five decades.

The report draws on the experiences of developing countries that dramatically alleviated poverty and grew their economies in past few decades, especially those in the Asia Pacific region. In every case, scientific and technical information was a crucial factor in their success. These countries and economies could and should help other developing countries meet the Goals by sharing their best practices and experiences in the spirit of South-South cooperation. These lessons are not offered as recommendations that can be readily adopted but as sources that can generate new ideas and evidence. (National governments have already used earlier versions of this report to carry out local assessments to identify specific actions.) Developing countries must have the courage to break with traditional approaches and explore the role of science, technology, and innovation in their development strategies. Doing so will demand a degree of intellectual courage that would resonate with the words of the Dutch philosopher Benedict de Spinoza (1632–77): "I do not know how to teach philosophy without being a disturber of established religion."

Acknowledgments

The task force worked closely with the UN Information and Communications Technologies task force, which made important contributions to the report. It also worked with international science and technical information organizations, such as the InterAcademy Council, which recently began conducting major studies on the importance of building scientific and technological capabilities worldwide.

In dealing with the operational implications of the report, the task force worked closely with several international development agencies, particularly the World Bank, the Inter-American Development Bank, and the Canadian International Development Research Centre. The report complements the work carried out by the InterAcademy Council and several UN agencies, in particular the UN Commission on Science and Technology for Development (UNCSTD), the UN Conference on Trade and Development (UNCTAD), the International Telecommunications Union (ITU), the United Nations Development Programme (UNDP), the United Nations Educational, Scientific and Cultural Organization (UNESCO), the Food and Agriculture Organization of the United Nations (FAO), the United Nations Industrial Development Organization (UNIDO), and intergovernmental bodies dealing with science, technology, and innovation.

An earlier draft of this report was circulated among science, technology, and innovation ministries, academies of sciences, academies of engineering, and national institutions of engineers in the Asia Pacific region, soliciting their support for collaboration with developing countries, especially those in Africa. The support they provided was critical. The task force also circulated the earlier draft to all heads of state and government around the world. It is grateful to those who responded with comments and additional information.

Many people contributed directly or indirectly to the preparation of this report. Enormous support was provided by the task force's host organizations, the Belfer Center for Science and International Affairs of Harvard University's

Kennedy School of Government and the World Federation of Engineering Organizations. Additional support was provided by the Rockefeller Foundation, the Science Advisor's Office of the Prime Minister of Malaysia, the Academy of Sciences Malaysia, the Kenyan Ministry of Planning and National Development, and the Kenya National Academy of Sciences, which hosted several task force meetings. We would also like to acknowledge with appreciation the financial and other support provided to members of the task force by UNCTAD, UNDP, UNESCO, UNIDO, the University of Toronto, Department of Communications, the Marine and Natural Resources of Ireland, and the SageMetrics Corporation. The team preparing the report also gained immensely from continuous interaction with the leadership and team of the UN Millennium Project, particularly Jeffrey Sachs, Guido Schmidt-Traub, John McArthur, and Alice Wiemers.

The comments and additional information provided by the many reviewers of this report played an important role in the report's evolution, content, and structure. The task force is grateful for the comments and additional information it received from heads of state and government from Argentina, Bolivia, Canada, Chile, Guyana, Israel, Kenya, Latvia, Malaysia, Monaco, Portugal, Spain, Trinidad and Tobago, and Zambia.

We would like to acknowledge with appreciation numerous people who made suggestions on how the options for action identified in this report could be funded. We are particularly grateful to George Atkinson (Science and Technology Advisor to the U.S. Secretary of State) for convening over a period of six months an informal roundtable on science, technology, and development. The other members of the roundtable whose contributions helped to shape our thinking regarding financial support for technological innovation include Mamphela Ramphele, Robert Watson, and Michael Crawford (World Bank, Washington, D.C.); Bruce Alberts (U.S. National Academies, Washington, D.C.), and Marta Cehelsky (Inter-American Development Bank, Washington, D.C.).

The task force is particularly grateful to the Department for International Development (DFID) and the Institute of Development Studies at Sussex University, which convened a meeting at which an earlier version of the draft was discussed. The workshop provided additional information and extremely valuable suggestions for improving the report. The team would like to thank in particular Masood Ahmed, Richard Martini, and Rachel Turner from DFID and Lawrence Haddad, Raphael Kaplinsky, and Catherine Gee from the Institute of Development Studies for their invaluable contributions to this effort.

The task force received valuable reviews, comments, and additional information from Karon Acon (EARTH University, Costa Rica); Ricardo Acosta (State Council for Science and Technology, Mexico); Abdul-Hakeem Ajijola Office of the Presidency, Abuja, Nigeria); Alkhattab AlHinai (King Fahd University of Petroleum and Minerals, Dhahran, Saudi Arabia); Abdalla Alnajjar (Arab Science and Technology Foundation, Sharjah, United Arab Emirates); Alice Amsden (Massachusetts Institute of Technology, Mass.); Daniele Archibugi (Italian

National Research Council, Rome); Rodrigo Arocena (Universidad de la Republica, Uruguay); Brigitte Baeuerle (University of Denver, Colo.); Audia Barnett (Scientific Research Council, Kingston, Jamaica); John Barton (Stanford University, Palo Alto, Ca.); B. Bowonder (Administrative Staff College of India, Hyderabad, India); Lewis Branscomb (Kennedy School of Government, Harvard University, Cambridge, Mass.); Christe S. Bruderlin (Los Angeles, Ca.) (freelance writer); Mark Cantley (European Commission, Brussels); Alfonso Carrasco (Intermediate Technology Development Group, Lima, Peru); Rosalba Casas (Universidad Nacional Autonoma de Mexico, Mexico City); Fidel Castro Díaz-Balart (Office of the Scientific Advisor, State Council, Havana, Cuba); Aurora Cebreros (National Science and Technology Council, Lima, Peru); Lennox Chandler (Science and Technology Division, Government of Barbados, Bridgetown); Pamela Chasek (Earth Negotiations Bulletin, New York); Shin-Horng Chen (Chung-Hua Institution for Economic Research, Taipei); Mbita Chitala (Ministry of Finance and National Planning, Lusaka, Zambia); Clara Cohen (National Academies, Washington, D.C.); William Clark (Kennedy School of Government, Harvard University, Cambridge, Mass.); Ismael Clark-Arxer (Cuban Academy of Sciences, Havana); Peter Collins (Royal Society, London); Gordon Conway (Rockefeller Foundation, New York); Susan E. Cozzens, Georgia Institute of Technology, Atlanta, USA).

Dana Dalrymple (U.S. Agency for International Development, Washington, D.C.); Louk de la Rive Box (Institute of Social Studies, The Hague); Tulio Abel del Bono (Ministry of Education, Science and Technology, Buenos Aires); Mateja Dermastia (Ministry of the Economy, Ljubljana); David Dickson (Science and Development Network, London); Paul Dufour (Office of the Science Advisor to the Prime Minister of Canada, Ottawa); Dieter Ernst (East-West Center, Honolulu); Henry Etzkowitz (State University of New York, Purchase); Jonathan Fanton (MacArthur Foundation, Chicago, Ill.); Sarah Farley (World Bank, Washington, D.C.); Eduardo A. Fernandez (Chamber of Commerce of Barranquilla, Atlantico, Colombia); Kenneth Fernandez (National Aeronautics and Space Administration, Marshall Space Flight Center, Huntsville, Ala.); Sergio Ferreira de Figueiredo (Ministry of Development, Brasilia); Sinesio Pires Ferreira (Institute for Statistics and Socioeconomic Research, São Paulo, Brazil); Janine Ferretti (Inter-American Development Bank, Washington, D.C.); Judith Francis (Technical Centre for Agricultural and Rural Cooperation, Wageningen, the Netherlands); Dan Glickman (Motion Picture Association of America, Washington, D.C.); Katherine Gockel (University of Denver, Colo.); Manuel Mira Godinho (Technical University of Lisbon); Langston "Kimo" Goree (Earth Negotiations Bulletin, New York); Xu Guanhua (Minister of Science and Technology, People's Republic of China); R.K. Gupta (Planning Commission, Government of India, New Delhi); Mongi Hamdi (UNCTAD, Geneva); Stephanie Hanford (Brazilian Business Council for Sustainable Development, Rio de Janeiro); Mohamed Hassan (Third World Academy of Sciences, Trieste, Italy); John Holdren

(Kennedy School of Government, Harvard University, Cambridge, Mass.); Jason Hsu (Industrial Technology Research Institute, Taipei); Barry Hughes (University of Denver, Colo.); Jack Huttner (Genencor International, Palo Alto, California, U.S.A.); Jung-Chiou Hwang (Ministry of Economic Affairs, Taipei); Patarapong Intarakumnerd (National Science and Technology Development Agency, Bangkok); Akira Iriyama (Sasakawa Peace Foundation, Tokyo); Travis Kalanick (Redswoosh Inc., Los Angeles, Calif.); Sergei Kambalov (United Nations Secretariat, New York); Sarbuland Khan (United Nations Secretariat, New York); Victor Konde (UNCTAD, Geneva); Regina Lacayo Oyanguren (Project for Innovation Technology Support, Managua); Helena Lastres (Economics Institute, Federal University of Rio de Janeiro); Doris Estelle Long (John Marshall Law School, Chicago, Ill.); Juan López Villar (Friends of the Earth International, Florence, Italy); Eugene A. Lottering (National Research Foundation, Pretoria, South Africa); Bengt-Åke Lundvall (Aalborg University, Denmark); Silas Lwakabamba (Kigali Institute of Science, Technology and Management).

Samuel Makinda (Murdoch University, Murdoch, Australia); Peter Matlon (Rockefeller Foundation, Nairobi); Lucky Maohi (Ministry of Communications, Science and Technology, Gaberone); Julia Marton-Lefèvre (LEAD-International, London); R.A. Mashelkar (Council of Scientific and Industrial Research, New Delhi); John A. Mathews (Macquarie University, Sydney, Australia); Janet Maughan (Rockefeller Foundation, New York); Akashambatwa Mbikusita-Lewanika (National Economic Advisory Council, Lusaka, Zambia); Patrick Messerlin (Institut d'Etudes Politiques, Paris); John Mugabe (New Partnership for Africa's Development, Pretoria, South Africa); Masafumi Nagao (Hiroshima University, Hiroshima, Japan); Thien Nhan Nguyen (People's Committee of Ho Chi Minh City); Julia Novy-Hildesley (Lemelson Foundation, Portland, Oregon, U.S.A.); Peter Anyang' Nyong'o (Minister of Planning and National Development, Nairobi); Osita Ogbu (Science and Technology Policy Studies Network, Nairobi); Gabriel Ogunmola (Nigerian Academy of Science, Ibadan); Geoffrey Oldham (University of Sussex); William Otim-Nape (National Agricultural Research Organization, Kampala, Uganda); Flora Painter (Inter-American Development Bank, Washington, D.C.); Phillip Feanny Paulwell (Minister of Ministry of Commerce, Science and Technology, Kingston); Carlo Pietrobelli (University of Rome III, Rome); Auliana Poon (Tourism Intelligence International, Bielefeld, Germany); Norris Prevost (Parliament of the Commonwealth of Dominica, Roseau); Esad Prohic (Office of the President, Zagreb); Igbal Quadir (Kennedy School of Government, Harvard University, Cambridge, Mass.); Peter Raven (Missouri Botanical Garden, St. Louis, Mo.); Harold Ramkisson (University of the West Indies, St. Augustine, Trinidad and Tobago); Andrew Reynolds (Office of the Science and Technology Advisor to the U.S. Secretary of State, Washington, D.C.); William J. Rourke (Canberra); Vincent Rugwizangoga Rubarema (Office of the President, Kampala).

Francisco Sagasti (Agenda: PERÚ, Lima, Peru); Zafar Saied Saify (University of Karachi, Pakistan); George Saitoti (Minister of Science, Technology and Education, Nairobi); Karl Sauvant (UNCTAD, Geneva); Susan Sechler (German Marshall Fund of the United States, Washington, D.C.); Ismail Serageldin (Library of Alexandria, Egypt); Tengku Mohd Azzman Shariffadeen (Malaysia Institute of Microelectronic Systems, Kuala Lumpur); Luc Soete (Maastricht University, The Netherlands); Paz Soriano (Secretariat of the Presidency in Chile, Santiago); Charlie Spillane (University College Cork, Cork, Ireland), Apiwat Sretarugsa (Ministry of Natural Resources and Environment, Bangkok); Robert Stowe (Kennedy School of Government, Harvard University, Cambridge, Mass.); M.S. Swaminathan (M.S. Swaminathan Research Foundation, Chennai, India); Chikako Takase (United Nations Secretariat, New York); Don Thornhill (Commission for Higher Education, Dublin); Monica Trejo de Salazar (Corte de Cuentas de La Republica, San Salvador); Alvaro Umaña (United Nations Development Programme, New York); Arnoldo Ventura (Office of the Prime Minister of Jamaica, Kingston); Eduardo Viotti (Institute for Applied Economics Research, University of Brasilia); Judi Wakhungu (African Centre for Technology Studies, Nairobi); Shem Wandiga (Kenya National Academy of Sciences, Nairobi); Philip Weech (Secretariat of the UN Framework Convention on Climate Change, Bonn, Germany); Kenneth E. Weg (Clearview Projects, Princeton, N.J.); Roy Widdus (World Health Organization, Geneva); Abiodun Williams (United Nations Secretariat, New York); Wei Xie (Tsinghua University, Beijing); Lu Yongxiang (Chinese Academy of Sciences, Beijing); Abdulqawi Yusuf (UNESCO, Paris); Zane Zeibote (Advisor on Economic Affairs, Presidency of Latvia); and Jacob Ziv (Israel Academy of Sciences and Humanities, Jerusalem).

We commend the outstanding editorial and production work undertaken by Meta de Coquereaumont, Barbara Karni, Bruce Ross-Larson, Christopher Trott, and Elaine Wilson of Communications Development Incorporated.

Wider distribution of this report in developing countries was made possible through the generous support of a number of institutions that strongly believe that innovation can be an engine of development. These include: Genencor International, USA; International Development Research Centre, Canada; Secretariat of the African Forum on Science and Technology for Development of the New Partnership for Africa's Development (NEPAD); and the Joint Centre for Bioethics, University of Toronto. We also want to single out the Government of Canada for providing leadership in promoting the application of emerging technologies to development.

Preparation of this report would not have been possible without the outstanding contributions of the task force research team and the continuous and generous support of the staff of the UN Millennium Project. Behind the whole enterprise was Brian Torpy, at the Belfer Center for Science and International Affairs, whose logistical support, organizational capabilities, and dedication to duty made it possible for the task force to operate smoothly and effectively.

Abbreviations

CGIAR	Consultative Group on International Agricultural Research
DFID	Department for International Development
EPZ	export processing zones
FAO	Food and Agriculture Organization
FNIH	Foundation for the National Institutes of Health
FUNDAEC	Foundation for the Application and Teaching of the Sciences
GeSCI	Global eSchools and Communities Initiative
IAC	InterAcademy Council
ICT	information and communication technology
IDRC	Canadian International Development Research Centre
IMF	International Monetary Fund
ISO	International Organization for Standardization
ITRI	Industrial Technology Research Institute
KIST	Kigali Institute of Science, Technology and Management
LAMAP	La Main à la Pate
MDG	Millennium Development Goal
MIGHT	Malaysia Industry-Government Partnership for High Technology
MIT	Massachusetts Institute of Technology
MSC	Multimedia Super-Corridor
NGO	nongovernmental organization
OECD	Organisation for Economic Co-operation and Development
PCR	polymerase chain reaction
PRSP	Poverty Reduction Strategy Paper
R&D	research and development
SAM	Academy of Science Malaysia
SARS	Severe Acute Respiratory Syndrome
SAT	Sistema de Aprendizaje Tutorial (Tutorial Learning System)

TRIPS	Trade-Related Aspects of Intellectual Property Rights
UNCSTD	United Nations Commission on Science and Technology for Development
UNCTAD	United Nations Conference on Trade and Development
UNDAF	UN Development Assistance Frameworks
UNESCO	United Nations Educational, Scientific and Cultural Organization
UNICAMP	University of Campinas, São Paulo, Brazil
UNIDO	United Nations Industrial Development Organization
WHO	World Health Organization
WSIS	World Summit on the Information Society
WSSD	World Summit on Sustainable Development
WTO	World Trade Organization

goals

Millennium Development Goals

Goal 1

Eradicate extreme poverty and hunger

Target 1.
Halve, between 1990 and 2015, the proportion of people whose income is less than $1 a day

Target 2.
Halve, between 1990 and 2015, the proportion of people who suffer from hunger

Goal 2

Achieve universal primary education

Target 3.
Ensure that, by 2015, children everywhere, boys and girls alike, will be able to complete a full course of primary schooling

Goal 3

Promote gender equality and empower women

Target 4.
Eliminate gender disparity in primary and secondary education, preferably by 2005, and in all levels of education no later than 2015

Goal 4

Reduce child mortality

Target 5.
Reduce by two-thirds, between 1990 and 2015, the under-five mortality rate

Goal 5

Improve maternal health

Target 6.
Reduce by three-quarters, between 1990 and 2015, the maternal mortality ratio

Goal 6

Combat HIV/AIDS, malaria, and other diseases

Target 7.
Have halted by 2015 and begun to reverse the spread of HIV/AIDS

Target 8.
Have halted by 2015 and begun to reverse the incidence of malaria and other major diseases

Goal 7

Ensure environmental sustainability

Target 9.
Integrate the principles of sustainable development into country policies and programs and reverse the loss of environmental resources

Target 10.
Halve, by 2015, the proportion of people without sustainable access to safe drinking water and basic sanitation

Target 11.
Have achieved by 2020 a significant improvement in the lives of at least 100 million slum dwellers

Goal 8

Develop a global partnership for development

Target 12.
Develop further an open, rule-based, predictable, nondiscriminatory trading and financial system (includes a commitment to good governance, development, and poverty reduction—both nationally and internationally)

Target 13.
Address the special needs of the Least Developed Countries (includes tariff- and quota-free access for Least Developed Countries' exports, enhanced program of debt relief for heavily indebted poor countries [HIPCs] and cancellation of official bilateral debt, and more generous official development assistance for countries committed to poverty reduction)

Target 14.
Address the special needs of landlocked developing countries and small island developing states (through the Program of Action for the Sustainable Development of Small Island Developing States and 22nd General Assembly provisions)

Target 15.
Deal comprehensively with the debt problems of developing countries through national and international measures in order to make debt sustainable in the long term

Some of the indicators listed below are monitored separately for the least developed countries, Africa, landlocked developing countries, and small island developing states

Target 16.
In cooperation with developing countries, develop and implement strategies for decent and productive work for youth

Target 17.
In cooperation with pharmaceutical companies, provide access to affordable essential drugs in developing countries

Target 18.
In cooperation with the private sector, make available the benefits of new technologies, especially information and communications technologies

Executive summary

Since their adoption at the United Nations Millennium Summit in 2000, the Millennium Development Goals have become the international standard of reference for measuring and tracking improvements in the human condition in developing countries. The Goals are backed by a political mandate agreed to by the leaders of all UN member states. They offer a comprehensive and multidimensional development framework and set clear quantifiable targets to be achieved by 2015.

Meeting the Goals will require a substantial reorientation of development policies to focus on key sources of economic growth, including those associated with the use of new and established scientific and technological knowledge and related institutional adjustments. Countries will need to recognize the benefits from advances in science and technology and develop strategies to harness the explosion in new knowledge.

This report describes approaches for effectively applying science, technology, and innovation to achieving the Goals. It outlines key areas for policy action, including focusing on platform (generic) technologies; improving infrastructure services as a foundation for technology; improving higher education in science and engineering and redefining the role of universities; promoting business activities in science, technology, and innovation; improving the policy environment; and focusing on areas of underfunded research for development. The report draws on experiences from throughout the world to show how developing and developed countries have used science, technology, and innovation to achieve their development goals.

Platform technologies are key

Most developing countries still distinguish between industrial policies, which emphasize building manufacturing capabilities, policies designed to generate

Developing countries need to adopt strategies to improve their infrastructure in ways that promote the technological development necessary for sustained economic growth

new knowledge through support for R&D, and those dedicated to education. Combining the three approaches would focus attention on the use of existing technologies while building a foundation for long-term R&D activities. This approach requires focusing on existing technologies, especially platform technologies that have broad applications or impacts in the economy. Developments in information and communications technology, biotechnology, nanotechnology, and new materials will have profound implications for long-term economic transformation and achievement of the Goals.

Infrastructure is the foundation for technology

One of the problems hindering reduction of poverty—and the achievement of other Goals—in the developing world is the absence of adequate infrastructure. Adequate infrastructure is a necessary, if not sufficient, requirement for enhancing the creation and application of science, technology, and innovation in development. Developing countries need to adopt strategies to improve their infrastructure in ways that promote the technological development necessary for sustained economic growth.

Infrastructure affects the production and consumption of firms and individuals while generating substantial positive and negative externalities. Because infrastructure services are intermediate inputs into production, their costs have a direct effect on firms' profitability and competitiveness. Infrastructure services also affect the productivity of other factors of production: electric power allows firms to shift from manual to electrical machinery, transportation networks reduce workers' commuting time, telecommunications networks facilitate the flow of information. Infrastructure may also attract firms to certain locations, which can create agglomeration economies and reduce factor and transactions costs.

Governments have traditionally viewed infrastructure projects from a static perspective. Although they recognize the fundamental importance of infrastructure, they seldom consider infrastructure projects as part of a technological learning process. In fact, infrastructure development provides a foundation for technological learning, because it involves the use of a wide range of technologies and complex institutional arrangements. Policymakers need to recognize the dynamic role infrastructure development can play in economic growth and take the initiative in acquiring the technical knowledge available through international and indigenous construction and engineering firms.

For infrastructure to become more effective and extensible, developing countries need to adopt and enforce infrastructure standards. Beginning in the early design stages, they need to promote the interoperability of infrastructure systems, not only nationally but also regionally and internationally. Standards should be designed and implemented so that they do not create barriers to innovation.

To build science, technology, and innovation capabilities, developing countries need to devote resources to helping more young people, especially women, receive higher education

Investment in science and technology education needs to increase, and the role of universities needs to change

Investment in science and technology education has been one of the most critical sources of economic transformation. Such investment should be part of a larger framework to build capacities in science, technology, and innovation worldwide. Improvements in higher education need to be accompanied by the growth of economic opportunities, so that graduates can apply their acquired capabilities.

To build science, technology, and innovation capabilities, developing countries need to devote resources to helping more young people, especially women, receive higher education. Although the education Goal is limited to achieving universal primary education, science education at the primary and secondary levels is also critical.

Higher education is more important than ever before in the developing world. The change reflects the increased demand for higher education due to improved access to schooling, pressing local and national concerns that require advanced knowledge to address, and a global economy that rewards technological expertise.

Universities can contribute to development in several ways. They can undertake entrepreneurial activities that aim to improve regional or national economic and social performance. They can get involved with their communities, gaining direct knowledge about social needs, some of which could be addressed through R&D activities. They can conduct industrial R&D; create spin-off firms; participate in capital formation projects, such as technology parks and business incubator facilities; introduce entrepreneurial training and internships into their curricula; and encourage students to take research from the university to firms. Universities need to be transformed to play these roles. Eventually, new institutions need to be created that focus on business incubation and community development.

Reshaping universities to contribute to development will require adjustments in curricula, changes in schemes of service, modifications in pedagogy, shifts in the location of universities, and the creation of a wider institutional ecology that includes other parts of the development process. National development plans will need to incorporate new links between universities, industry, and government. These changes are likely to have an impact on the entire national innovation system, including firms, R&D institutes, and government organizations.

Government needs to promote business activities in science, technology, and innovation

Economic change is largely a process by which knowledge is transformed into goods and services. Creating links between knowledge generation and enterprise development is thus one of the greatest challenges facing developing countries.

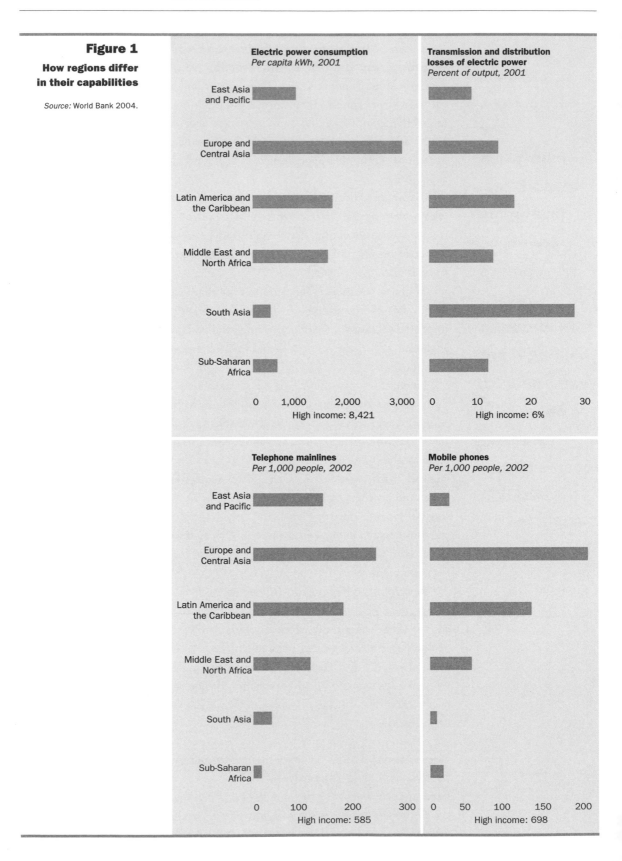

Figure 1

How regions differ in their capabilities

Source: World Bank 2004.

Electric power consumption
Per capita kWh, 2001

East Asia and Pacific

Europe and Central Asia

Latin America and the Caribbean

Middle East and North Africa

South Asia

Sub-Saharan Africa

0   1,000   2,000   3,000
High income: 8,421

Transmission and distribution losses of electric power
Percent of output, 2001

0   10   20   30
High income: 6%

Telephone mainlines
Per 1,000 people, 2002

East Asia and Pacific

Europe and Central Asia

Latin America and the Caribbean

Middle East and North Africa

South Asia

Sub-Saharan Africa

0   100   200   300
High income: 585

Mobile phones
Per 1,000 people, 2002

0   50   100   150   200
High income: 698

Policymakers need to develop, apply, and emphasize the important role of engineering, technology, and small enterprise development

If developing countries are going to promote the development of local technology, they need to improve their incentive structures. A range of structures—from taxation regimes and market-based instruments to consumption policies and changes within the national system of innovation—can be used to create and sustain enterprises. Government procurement can be used to promote technological innovation and generate markets for new products in areas such as environmental management.

Stimulating the creation and expansion of small and medium-size businesses

Small and medium-size enterprises need to play leading roles in the development of new opportunities and the use of technology. To help them do so, governments can support regional and national road shows, technology days, trade shows, advertising, workshops, and online discussions. Policymakers need to develop, apply, and emphasize the important role of engineering, technology, and small enterprise development in poverty reduction and sustainable social and economic development. They need to support business and technology incubators, export processing zones, and production networks.

Business and technology incubators. Incubators play an important role in fostering the creation and growth of small and medium-size businesses. Their roles range from providing affordable space to providing core business support functions, such as business development, financing, marketing, and legal services. Factors considered important to success include public policy that facilitates the creation of venture capital and provides business infrastructure, private sector partnerships for mentoring and marketing, community involvement, a knowledge base of university and research facilities, and professional networking.

Export processing zones. Export processing zones (EPZs) are areas in developing countries in which firms can acquire imported inputs duty free as long as they export 100 percent of their output. If they are designed with long-term technological development in mind, EPZs can help firms acquire technology and diffuse it throughout the local economy.

Production networks. Networking helps small and medium-size enterprises access skills, find highly educated labor, and pool business services. The rapidly changing technological and global environment makes networking particularly important in fostering incubation activities.

Unlocking financial capital

Banks and financial institutions can play an important role in fostering technological innovation. But their record in this field has been poor in developing

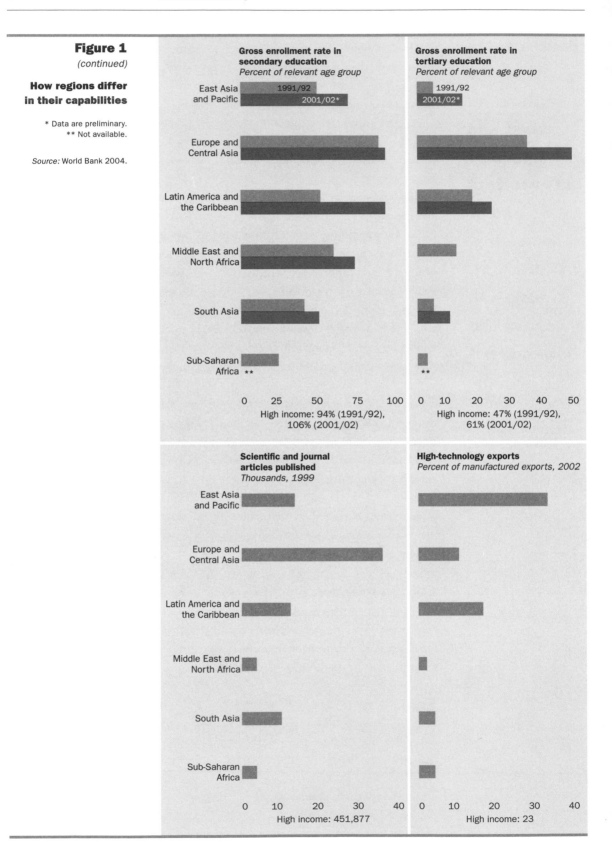

Figure 1
(continued)

**How regions differ
in their capabilities**

* Data are preliminary.
** Not available.

Source: World Bank 2004.

**Gross enrollment rate in
secondary education**
Percent of relevant age group

East Asia and Pacific
1991/92
2001/02*

Europe and Central Asia

Latin America and the Caribbean

Middle East and North Africa

South Asia

Sub-Saharan Africa **

0   25   50   75   100

High income: 94% (1991/92),
106% (2001/02)

**Gross enrollment rate in
tertiary education**
Percent of relevant age group

1991/92
2001/02*

0   10   20   30   40   50

High income: 47% (1991/92),
61% (2001/02)

**Scientific and journal
articles published**
Thousands, 1999

East Asia and Pacific

Europe and Central Asia

Latin America and the Caribbean

Middle East and North Africa

South Asia

Sub-Saharan Africa

0   10   20   30   40

High income: 451,877

High-technology exports
Percent of manufactured exports, 2002

0   10   20   30   40

High income: 23

Bringing venture and other forms of risk capital into developing countries could help create new businesses and improve their sustainability

countries. Reforming some banking and financial institutions would allow them to help promote technological innovation.

Capital markets (and venture capitalists) have played a critical role in creating small and medium-size enterprises in developed countries. Venture capitalists do not just bring money to the table; they help groom small and medium-size start-ups into multinational institutions. Bringing venture and other forms of risk capital into developing countries could help create new businesses and improve their sustainability.

Using government procurement to stimulate technological development

Government procurement can be an important tool for stimulating technological development in countries in which demand for technology is weak. Although there is an ideological debate about the role of public procurement, many countries have created and nurtured entire new industries or lagging old ones on this basis. In many of these countries, technological capability was created and firms became globally competitive over time.

Increasing participation in international trade

Developing countries need to participate more actively in international trade to acquire technological and other capabilities. Doing so does not mean that they need to completely liberalize their economies; selective industrial policies are still necessary to foster domestic technological capabilities. Global trade rules should be differentiated to take into account the different needs of countries at varying levels of development.

To participate more fully in international trade, developing countries need to develop their standards-related facilities and capabilities, including those for metrology, product testing, quality assessment, and certification. The recent proliferation of standards and technical regulations in industrial countries makes it more important than ever for developing countries to develop these capabilities.

Protecting the rights of inventors while promoting technological development in developing countries

Protecting intellectual property rights is a critical aspect of technological innovation. But overly protective systems can constrain creativity. Intellectual property protection systems need to be designed to take into account the special needs of developing countries. Provisions in international intellectual property agreements that promote technology cooperation with developing countries need to be identified and implemented.

Developing countries need to acquire global knowledge. The process of technological innovation has become intricately linked to the globalization of the world economic system. The shift from largely domestic activities to more complex

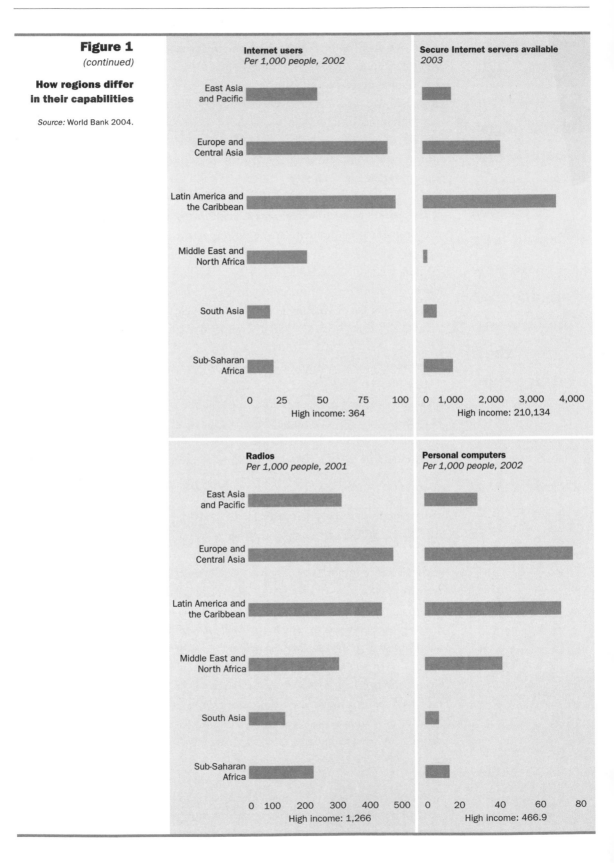

Figure 1
(continued)

**How regions differ
in their capabilities**

Source: World Bank 2004.

Internet users
Per 1,000 people, 2002

East Asia and Pacific

Europe and Central Asia

Latin America and the Caribbean

Middle East and North Africa

South Asia

Sub-Saharan Africa

0   25   50   75   100
High income: 364

Secure Internet servers available
2003

0   1,000   2,000   3,000   4,000
High income: 210,134

Radios
Per 1,000 people, 2001

East Asia and Pacific

Europe and Central Asia

Latin America and the Caribbean

Middle East and North Africa

South Asia

Sub-Saharan Africa

0   100   200   300   400   500
High income: 1,266

Personal computers
Per 1,000 people, 2002

0   20   40   60   80
High income: 466.9

In many countries science advisors report to the president or prime minister and national scientific and engineering academies provide political leaders with advice

international relationships demands a fresh look at policies that seek to integrate science, technology, and innovation into economic strategies.

Attracting foreign direct investment and becoming part of global value chains

Creating incentives and promoting an enabling environment for foreign direct investment is one of the most important mechanisms for building domestic technological capacity. Global production systems have changed the ways funds flow and can be used for long-term growth. Foreign direct investment needs be used as a vehicle for diffusing tacit knowledge and helping enterprises learn where the world technological frontiers and aspire to reach them.

Today's global economy consists of many product value chains that encompass the full range of activities—R&D, design, production, logistics, marketing, distribution, support services—that bring products from conception to end use and beyond. Firms in developing countries need to gradually move up these chains to perform higher value-added activities.

Promoting regional markets

Creating regional markets through economic integration is emerging as one of the key measures used to promote the application of technology to development. Regional integration increases the potential to benefit from economies of scale, provides the space needed for product diversification, and increases the scope for research cooperation, which enhances the prospects for innovation.

Mechanisms for advising governments on science, technology, and innovation need to be improved

Advice on science, technology, and innovation needs to reach policymakers. For this to happen, an institutional framework needs to be created and commitment needs to be garnered to support it.

Setting up an advisory structure

Advisory structures differ across countries. In many countries science advisors report to the president or prime minister and national scientific and engineering academies provide political leaders with advice.

Whatever structure is adopted, the advising function should have some statutory, legislative, or jurisdictional mandate to advise the highest levels of government. It should have its own operating budget and a budget for funding policy research. The advisor should have access to good and credible scientific or technical information from the government, national academies, and international networks. The advisory processes should be accountable to the public and be able to gauge public opinion about science, technology, and innovation.

Successful implementation of science, technology, and innovation policy requires civil servants with the capacity for policy analysis

Strengthening the capacity of scientific and technical academies to participate in advisory activities

Science, technology, engineering, medicine, and agriculture academies can play important roles in providing advice to governments. But they need to be strengthened or reformed in order to play this function. Scientific and technical academies need to cooperate with other institutions—especially judicial academies—whose activities influence scientific and technological development. Where they do not exist, efforts should be made to create them.

Training decisionmakers in science, technology, and innovation

Successful implementation of science, technology, and innovation policy requires civil servants with the capacity for policy analysis—capacity that most civil servants lack. Providing civil servants with training in technology management, science policy, and foresight techniques can help integrate science, technology, and innovation advice into decisionmaking. Training diplomats and negotiators in science and technology can increase their capacity to handle technological issues in international forums.

Using foresight techniques to set priorities for funding and crafting policy

Originally used to identify new technologies, foresight is now used to help understand the full innovation system. Crafting policy based on the analysis of current trends and expectations of future developments is particularly important for emerging fields, such as genomics, new materials, and nanotechnology.

Governance mechanisms need to be put in place for managing global technology

International organizations can play a critical role in promoting the application of science, technology, and innovation to achieving the Goals. These organizations—especially the organs of the United Nations and allied intergovernmental bodies—have extensive influence on the development agenda.

Strengthening the United Nations' capacity to use scientific and technical advice in its operations

The United Nations should strengthen its capacity to advise countries on the linkages between technological innovation and development. Doing so will entail building competence in science, technology, and innovation advice in the United Nations' executive offices. The UN Secretary-General has set a pioneering example by encouraging and nurturing the development of the Inter-Academy Council of world science academies in providing science, technology, and innovation advice on global issues of pressing concern to him. He could do more to incorporate science, technology, and innovation advice into policy formation and encourage other UN agencies to do the same.

Managing the risks and responding to public concerns are necessary if science and technology are to be effectively deployed to meet the Goals

Examining the impact of rule-making and standards-setting organizations on developing countries' capacity to use technology to promote development
International rule-making and standards-setting institutions, such as the World Trade Organization, the International Organization for Standardization, and the Bretton Woods institutions, have established a wide range of rules that affect the capacity of developing countries to build domestic scientific and technological capabilities. These rule-making and standard-setting activities need to be reviewed to determine how they could be adjusted to better meet the needs of developing countries.

Increasing the capacity of multilateral and bilateral institutions to promote technological innovation
Multilateral financial institutions, led by the World Bank and the regional development banks, should play a leading role in promoting technological innovation in developing countries. Bilateral aid agencies should place science, technology, and innovation at the core of their development assistance programs. For this to happen, units within multilateral and bilateral agencies that can provide science, technology, and innovation advice need to be created and strengthened.

Resources need to be channeled to pressing development problems of widespread importance that are currently underfunded. To help do so, bilateral donors could increase their official development assistance to fund research that both meets local needs and is of broader significance. Bilateral and multilateral donors could join forces to support international research centers, individually or through consortia that work closely with developing countries. Donor support for research could be funded through international cooperative projects in which funds are provided to teams that propose world-class research projects that focus on underrepresented research activities.

Expanding open access for scientific publishing
Open access publishing has the potential to make all published knowledge available to anyone with an Internet connection. The United Nations has been at the forefront in the drive to establish open access to information and technology.

Manage the benefits and risks of new and existing technologies
Perceptions about the benefits and risks of technological innovation have become a major aspect of international discussion and dialogue. Managing the risks and responding to public concerns are necessary if science and technology are to be effectively deployed to meet the Goals. New technologies have been credited with creating new industrial opportunities but also with disruptions to the status quo. While investors focus on the benefits of new and existing technologies, others worry about their risks.

**A few
strategic
measures
need to be
taken at the
national and
international
levels in the
short run**

Managing technological uncertainty will require increased investment in innovative activities at the scientific and institutional levels. At the technical level, technological diversity is essential to ensuring that society is able to respond to emerging challenges with the knowledge at its disposal. Technological diversity demands greater investment in scientific enterprises as well as the creation of measures to promote access to available technical options. More fundamentally, much of the effort should be focused on building trust in technology and in those who promote it.

Forging ahead

Many of the options for action in this report are already part of the development strategies of most countries. They may not have been formulated with the sense of urgency and priority that has informed this report, however. Indeed, most of these options will be implemented over the long run or are contingent on complementary adjustments in other countries, regions, or the international economic system. There are, however, a few strategic measures that need to be taken at the national and international levels in the short run.

Developing countries need to create and improve science and technology advisory institutions at the national and international levels. Multilateral and bilateral institutions, including various organs of the United Nations, should be involved in this process. Developing countries also need to initiate reviews of their educational systems to examine the degree to which they address the challenges of development. The review process should focus on the role of higher education in development and the place accorded to training in science, engineering, and technology within the higher education curricula. Finally, developing countries should review and strengthen national programs designed to promote business development. These measures, which can be achieved in the next five years, will pave the way for the more systematic implementation of additional measures aimed at achieving the Goals in particular and sustainable development in general.

1

Mapping the terrain

Chapter 1

Development as learning

This report outlines strategic options for using science, technology, and innovation to meet the Millennium Development Goals arising from the UN Millennium Declaration adopted in 2000 (see Goals on p. xxii).[1]

This report argues that economic improvement is largely a result of the application of knowledge in productive activities and the associated adjustments in social institutions (Rosenberg and Birdzell 1986; Mokyr 2002). It uses an innovation systems approach that attributes economic growth to interactive learning involving government, industry, academia, and civil society (Edquist 1997). It focuses on the importance of learning or continuous improvement in the knowledge base and institutional arrangements for development (Conceição and Heitor 2002). Technological innovation is therefore not simply a matter of installing devices, but of transforming society and its value systems (Sagasti 2004).

Transformational nature of technological innovation

This report defines "new technologies" in two ways. First, new technologies include applications in new areas, irrespective of whether the technologies have been used in other parts of the world. Second, the concept of "new technologies" is used to denote the use of emerging technologies, including information and communications technologies (ICTs), biotechnology, nanotechnology, and new materials. While the report outlines ways in which these emerging technologies can be applied to implement the first seven Goals, the overall strategic options presented in the report focus on introducing new technological systems or applications in economic systems.

This transformational nature of technological innovation involves a shift in traditional relationships in society. Imbuing society with a science culture involves valuing openness, encouraging criticism and exploration, and

Science, technology, and innovation underpin every one of the Goals

broadening access to science education for women. Educating women in the sciences is not simply a matter of meeting international obligations related to equality, it has a practical purpose of changing social attitudes and preparing the next generation to adapt to changing world conditions (Everts 1998). Technological learning is a wider process that involves the building of capabilities at the personal, organizational, and societal levels.

Technological innovation is not the only source of economic transformation, but its importance will increase over time. The report rejects the view that technology determines socioeconomic change, but it notes the co-evolution between technical change and social adjustment. It therefore stresses the importance of aligning structures of governance with development goals and the associated technological missions. While specific strategies may vary across countries, most of the institutional measures needed to promote technological innovation are similar. This is not to suggest that the relations between technological change and institutional adjustment are deterministic. To the contrary, the report underscores the fact that building a knowledge-based economy in developing countries will require the creation of governance structures that reflect the co-evolutionary dynamics of technology and institutions.

Governance structures will need to be realigned to reflect technological imperatives. In some cases technological choices will need to be sensitive to social factors. A learning approach will demand major changes in international development cooperation, which will include increased mutual trust and the adoption of norms of interaction that are consistent with the demands of mentoring and learning. Current practices that emphasize cumbersome accountability mechanisms are a symptom of the lack of trust. They cannot be effective vehicles for promoting learning.

Science, technology, and innovation underpin every one of the Goals. It is inconceivable that gains can be made in health and environmental concerns without a focused science, technology, and innovation policy. A well-articulated and focused science, technology, and innovation policy can also help make progress in education, gender equality (which is often tied to education and health care), and living conditions.

This report uses the term *policy* to include both explicit technology policies designed to promote technological innovation and implicit technology policies that have an indirect impact on technological innovation. Macroeconomic policies that reduce public expenditure may promote technological innovation but indirectly undermine the functioning of public research institutions needed to develop new crop varieties. The globalization of financial markets has had a similar impact on national technological capabilities (Katrak 2002; Cassiolato, Szapiro, and Lastres 2002). The report advocates more systematic examination of opportunities for promoting technological innovation in fields that are often considered outside the domain of government agencies concerned with science and technology.

Much of the improvement in human welfare over the past century can be accounted for by technological innovation in public health, nutrition, and agriculture

Much of the improvement in human welfare over the past century can be accounted for by technological innovation in public health, nutrition, and agriculture. These improvements have reduced mortality rates and increased life expectancy. Improvements in areas such as environmental management will also increasingly rely on the generation and application of new knowledge. Achieving the Goals will require the application of existing and new knowledge and the associated institutional adjustments.

Science, technology, and innovation policy cannot be viable unless it is underpinned by well-designed measures for addressing such issues as learning, research and development (R&D), and the diffusion, transfer, and commercialization of technology (Cantner and Pyka 2001). This is particularly true in areas that have an impact on education, health, and environmental issues, areas such as agricultural and medical biotechnologies, pharmaceuticals, computer networks, and telecommunication systems. These technologies can also affect water and energy usage in developing countries. Meeting the Goals requires focusing on creating policies and institutions that facilitate the cumulative application of science, technology, and innovation to each of the Goals (often expressed in the form of building scientific and technological capabilities).[2] It is this process of *technological learning* associated with *technological competence building* that forms the basis of this report (Kim and Nelson 2000).

The report adopts a systems approach, within which it is difficult to discern the impact of individual technologies on the economy. The approach highlights how these emerging technologies interact with one another and create new production combinations. The approach adopted here encourages the upgrading of current production practices in developing countries, which will necessarily involve the integration of new knowledge into existing technologies.

The report provides policy guidance that can be adapted by policymakers at the local, national, regional, and international levels. It draws from a diversity of sources and experiences and does not restrict itself to particular countries. The report's broad coverage is informed by the view that responses to development tend to have more in common than is usually acknowledged. The tendency to categorize countries into certain groups has often deflected attention from a more systematic identification of common features of development lessons that can be shared across countries and regions. Many more important and pertinent lessons that can inform development activities are emerging from Brazil, Chile, China, India, and Thailand.

The choice of lessons should be guided by a deeper understanding of the nature of problems facing society, not by theoretical constructs that limit the scope of social learning. Examples of best practices come from all around the world. The acid test should be whether they have contributed to the overall economic and social uplifting of their own countries. Best practices must be viewed in the proper context, a context that includes the enabling policy environment. Developing countries should consider all existing and historical development

**The limits
to learning
are not in
the lessons
available but
in theoretical
frameworks
that
undermine
open
inquiry and
experimental
thought. The
inquiring
mind knows
no limits**

lessons in designing their own solutions. The limits to learning are not in the lessons available but in theoretical frameworks that undermine open inquiry and experimental thought. The inquiring mind knows no limits.

Scope of the report

This report does not deal with the role of specific technologies, partly because technological choices and combinations are usually site specific or industry specific and therefore better dealt with at the appropriate levels. The report emphasizes that the general tendency to identify certain groups of technologies as more important than others is often misguided. That said, some generic technologies—such as ICT, biotechnology (or genomics), nanotechnology, materials science, and spatial information technology—are pervasive in scope and hold great promise for the Goals. These technologies deserve special attention. Ultimately, however, it is the confluence between different technological systems and the associated institutional arrangements that matter, not the individual impact of particular technologies.

In selecting the scope of coverage, the task force was guided by the need to avoid repetition and to identify significant themes that have received little policy attention. The report should be read in conjunction with other important reports on science, technology, and innovation, such as the *Human Development Report 2001: Making Technologies Work for Human Development* (UNDP 2001); *Industrial Development Report 2004: Industrialization, Environment and the Millennium Development Goals in Sub-Saharan Africa* (UNIDO 2004); *Strategic Approaches to Science and Technology in Development* (Watson, Crawford, and Farley 2003); *Inventing a Better Future: A Strategy for Building Worldwide Capacity in Science and Technology* (InterAcademy Council 2003); *World Report on Knowledge for Better Health: Strengthening Health Systems: Changing History* (WHO 2004); *World Telecommunication Development Report 2003* (ITU 2003); *The State of Food and Agriculture 2003–2004* (FAO 2004); *Unleashing Entrepreneurship: Making Business Work for the Poor* (UNDP 2004); *A More Secure World: Our Shared Responsibility* (UN 2004); and the reports of the other UN Millennium Project task forces.

The main contribution of this report lies in defining development as a learning process. The report focuses on institutional aspects of this process, which include providing advice on science, technology, and innovation; building human capabilities (especially by improving education in science, technology, and innovation); and promoting enterprise development. It also seeks to redefine infrastructure as a foundation for technological innovation. It recognizes the importance of designing policies that respond to the challenges of globalization. With appropriate modifications, the guidance provided in this report can be applied to the relevant aspects of thematic activities or sectors, such as water and sanitation, energy, health, agriculture, biological diversity, and environmental management, as elaborated by the 2002 World Summit on Sustainable Development.

The report highlights the interactions between government, industry, and knowledge-generating institutions as a central feature of economic change

This report is divided into three parts. Part 1 reviews the status of development trends and identifies the associated challenges. It provides an illustrative assessment of how platform (generic) technologies, particularly information and communications technologies and biotechnology, can help countries meet the Goals. It offers a conceptual framework within which economic change is viewed as a learning process in which knowledge is transformed into goods and services through systemic interactions between various parts of the economy.

Within this framework, emphasis is placed on the role governments can play as facilitators of technological learning and the role enterprises can play as the focal point at which learning occurs and technological capability accumulates. The report highlights the interactions among government, industry, and knowledge-generating institutions as a central feature of economic change. This part of the report also stresses the linkages between development and national and global security. It notes that durable national and global security cannot be achieved without improving the living conditions of the poor.

Part 2 outlines priority areas that require immediate policy focus. These include redefining infrastructure development as a foundation for technological innovation; using institutions of higher learning to increase scientific and technical capabilities in developing countries; enhancing entrepreneurship by creating and expanding businesses and industries (by effectively using intellectual, human, financial, and social capital); and managing technological innovation in a rapidly globalizing world.

Part 3 deals with the policy innovations needed to bring science, technology, and innovation to the core of development efforts. It examines how advice on science, technology, and innovation can play a more important role at the national level and how the activities of international institutions can be realigned to reflect the technological imperatives of the Goals. Part 3 also explores ways in which the United Nations and other multilateral organizations can address science, technology, and innovation as the international community prepares for the five-year review of the implementation of the Goals. It also addresses the importance of adopting strategies that maximize the socioeconomic benefits of technological innovation while minimizing its wider risks.

Chapter 2

How science and technology can contribute to achieving the Goals

At the Millennium Summit in September 2000, world leaders passed the Millennium Declaration, which formally established the Millennium Development Goals. Since then the Goals have become the international standard of reference for measuring and tracking improvements in the human condition in developing countries. The Goals are important because they are backed by a political mandate agreed upon by the leaders of all UN member states, offer a comprehensive and multidimensional development framework, and set clear quantifiable targets to be achieved in all countries by 2015.

Contribution to human welfare

A nation's ability to solve problems and initiate and sustain economic growth depends partly on its capabilities in science, technology, and innovation.[1] Science and technology are linked to economic growth; scientific and technical capabilities determine the ability to provide clean water, good health care, adequate infrastructure, and safe food. Development trends around the world need to be reviewed to evaluate the role that science, technology, and innovation play in economic transformation in particular and sustainable development in general (Juma and others 2001).[2]

Improving the welfare of developing countries is not only an end in itself, it is also intricately intertwined with the security of all countries, making development a truly global venture. Indeed, countries such as the United States have started to classify human development challenges that are prevalent in developing countries, such as HIV/AIDS, as national security issues. This is the beginning of a process that recognizes the emergence of a globalized world that requires collective action to deal with issues once considered strictly national (UN 2004).

This report addresses Goal 8 ("Building global partnerships for development") and target 18 ("In cooperation with the private sector, make available the

Many technologies hold the promise of significantly improving the condition of women in developing countries

benefits of new technologies, especially information and communications"). Its remit has been broadened to include how science, technology, and innovation can be enhanced and put to use to help all countries achieve the Goals. The task force's mission is guided by the understanding that most Goals cannot be achieved without a framework of action that places science, technology, and innovation at the center of the development process.

Experts from anywhere in the world can help apply science and technology to assist developing countries meet the Goals. But if long-term goals are to be achieved and growth and problem-solving are to become indigenous and sustainable, developing countries need to develop their own capabilities for science, technology, and innovation. This goal is the focus of this report. Meeting it requires an approach that views science, technology, and innovation as a system of interconnecting capabilities, including governance, education, institutions, advice, and collaboration.[3]

The strategies proposed by the task force are meant to complement, not replace, other approaches. For example, science, technology, and innovation play an important role in addressing the challenges associated with eliminating poverty and hunger, as the case of Southeast Asia demonstrates (box 2.1). They reduce poverty by contributing to economic development (by creating job opportunities and raising agricultural productivity, for example). They alleviate hunger by improving nutrition, increasing yields of cash and subsistence crops, improving

Box 2.1

Why did Southeast Asia and the Asian Pacific grow so quickly?

At least three critical elements contributed to the rapid economic transformation of Southeast Asia and the Asian Pacific. These features are critical to achieving the Goals throughout the world:

- Basic infrastructure, including roads, schools, water, sanitation, irrigation, clinics, telecommunications, and energy.
- Small and medium-size enterprises that supply goods and services to the agriculture and natural resources sectors. Developing these enterprises requires developing indigenous operational, repair, and maintenance expertise and a pool of local technicians. Without this base, indigenous industries cannot scale up and the economy cannot benefit from technology.
- Government support and funding to establish and nurture academies of engineering and technological sciences, professional engineering and technological associations, and industrial and trade associations. These human resource and supporting institutional frameworks spur sectorwide innovations in development processes.

Science and technology can also play an important role in facilitating implementation of the Goals on education, gender, health, and sustainable development. The World Summit on Sustainable Development affirmed the importance of science and technology. But the scientific, engineering, and technology communities have yet to be fully integrated into a system that encourages and enables development. Very capable engineering organizations and expertise are available to address acute problems, such as natural or other disasters. But the ability to put these resources to use for long-term sustainable development in developing countries is lacking.

Considerable technological innovation is taking place in energy generation and use, which will continue to be of strategic policy interest for all countries

soil management, and creating efficient irrigation systems.[4] In themselves, however, these scientific and technological measures do not solve the challenges of poverty and hunger; they need to be part of an integrated strategy aimed at improving overall human welfare.

ICTs can increase primary, secondary, and tertiary education by facilitating distance learning, providing remote access to educational resources, and enabling other solutions. Many technologies hold the promise of significantly improving the condition of women in developing countries (by improving energy sources, agricultural technology, and access to water and sanitation, for example).

Many health interventions—including the treatment and prevention of malaria, HIV/AIDS, drug-resistant tuberculosis, and vitamin and other micronutrient deficiencies—require new treatments and vaccines. The production of generic medicines holds the promise of improving poor people's access to essential medicines. Science and technology can also improve the monitoring of drug quality.

Improved scientific as well as traditional or indigenous knowledge at the local level will be indispensable for monitoring and managing complex ecosystems, such as watersheds, forests, and seas, and for helping to predict (and thereby manage) the impact of climate change and the loss of biodiversity. Access to water and sanitation will require continuous improvement in low-cost technologies for water delivery and treatment, drip irrigation, and sanitation.

Contribution to energy

Increasing access to energy is not a Goal, but it is one of the five priority areas identified by the World Summit on Sustainable Development. Energy is an important input into the development process. Considerable technological innovation is taking place in energy generation and use, which will continue to be of strategic policy interest for all countries.

Over the long term, the use of fossil fuels is unsustainable. Burning fossil fuel results in the emission of carbon dioxide and exacerbates the greenhouse effect. About 80 percent of all climate warming is caused by emissions of carbon dioxide.

One promising solution for reducing these emissions is the development of small, environmentally benign power plants, units, and systems. The medium-term prospects for doing so are promising. Hydrogen fuel cells and gas-fueled microturbines could be economically viable in the medium term (see chapter 4), opening up new opportunities for expanding the base for energy sources. Venture capital investment in these technologies has increased dramatically in the United States, and giant power manufacturers and large oil corporations are investing in fuel cells and renewable energy.

Contribution to health

HIV/AIDS and tuberculosis are severe problems in many African and South Asian countries, where HIV/AIDS is exacerbating what was thought to be a relatively well controlled tuberculosis phenomenon. Malaria also remains a serious

Technological innovation is becoming critical in the management of freshwater resources

problem, with high mortality rates in most tropical regions (and rising rates in parts of Africa). Science, technology, and innovation policy needs to be oriented toward finding vaccines and cures for these diseases, while creating new institutional frameworks from which new research collaborations can spring (box 2.2).[5]

Contribution to water and sanitation

Technological innovation is becoming equally critical in the management of freshwater resources. So far much of the attention on freshwater has focused on market-related issues, such as privatization. Innovation-related responses are just starting to emerge. For example, concern over water scarcity in agriculture is generating interest in alternative approaches that reduce the amount of water used to produce a unit of grain. Attention is also now turning to the development of drought-tolerant crops using both conventional breeding methods and genetic engineering. These technologies need not rely only on modern technologies. The development of the Autonomous Potable Water Unit in Uruguay illustrates the potential for creativity in the water sector in developing countries (box 2.3).[6]

Contribution to political stability and global security

Scientific and technical innovations can enhance national stability and international security.[7] Over time economic growth fuelled by innovations in science, technology, and innovation can increase social cohesion, stability, and democratization.

In Brazil and the Republic of Korea, for example, economic growth over the past 40 years led to a virtuous cycle in which first labor and then an emerging middle class began to insist on greater social, economic, and political participation. Advances in education, science, technology, and economic growth in these and similar economies are improving the prospects for both democracy and stability.

Increases in democratic practices, economic growth, and innovation normally lead a nation to increase its participation in international trading regimes.[8] As this occurs, the trading countries must establish a wide range of harmonized practices, such as standards, regulations, and tariffs. Trade ties usually have positive

---

Box 2.2

Working together researchers from Canada and Cuba developed a synthetic flu vaccine

Source: Verez-Bencomo and others 2004.

An encouraging example of what can be achieved through a good mix of political determination and international collaboration is the recent development of a synthetic vaccine against *Haemophilus influenzae* B Type (Hib), one of the worst pathogens affecting children. The vaccine, developed by research groups at the Universities of Havana and Ottawa, represents the first joint patent by Cuban and Canadian scientists The breakthrough was not the development of the vaccine itself, which was already available, but the invention of a synthetic version of the vaccine, which is substantially cheaper and much easier to manufacture than the nonsynthetic vaccine currently on the market. Pharmaceutical companies currently can produce just one-fifth of the 500 million doses needed a year. With the new synthetic vaccine, Cuba alone may be able to manufacture 50 million doses a year.

Box 2.3

**Basic technology
is helping people
in Uruguay meet
their water needs**

The Autonomous Potable Water Unit (APWU) was developed to convert "dirty" water into potable water without using large water treatment installations. The device comes in three models. The smallest one is 6 meters long and can be put into operation in 24 hours. The large units are 13 and 18 meters long and require 48 hours to be put into operation.

The APWU was designed in 1992 by engineers from the Uruguayan public water supply enterprise at the request of army engineers concerned about the sanitary conditions faced by Uruguayan soldiers serving as UN peacekeepers in Africa. The challenge was to create an inexpensive mobile, portable, and autonomous water treatment plant able to meet the basic requirements of a traditional treatment plant. The first unit was installed in the Democratic Republic of the Congo in 1993. Once the technology proved viable, the Uruguayan government financed the construction and installation of 120 units across Uruguay, where the device has reduced waterborne diseases, especially cholera.

Following Hurricane Mitch, the Uruguayan government donated some units to Nicaragua and El Salvador; it donated another unit to Venezuela after the mud avalanche in the La Guaira region. A small unit was donated to the village of Talwandi Sabo, in Punjab, India, in 2002, leading to hopes that India's demand for such units could reach 1,000 in five years. Hungary and South Africa have also expressed interest in the technology. Negotiations between Uruguay and Brazil are also underway. The two countries hope to use the technology to revitalize the metalworking industry and promote employment.

effects on political relationships between countries. Indeed, democratic countries with trade interdependencies are usually less likely to go to war with one another (Maital 1995).[9]

As scientific and technological innovations work to foster economic growth and political stability and democracy, countries become better international citizens and stakeholders in security (Commission on Human Security 2003). They also become more open to understanding that security often has important non-military dimensions. The recent redefinition of HIV/AIDS by the United States as a security crisis is one example of this broadened view of security in the twenty-first century.

Most international disputes and conflicts have revolved around access to land, commodities, and natural resources. These economic factors continue to play a role today. But increasingly, the world will be made up of societies in which economic value will be derived from knowledge, especially scientific and technical knowledge. Unlike traditional sources of wealth, knowledge is not scarce and can therefore grow at exponential rates. Knowledge-based societies will not develop without conflicts of their own, but warfare based on mercantilism or land grabs will take different forms.

One of the major new forces emerging today is global civil society, which promises to become even more important a force. Many of the nongovernmental organizations (NGOs) and NGO networks that make up this global civil society derive their capacity from their use of advanced ICTs; many have a keen interest in seeing science and technology serve peaceful democratic purposes and

The rise of globalization is changing the rules that govern innovation

create open societies. One of the key challenges ahead is to better integrate NGOs into policymaking mechanisms and forums at the local and international levels, forums that have been traditionally dominated by state and corporate actors.

Technology in today's global setting

Countries' achievements in creating and diffusing technologies and building human skills to master new innovations can be gauged in three areas: technology creation (measured by patent and royalty receipts), the diffusion of new technologies (measured by Internet use and exports of medium- and high-tech goods) and old technologies (such as telephony and electricity), and human skills (measured by mean years of schooling and the gross tertiary science enrollment ratio).

A host of success stories has been analyzed and widely advertised, but the global rules governing market exchange and intellectual property rights have changed, causing developing countries today to face constraints (as well as opportunities) that their predecessors did not. The Republic of Korea, for example, used a vast array of import-protecting measures and the selective use of foreign investments to develop its economy. Adopting these measures would be difficult under the current global trading regime. India developed its chemical and pharmaceutical sectors partly under the umbrella of a patent regime that recognized only process patents. As a result of the tightening of intellectual property protection and other factors that limit technological spillovers, that protection is no longer available.

The rise of globalization (involving greater mobility, connectivity, and interdependence) is changing the rules that govern innovation. Technological change is thus occurring in a vastly different global structural environment today. One manifestation of this change is the existence of globalized production networks that are dependent on geographically dispersed cost and logistical differences. These networks represent a big shift from a few decades ago, when foreign direct investment took different forms. Another factor affecting the global structural environment is the changed geopolitical climate, which has provided certain countries with preferential access to the United States and other advanced markets for new technologies, access to new export markets, and significant amounts of development assistance. A third factor is the changed intellectual property regime, which played such a critical role in the early development of certain industries in advanced and newly industrial countries. A fourth is the fact that revolutions in ICT and biotechnology have created new opportunities and put new pressures on skill sets and organizational practices within enterprises, universities, and other R&D and manufacturing sites.

A country's induction into privileged circles of trade negotiation, economic treaties, and preferential status depends partly on its technological capability. Countries with rapid economic growth rates attract foreign attention, because they represent new markets for goods and services from leading industrial powers and are considered important players with regional political power. Brazil, China, and India gained entry into select economic and political clubs as a result of their

Technological innovation is one of the least studied but most critical sources of productivity growth

economic growth and advanced technological capabilities. There is no substitute for scientific and technological bases, which undergird everything from agricultural self-sufficiency to public health coverage to lucrative licensing options for indigenous technology advances.

Natural disasters such as earthquakes, tsunamis, floods, locusts, and droughts can erode important gains made in development. The tragic loss of lives and property caused by the Indian Ocean tsunamis at the end of 2004 illustrate this point. Scientific advance and technological innovation can be used to reduce the risks caused by such disasters. Early warning systems based on earth observation systems and other techniques can play a key role in enhancing preparedness. Other technological innovations in construction, infrastructure, and civil engineering projects, accompanied by relevant institutional innovations, are also important. Natural disasters also cause untold damage to agriculture and aquaculture by destroying genetic material used for breeding crops, livestock, trees, and fish. New technologies such as tissue culture propagation can be used to reproduce seed for agricultural rehabilitation. Technological diversity helps society to reduce the impact of natural disasters and reestablish economic activity. Making effective use of technological innovation to manage disaster risks will require closer cooperation between disaster management and development communities.

But as the case of China demonstrated, the first priority for developing countries is to build indigenous scientific and technological capacity, including research infrastructure, as part of the national planning strategies (Y. Lu, Chinese Academy of Sciences, personal communication, 2004). It is through the existence of such capacity that developing countries will be able to manage technology acquisition, absorption, and diffusion activities relevant to development. In other words, their capacity to utilize imported technology will depend largely on the existence of indigenous technological capacity and the learning strategies they put in place (Gallagher forthcoming; Peilei forthcoming; Xie and White 2004).

Conclusion

Technological innovation is one of the least studied but most critical sources of productivity growth. Indeed, economic historians are currently changing our understanding of human history, placing greater emphasis on the role of technology and the associated institutional innovations. Technological innovation has played a critical role in spurring growth in the industrial countries. But lessons derived from these experiences have not been applied in developing countries, where technological change remains a marginal part of national growth strategies. The Goals offer an opportunity for the international community to plug this policy deficit.

Chapter 3

Innovation and economic advance

Economic historians suggest that the prime explanation for the success of today's advanced industrial countries lies in their history of innovation along different dimensions: institutions, technology, trade, organization, and the application of natural resources (Rosenberg and Birdzell 1986; Mokyr 2002). These factors also explain the economic transformation of developing countries that have recently industrialized.

Scientific and technological innovations come about through a process of institutional and organizational creation and modification. Defining characteristics of the West have been the institutionalization of private enterprise, continuous reductions in the cost of production, the introduction of new products, and the exploitation of opportunities provided by trade and natural resources. These achievements are a tribute to the private sector and the state's ability to recognize new opportunities and the ways in which to exploit them.

Economic growth and innovation

Since the pathbreaking work of Solow (1956, 1957), economists have recognized the critical importance of innovation and capital accumulation for growth. Empirical evidence and the modern theory of economic growth provide strong support for the thesis that long-term economic growth requires not only capital but also an understanding of innovation (Clark and Juma 1992). As the Millennium Project's *Investing in Development: A Practical Plan to Achieve the Millennium Development Goals* (UN Millennium Project 2005) shows, countries that are not on track to meet the Goals lack sufficient levels of physical, human, social, and other forms of capital. An important element of any Goal strategy must therefore be to raise the stock of these different forms of capital. (These interventions are described in more detail in *Investing in Development* and the reports of other Millennium Project task forces.)

Innovation and technology are needed to transform countries from reliance on the exploitation of natural resources to technological innovation as the basis for development

Focusing only on accumulating capital will not be sufficient to ensure long-term growth rates that can reduce poverty and help achieve the other Goals, however—as the case of Latin America, where income and capital levels are relatively high and growth rates persistently low, suggests. Innovation and technology are also needed to transform countries from reliance on the exploitation of natural resources to technological innovation as the basis for development.

Finland has transformed its economy from one dependent on natural resources to one at the top of the list of most indices of global competitiveness. This transformation began in the 1980s, with efforts aimed at aligning governance structures with long-term technological goals. Finland's success reflects its ability to combine science and technology policies aimed at promoting research with industrial policies geared toward manufacturing and export into a comprehensive innovation policy (Lemola 2002). The focus on Nokia as a national symbol conceals innovations in other sectors of the economy such as wood processing, opto-electronics, and biotechnology.

Finland focused on reforming its policies in education, research, innovation, and support for entrepreneurship. While the private sector is acknowledged as the locus of competitiveness, a wide range of public sector bodies play key roles. For example, the Ministry of Education and the Ministry of Trade and Industry are critical components in the Finnish innovation system. In 2003 the Ministry of Education controlled some 42 percent of the public research budget, while the Ministry of Trade and Industry accounted for nearly 35 percent. Other ministries also fund research.

The Ministry of Education oversees 20 regular universities, 29 universities of applied science, and the Academy of Finland. The Academy is the most important planning and basic research funding agency in basic research. The Ministry of Trade and Industry formulates innovation policy, supports private sector R&D, and oversees the country's Technology Development Agency (Tekes). Tekes is the main planning and funding organ for applied technology research and private sector R&D. It allocates nearly 30 percent of the country's public research funding. The Technical Research Centre (VTT), part of the Ministry of Trade and Industry, conducts contract research in partnership with the private sector (Berwert and others 2004).

The main policy body is the Science and Technology Policy Council, founded in 1987 to succeed the Science Policy Council, established in 1963. The Council brings together key science and technology players to develop visions and reach consensus on specific actions. Its members include the Prime Minister, who chairs the council; the Minister of Trade and Industry and the Minister of Education, who serve as vice-chairs; the Minister of Finance; and leading actors in the fields of science and technology. The council reports to Parliament.

Other components of the Finnish innovation system include Sitra, an independent public foundation that explores new technological directions.

The return on investments in science, technology, and innovation is likely to be lower in developing countries than in developed countries

Supervised by Parliament, it operates in the fields of venture capital, research, education, and innovation. Complementary institutions deal with investment, employment, and inventions that are part of the Finnish ecology of innovation. These institutions have benefited from the realignment of institutions with technological innovation goals.

Advances in economic theory, notably the development of endogenous growth models (Lucas 1988; Romer 1990; Aghion and Howitt 1992), lend strong support to this report's focus on the need for institutions and policies to promote science, technology, and innovation. The models and their empirical applications show that innovation and adoption of technologies is endogenous and driven largely by the combination of investments in science, technology, and innovation and adequate policy frameworks.

The rise of science and technology, particularly the institutionalization of the scientific method in the seventeenth century, created a forum for experimentation, the exchange of findings, and advancement and refinement of method. Experimentation and uncertainty were encouraged through the support of risk-taking and the rewarding of discovery. Eventually, transformation of organizational types took place in the private sector as well as in new public institutions that could weather economic uncertainty over time. Incentives for investment followed. This environment produced a diversity of products, services, organizations, and institutions suited to different conditions. But dependence on local market niches has been complemented by the emergence of global markets. In today's increasingly global environment, developed countries and their corporations tap the world's natural resources, have access to the best and brightest human resources from around the globe, manufacture in the most cost-effective locations, and sell their products throughout the world.

The most recent successes lie in the newly industrial economies of East Asia. High growth rates were certainly a necessary part of the story, but they were buttressed by diverse and adaptable institutions that oversaw new production regimes, export orientation, and compacts between state and private enterprise (Hobday 1995). Choices made by governments and the rapid adaptation to changed economic circumstance allowed producers to reap significant rewards while requiring them to demonstrate a certain commitment to national goals. Legitimacy for governments in this region was derived in part by higher economic growth rates. Economic development became a vehicle for buttressing democracy—both the Republic of Korea and Taiwan (China) elected and are now governed by presidents from parties that were once in the opposition.

Technological divergence across countries

The productivity of and return on investments in science, technology, and innovation is likely to be lower in developing countries than in developed countries. Increases in R&D funding will not increase capacity if only a few scientists are available to put those resources to work.

**Innovation
can directly
increase
the ability
of existing
science,
technology,
and
innovation
programs
to reduce
poverty
and expand
human
capabilities**

As part of a World Bank project, the RAND Corporation developed four broad categories of countries: scientifically advanced, scientifically proficient, scientifically developing, and scientifically lagging countries (Wagner and others 2001).

These categories provide a framework within which to consider research collaboration, teaming for capacity building, joint research, technology transfer, funding and investment priorities, and the productivity and effectiveness of aid. Collaborative research is shown to contribute most to capacity building, for example, when the subject is tied to a problem or issue in which the developing country has direct experience and some indigenous capacity exists.

Scientifically advanced countries

Scientifically advanced countries are countries with an above average capacity for science, technology, and innovation. These countries generally have capacity in all major areas of science and technology. They are responsible for the vast majority of all scientific articles published in internationally recognized journals, and they fund more than 80 percent of the world's R&D. Most of these countries have made investment in science, technology, and innovation a national priority for more than 50 years, in some cases for more than 100 years.

Scientifically proficient countries

Scientifically proficient countries are countries with an average or above average capacity for science, technology, and innovation capacity. In some of these countries, investment exceeds the international average, in others it falls below the mean. Countries in this category may display world-class strength in particular disciplines or subfields. These countries have made investments in the infrastructure and R&D required to build a science base, and their investments are showing results. Some of these countries have experienced significant gains in their roles in international science and technology. Some scientifically proficient countries have been making investments in science, technology, and innovation for more than 20 years. Others have a longer tradition of national science and technology that was disrupted by war or another type of catastrophe.

Scientifically developing countries

Scientifically developing countries have below average capacity in science, technology, and innovation, although some of them are able to participate in some international science, technology, and innovation. Some of these countries have good capabilities that attract international partners. Some countries in this category might be able move into the "proficient" category if they can improve their infrastructure and increase GNP.

Scientifically lagging countries

Scientifically lagging countries are countries that have not invested in science, technology, and innovation (or for which adequate data are not available).

Technology can indirectly affect human well-being by enhancing productivity and increasing economic growth and incomes

These countries fall below—in most cases well below—the international mean for all the components that reflect science, technology, and innovation capabilities. They fail to translate knowledge, education, and learning into institutions or activities that promote science and technology.

Technology, innovation, and income levels

Technology affects human development along two major paths. First, innovation can directly increase the ability of existing science, technology, and innovation programs to reduce poverty and expand human capabilities. This is most evident through technological innovations in public health, agriculture, energy use, and ICT. Second, technology can indirectly affect human well-being by enhancing productivity and increasing economic growth and incomes. Productivity can be enhanced by increasing the output of workers, raising agricultural yields, and improving the efficiency of services; higher incomes can help people meet their basic needs. Increased productivity helps overcome the barriers of low-incomes and weak institutions.

Science, technology, and innovation capacity is often associated with economic growth. The extent to which the two are linked is not clear, however. Many fields of science have little connection to economic development, and many areas of economic growth do not rely on science and technology. Others, such as agricultural research, directly contribute to growth and development (Thirtle, Lin, and Piesse 2003). Human development strengthens technology development: the productivity of industry, agriculture, or services depend on people and their knowledge.

An important force driving the adoption of technology is income. But technology may be a cause, not a result, of increased consumption. Innovation itself may be a result of the adoption of certain technologies. It is thus not clear whether higher incomes are a cause or a result of technology use and diffusion.

Major technological innovations rarely occur without financial investment. But funding alone is not sufficient for science and technology. The institutional mix of actors—individuals, firms, the state, and other organizations—all determine the milieu in which a technological innovation occurs.

Technologies have direct effects on human development. Medical breakthroughs are linked to basic health, less expensive medicines, and lower mortality rates. Higher agricultural production is linked to better seeds, better water use, and the use of more efficient and less toxic fertilizers. ICT enhances information and participation. Manufacturing technologies drive industrial expansion, employment, and incomes.

Technological advances in one field reinforce advances in others. This is especially visible in medical technologies, where breakthroughs in genetics coupled with computing advances have helped facilitate the process of drug discovery and created new fields of research, such as bioinformatics. Advances in

The
technological
knowledge
system is a
set of inter-
connecting
networks
embedded in
a wide array
of global
institutions

ICT have facilitated technological advances in the agricultural, manufacturing, and service sectors.

Technological learning and public policy

The technological knowledge system is a set of interconnecting networks embedded in a wide array of global institutions. These networks include communications (both written and verbal), knowledge (both tacit and explicit), and actors. The complexity of the interaction of these networks means that no single group (governments, NGOs, corporations) controls the outcomes. Defining the scope and use of new technologies is influenced heavily by the dynamics of these networks. Countries are not in full control of how they channel technologies to certain domestic sectors; they do not control the markets in which they will sell the technologies they develop. Understanding the dynamics operating at the regional, national, and global levels is important to moving the development agenda into the twenty-first century.

Broadening the concept of technology transfer

The 1960s and 1970s generated a somewhat utopian view of technology transfer from industrial to industrializing countries. Subsequent evidence has highlighted the need to broaden the concept to include emerging perspectives on technology and development.

The classical view of technology transfer as flowing from industrial countries to developing countries is being replaced by new approaches that emphasize complex interactions between countries. This systems view allows countries to think strategically of different ways in which scientific and technological knowledge is acquired, retained, diffused, and improved.

Transfers from industrial countries to developing countries are limited, due to a variety of factors, including the lack trained people, the inability to supply spare parts, and different ecological conditions, which require technological adaptation. For this reason, both industrial and developing countries are seeking ways of spurring endogenous innovation in developing countries while ensuring that these countries have access to mature technologies.

International policy discussions of technology continue to focus on new technologies without considering the economic context in which these technologies could be applied. These debates have focused on potential barriers to the transfer of such technologies, ignoring the fact that new technologies cannot benefit countries that lack the basic technological capabilities to absorb them.

The immediate problem facing developing countries, at least in the manufacturing sector, is not the creation of new knowledge but the efficient application of existing technologies. A cornucopia of technologies is available for industry that, if used by developing countries, could significantly enhance their incomes, employment, and exports. This technology is partly embodied in machinery and equipment, patents, and blueprints, and is partly "tacit,"

Adopting appropriate technology in the developing world requires a paradigm shift that favors mature technologies rather than cutting-edge technologies and related R&D

contained in the skills, knowledge, and experience of industrial employees, in both advanced industrial countries and industrializing countries.

The challenge is not simply to transfer and apply existing technologies in developing countries. The process of technology acquisition involves domestic modifications and adaptations that are not cost free. The efficient application of existing technologies involves considerable technical efforts. For less developed countries, pure scientific research has limited application. This research becomes relevant to technology only at the higher stages of development achieved by countries such as Brazil, China, India, the Republic of Korea, and Taiwan (China). The economic success of the newly industrializing countries of East Asia is associated with the effort to use existing technologies efficiently rather than to make scientific advances. Using new knowledge requires additional investment that may not be within the reach of developing countries.

Adopting appropriate technology in the developing world requires not only increased funding from developed countries but also a paradigm shift that favors mature technologies rather than cutting-edge technologies and related R&D. These technologies—mechanization of small farms, small-scale irrigation and potable water installation, small energy systems, rural roads, basic ITC—will do most to help developing countries meet the Goals. Creative approaches need to be developed for blending new technologies with old ones to provide the best solutions to pressing problems. Learning from countries that have had success in technological transitions would also enhance South-South cooperation.

Technology is a knowledge system, not simply physical technology and equipment. It relies heavily on modes of learning; adaptation to new technologies; educational systems; industrial policies and policies on science, technology, and innovation; the nature and composition of the private sector; and the capabilities inherent in the public sphere.

Technology relies heavily on demand: strong demand for technological solutions directed to local capabilities can be one of the strongest incentives to learning accumulation. Technology also depends on the flows of knowledge, resources, and people between public and private domains of knowledge and the mechanisms by which information on specific innovations is shared, developed, commercialized, and diffused. The incentive structure that causes different parties to become involved and stay committed to technological enterprises also needs careful attention from policymakers.

Innovation systems

The process of technological innovation involves interactions among a wide range of actors in society, who form a system of mutually reinforcing learning activities. These interactions and the associated components constitute dynamic "innovation systems" (Freeman 2002). Innovation systems can be understood by determining what in the institutional mixture is local and what

Informed science, technology, and innovation policy needs to account for the fact that universities need to continue to have local relevance

is external. Open systems are needed, in which new actors and institutions are constantly being created, changed, and adapted to suit the dynamics of scientific and technological creation.

The notion of a system offers a good framework for conveying the notion of parts, their interconnectedness, and their interaction and changes over time. Within countries the innovation system can vary across regions (box 3.1). Regional variations in innovation levels, technology adoption and diffusion, and the institutional mix are significant even in the most developed countries.

Government, the private sector, universities, and research institutions are important parts of a larger system of knowledge and interactions that allow diverse actors with varied strengths to come together to pursue broad common goals for innovation. In many developing countries, the state has much greater capabilities than the private sector, capabilities built up as a result of import substitution policies adopted when the public sector played the dominant role in the country's economy. Private sector capacity for adapting tacit knowledge and mature technology, and absorbing new knowledge, varies by country, region, and sector.

The role of universities in innovation. In many developing countries, universities suffer from unclear mandates and limited funds. They lack the flexibility to meet basic needs (often dealt with by public research centers in "mission mode") or promote competitiveness (dealt with by the private sector or government training institutes).[1]

Universities often lack the resources and the demand from a sound productive economic sector that is eager to benefit from the knowledge these universities and their students could create. They suffer from a "loneliness syndrome." Reversing this syndrome is one of the challenges for development, one that cannot be fulfilled by pushing universities to change while everything else remains the same. A better approach is to channel energies within the university environment to carry out a combined research, teaching, and application mandate, with different types of universities taking on different challenges and government and industries engaging in effective interaction with them.

Box 3.1

India has created hubs of technological excellence

Skilled high-tech professionals in India gravitate to Bangalore and Hyderabad, regions with adequate facilities and enabling environments. The national policy environment, which established the basis on which these city centers became competitive, has given way to an increasingly innovative local policy and an entrepreneurial climate that have generated significant advances in ICT, pharmaceuticals, and biotechnology. Large and small firms, universities, and government laboratories have all played a part in creating these centers.

Facilitating technological innovation will require governments to function as active promoters of technological learning

This path is not without dangers. One potential problem is that the pendulum could swing too far, so that universities become outposts for government or private sector service functions or engage only in applied research. Incentives need to be calibrated so that as universities continue to produce knowledge, they also seek to transfer that knowledge to useful applications where appropriate. Informed science, technology, and innovation policy needs to account for the fact that universities need to continue to have local relevance while fulfilling broader mandates of education and knowledge acquisition and diffusion.

The need to meet international standards. Local environments are important for technological innovations such as malaria vaccines. But these innovations must keep up with increasingly stringent global regulatory environments. In the pharmaceutical industry, for example, these regulations may be reflected in food safety rules, regulatory requirements, and certification for manufacturing facilities and output quality, based on new trading rules and WTO guidelines (see chapter 7). In the ICT industry, these regulations may take the form of pressure from network externalities and the need to tie into critical mass usage of a certain system or standard. Innovations do not determine the eventual market uptake of the technology or the ability to keep up with regulatory pressures.[2]

Adopting a working mix of institutional, technological, and organizational elements. In both East Asia and the West, successful countries adopted a working mix of institutional, technological, and organizational elements (Lall 2000). The challenge for developing countries is to examine this approach and adapt it to their own conditions. This approach is well suited for development purposes, because it explicitly acknowledges the political as well as institutional and cultural aspects of innovation processes; it stresses the importance of interactions between actors and organizations; it takes into account multiple actors with different roles and goes beyond the "state or market" dichotomy, making room for more "bottom-up" and associative networks; and it highlights interactions between users and producers, assigning an important role to usually neglected actors, such as workers or consumers.

Government as a learning facilitator

Government plays an important role as a facilitator of technological learning. But most governments do so in an implicit way. Facilitating technological innovation will require governments to function as active promoters of technological learning.

There are at least three ways to think about the government's involvement in promoting technological learning. The first, the market mechanism, deals with the supply and demand of technological development. Although science, technology, and innovation policy is often thought of as a manifestation

Developing countries need to create indigenous capacity by training scientists, technologists, and engineers in relevant fields

of the supply side, it has a significant effect on demand-side policies (more traditionally thought of as industrial policy) as well.

Even if indigenous capabilities exist, they may remain uncommercialized. Those who envision and design innovative products and processes need to commercialize them. It is often insufficient for inventors to hand over their findings to the private sector, because the proof of concept itself is not easily transferred. The people who commercialize innovations must not be cut off from research personnel once a project is past the prototyping stage. The web of capabilities needs to remain enmeshed. Effective "systems" of innovation use a variety of skills from many sources at every stage.

Science, technology, and innovation policies must become a core of industrial, agricultural, and services policies. They must create explicit links between market and nonmarket institutions—linking universities and state R&D laboratories to unions, community development organizations, and firms, for example. Technology licensing offices may be one form of link between universities and firms; agricultural extension services may link farmers and companies producing seeds or animal vaccines. The extension approach has worked in developed countries in both the agricultural and the manufacturing sectors. It should be encouraged in developing countries.

Successes and failures, particularly in agriculture and industry, must be documented. These "good" learning practices need to be institutionalized into structured relationships between market and nonmarket organizations.

The second aspect of government facilitation of technological learning is the creation of technology flows—transfers of foreign technologies, domestic diffusion of foreign technologies, or indigenous R&D efforts to innovate. While industrial policy usually covers these, science, technology, and innovation policy often does not, leaving critical elements of acquisition, absorption, and generation of technologies with no immediate link to the marketplace. Countries in which science, technology, and innovation policies form the basis for industrial and agricultural policies or in which the technological frontiers of the sector are moving rapidly can adapt better to global economic fluctuations.

The third way in which government can enhance learning is by strengthening a variety or diversity of learning institutions. The mix of firms, universities, and government can play a significant role. Community development organizations are important sources of innovation and diffusion. They also articulate future directions of governmental science, technology, and innovation policies. Particularly important is government procurement of technology (see chapter 7).

Science, technology, and engineering education
Developing countries need to create indigenous capacity by training scientists, technologists, and engineers in relevant fields. Such a strategy would help address

Business and industrial enterprises are the most critical locus at which learning of economic significance takes place

local concerns (health, food security, infrastructure, and manufacturing). Universities can play a vital role in development, by developing their countries' national innovation systems and their human resources. It is therefore imperative for universities in developing countries to focus on engineering as well as other advanced technological fields. It is necessary to focus on certain key national priority areas and design an action plan accordingly. International organizations, especially UNESCO, should play a leading role in promoting science, technology, and engineering education in developing countries.

The growing presence of multinationals and foreign firms in developing countries provides an additional impetus for these countries to focus on technical education, since these organizations require increasingly skilled and educated workers. Participation in the global economy—through trade, foreign direct investment, and firm location—requires that developing countries hire and train more educated workers in local firms as well, so that new technology can be adopted and adapted.

With the notable exception of some East Asian countries, most developing countries have given education in science and technology low priority. Many developing countries view science and technology as luxuries that are irrelevant to their immediate needs. Another misconception is that technology destroys jobs. Technology has merely changed employment patterns, reducing the number of jobs in production of goods relative to services, increasing the relative importance of high-skill occupations within sectors, and broadening skills within occupations.

Enterprises as the locus of learning

While learning occurs in a variety of institutions, business and industrial enterprises are the most critical locus at which learning of economic significance takes place (box 3.2). Government acts as a facilitator of institutionalizing knowledge acquisition, but the locus of that learning rests in enterprises, both public and private. The structure of industrial organization and the nature of the production process provide returns of varying amounts based on input factors of skilled labor, robust management practices, and other factors of production. The returns to investments that build innovative capacity vary, depending on the resource base, the institutional environment, and other factors.

Enterprises, particularly those involved in manufacturing, show great promise as centers of upgrading technology and organizational practices for developing countries. Enterprises that develop capabilities in design, research, and product development establish themselves along a global value chain that allows for more opportunities and increased profit margins through innovation and product differentiation. Yet manufacturing remains a core skill important to long-term enterprise learning. Historically, industry has been a critical source, user, and diffuser of technological progress and associated skills and attitudes. Industry is therefore not just an input, but also a critical node in

Box 3.2

What do we know about developing firm-level technological capability?

Source: Lall 2000.

1. Technological learning is a conscious and purposive process, not an automatic or passive one. Firms using a given technology need not be equally proficient.

2. Firms do not have full information about technical alternatives. They function with imperfect, variable, and hazy knowledge of the technology they use. There is no uniform, predictable learning curve for a given technology. Each is associated with different risks, uncertainties, and costs. Differences in learning are larger between countries at different levels of development.

3. Firms may not know how to build up the necessary capabilities; learning itself often has to be learned. In a developing country, knowledge of traditional technologies may not be a good base from which to learn how to master modern technologies.

4. Firms cope with uncertain conditions not by maximizing a well-defined function but by developing organizational and managerial routines. These routines are adapted as firms collect new information, learn from experience, and imitate other firms. Learning is path dependent and cumulative.

5. The learning process is highly technology specific, since technologies differ in their learning requirements. Some technologies are more embodied in equipment, while others have greater tacit elements. Process technologies (like chemicals) are more embodied than engineering technologies (machinery or automobiles) and demand different (often less) effort.

6. Different technologies have different degrees of dependence on outside sources of knowledge or information, such as other firms, consultants, capital goods suppliers, or technology institutions.

7. Capability building occurs at all levels—shop floor, process or product engineering, quality management, maintenance, procurement, inventory control, and sound logistics and relations with other firms and institutions.

8. Technological development can take place at different depths. The attainment of a minimum level of operational capability (know-how) is essential to all activity. This may not lead to the development of deeper capabilities. An understanding of the principles of the technology (know-why) requires a discrete strategy to invest in deepening.

9. Technological learning is rife with externalities and interlinkages. It is driven by direct interactions with suppliers of inputs or capital goods, competitors, customers, consultants, and technology suppliers. Other linkages are with firms in unrelated industries, technology institutes, extension services, universities, industry associations, and training institutions.

10. Technological interactions occur within a country and with foreign countries. Imported technology provides the most important input into technological learning in developing countries. Since technologies change constantly, access to foreign sources of innovation is vital to continued technological progress.

the development process. The fact that manufacturing can experiment with endless permutations of inputs in the production process and benefit from the increasing returns to scale of many industrial technologies give it a special place in economic development.

Manufacturing is also an engine of innovation because relative to formal R&D processes, it affords much greater opportunity for experimentation in engineering and production, as well as innovation in the procurement, quality, and

One of the biggest challenges for developing countries is the lack of participation of researchers in enterprises

other management aspects of the organization. Enterprises with manufacturing capability have been critically important historically, not only for creating new products but also for diffusing new processes, organizational practices, and learning opportunities for the labor force. Manufacturing enterprises act as a locus for spreading innovation outward into the agricultural and service sectors.

At the outset, the scope of an enterprise is to master imported technologies and to gradually improve upon them in ways that benefit local production. This process is not simply one of replication (Kim 1997). It involves complex learning activities and interactions with other players in the economy, including the original source of innovation.

Perhaps most important from an institutional and learning standpoint is the historical role played by manufacturing enterprises in spearheading institutional changes, particularly financial and legal changes, to support production processes worldwide. The extent to which these national institutions conform with or diverge from global practice or practices in first-mover countries defines the extent of convergence of learning speeds and economic development across countries.

This is not to say that institutions should be homogeneous. The more national institutions are compatible with or open to other external institutional changes, such as regulatory changes or trading rules, the more governments and local enterprises will be able to make decisions that quickly transform local conditions to reflect the external economic and geopolitical climate. The modernizing environment that was created by governments and firms in East Asia accelerated the investments made and the type of learning that took place across manufacturing enterprises.

The extent to which enterprises, particularly small and medium-size enterprises, can play a role in innovation and social well-being depends largely on the internal skills they have at their disposal. One of the biggest challenges for developing countries is the lack of participation of researchers in enterprises. Programs to help small and medium-size enterprises hire young engineers and other professionals—such as programs implemented in many European countries—can help redress this weakness.

Policy needs in an era of technical change and globalization
Science, technology, and innovation policies for competitive industrialization need to be responsive to rapid technical change and globalization.

Technical change. The rapid spread of information technology, the shrinking of economic distance, and the skill and institutional needs required to use new technologies make the competitive environment more demanding for firms in developing countries. Minimum entry levels in terms of skills, competence, infrastructure, and "connectivity" are higher than they used to be. Specialized education and training are more important and technology support more essential. All these factors increase the need for support of learning by local enterprises. Low wages matter, but they matter less in many industrial activities. Natural protection from large distance and information gaps is diminishing rapidly. The only industry in which competitive capabilities are not necessary is the extraction of natural resources.

Policy needs are direct (allowing enterprises in infant industries time to master new technologies and skills) and indirect (ensuring that skill, capital, technology, and infrastructure markets meet new needs). There is also a need to coordinate learning across enterprises and activities when these are linked in the production chain (imports cannot substitute effectively for local inputs).

The pace of technological change makes it necessary to provide more open access to international technology markets; it also makes it more difficult to anticipate which activities are likely to succeed. The information needs of industrial policy rise in tandem with technological change and complexity.

By raising entry thresholds for competitive industrial activity, technological change increases the need for policy support. Globalization reduces the need for some local capabilities but not others, and it cannot cover a large portion of the industry or countries involved. It makes access to markets and information easier. Governments have to exploit this fully. But the bottom line remains local capabilities. The case for interventions—direct and indirect—remains unchanged. Interventions have to be functional and selective; without promoting technology-specific learning, creating generic skills, infrastructure will not allow countries to develop and use complex technologies.

Does the complexity of technology make this infeasible? Not necessarily. Targeting particular technologies or products may be impractical because of the speed of change and the relocation of production, but targeting at higher levels is feasible—and more important. Such targeting has to be based on careful judgment and on observation of other countries. Technological progress may make the crafting of industrial policy easier if policy is directed at the right level.

Leaving capability development to free market forces alone is likely to result in slow and truncated technological development, with the gap between leaders and laggards rising as technical change accelerates. Some upgrading may take place over time, but it will be slower and more limited than it could be without promotion. Given the speed at which technologies are moving, and path dependence and cumulative causation in capability building, it can mire backward countries in low-growth traps (with inadequate learning and lagging competitiveness), from which market forces will not extract them.

Globalization. Globalization refers here to the spread of integrated production systems that fragment processes and functions and locate them in different countries. This trend poses different challenges to industrial policy from those discussed above, although globalization is closely related to technical change and the narrowing of economic distances.

Multinational corporations are much less willing to share valuable technologies with independent firms that might become competitors

Fragmentation allows countries to develop competitive industrial activities in small niches—one small component or process—and reach huge overseas markets in ways that were not possible just decades ago. The capabilities needed are narrower and more specialized than those required of broader activities. Multinational corporations are prepared to transfer the missing elements of technology, skills, and capital needed to complement local capabilities if they see a competitive product or component for global sourcing at the end of the investment. In the process, they develop new capabilities—mainly production skills—in the affiliates, to the extent needed for efficient production.

The spread of integrated systems, primarily (but not exclusively) under the aegis of multinational corporations, makes it more difficult and risky to adopt the autonomous strategies pursued successfully by Japan, the Republic of Korea, and Taiwan (China). It is much easier for countries to attract particular segments of transnational corporation activities and build on that than to develop local capabilities to match those of affiliates.

Even if they wanted to, local firms today would find it extremely difficult to enter export markets in a major way by emulating the example of original equipment manufacturing (OEM) contractors from the Republic of Korea and Taiwan (China). All of the later entrants into globalized systems—Costa Rica, Malaysia, Mexico, Thailand—have gone the foreign direct investment route. The foreign direct investment regime is less liberal today, and multinational corporations are much less willing to share valuable technologies with independent firms that might become competitors (box 3.3).

Box 3.3

Foreign direct investment alone cannot drive development

While the internationalization of industry is increasing the importance of foreign direct investment in all economies, it is difficult to see how foreign direct investment alone can drive industrial growth in much of the developing world. First, foreign direct investment is concentrated in technology- and marketing-intensive activities, where it is possible for enterprises to develop ownership-specific assets. It does not cover large areas of manufacturing with mundane skill, branding, and technological requirements—the heartland of industrial growth in latecomers to innovation. In countries with solid industrial sectors and liberal foreign direct investment policies, foreign affiliates account for one-third to one-half of manufacturing value-added (their shares are higher in sophisticated activities). Second, attracting foreign direct investment in manufacturing beyond the simplest resource extractive and labor-intensive activities needs strong local capabilities. Third, retaining an industrial base with a strong foreign presence requires rapidly rising capabilities that allow investors to operate competitively with changing technological and skill needs. Fourth, foreign direct investment is attracted increasingly to efficient agglomerations of industrial activity, which require strong local capabilities. Finally, the cumulative nature of capabilities means that once foreign direct investment takes root in particular locations and global sourcing systems become established, it becomes more difficult for newcomers to break in, particularly in more complex activities and functions. First-mover advantages mean that latecomers face increasing entry costs. Without strong local capabilities they will find it difficult to overcome these costs.

Attracting export-oriented foreign direct investment in a very competitive field requires selective policies that promote and target foreign direct investment

Globalization does not do away with the need for selective industrial policies, it simply reduces the scope and raises the potential cost of some. Foreign direct investment is not a substitute for local enterprises or capabilities; beyond a certain level of development the two are complements. Strong local capabilities raise the possibility of attracting high-value systems and capturing skill and technology spillovers from them; developing these capabilities requires selective policies.

Attracting export-oriented foreign direct investment in a very competitive field requires selective policies that promote and target foreign direct investment. The most effective targeting is probably undertaken by investment promotion agencies in industrial economies.

How far can globalized production systems spread across the developing world, and how much do they offer to industrial development in poor countries with low capabilities? Fragmented production is characteristic of only some industries, in which production processes can be readily separated in technological and geographical terms and where differences in labor costs significantly affect the location of each process. In low-technology industry fragmented production is important in clothing, footwear, sporting goods, and toys. In medium-technology industry fragmented production is important in automobiles, but the weight of the product and its high basic capability requirements mean that production takes place in only a few proximate, relatively industrial locations. In high-technology industry fragmented production is important in electronics. This leaves a broad range of industries in which foreign direct investment and exports are not driven by global production systems.

Where such systems do exist, they are likely to continue relocating to lower-wage countries in only some activities. Low-technology industries are the most likely candidates, because of relatively low entry levels, but the abolition of the Agreement on Textiles and Clothing (formerly the Multi-Fibre Agreement) raises the specter that apparel production will shift back to East Asia rather than spread across other developing countries. Trade liberalization will probably deprive many newer entrants of their most important manufactured exports. The U.S. African Growth and Opportunity Act (AGOA), which liberalized trade between the United States and Sub-Saharan Africa, has stimulated the growth of clothing exports by several countries, led by Lesotho. In the absence of strong local capabilities, however, it is not clear that such protection will have a lasting effect on industrial development.

In high-technology production systems like electronics, the picture is different. It is more difficult to enter this sector today than it was in the late 1960s, when the industry sought low-wage, semi-skilled labor in East Asia. Production techniques have advanced and systems have settled into their new locations, with established facilities, logistics, infrastructure, and support institutions. These systems are unlikely to spread to less industrial

Technological learning involves bringing together a wide variety of disciplines, research cultures, and traditions

sites. New entry is possible—China entered the field, for example—but most poor countries lack the capability, size, and other advantages of China, which continues to promote selective industrial policies that are beyond the reach of many other countries. Most observers agree that the prospects of complex global production systems spreading to Africa, parts of Latin America, or the Middle East and North Africa region are dim.

It is possible that new globalizing systems will emerge in other industries to catalyze the growth of production driven by foreign direct investment in new sites. But these industries may have even more demanding needs in terms of skills, technology, and infrastructure.[3] Given the advantages of clustering in locations with established capabilities, new systems are likely to congregate in successful countries rather than in countries without solid industrial bases.

The contrasting experiences of Sub-Saharan Africa (excepting South Africa) and Latin America and the Caribbean suggest that significant value-addition will occur only where a base of industrial capabilities exists.

Industrialization in the developing world continues to face many of the same constraints it did before the spread of integrated production systems. The need to foster the development of local capabilities remains the bottom line. Globalization offers an alternative route only in some activities in some countries—and even to them only for some time. Selective and functional policies are required, but their design must take account of the real lessons of the Asian Tigers and of the broad range of possible choices, and they must reflect local economic conditions and government capabilities.

Technological convergence and institutional change

Technological learning involves bringing together a wide variety of disciplines, research cultures, and traditions. It is largely a product of convergence between different technological traditions (covering modern and traditional knowledge) and therefore demands significant investment in coordination and management. A major hurdle preventing the commitment of the science, engineering, and technology community to sustainable development is its preoccupation with maintaining and strengthening its own disciplinary turf. Achieving the Goals requires a cross-disciplinary and holistic approach. Science, engineering, and technological knowledge is not created within a single office or laboratory; an active process of sharing insights, problems, issues, experimental approaches, and outcomes creates knowledge. This occurs among people who have common interests but who may not be in the same field.

The most interesting findings are increasingly emerging from the nexus of two or more fields of science and technology. As science, technology, and innovation institutions are created, nurtured, and encouraged in developing countries, it is important to tie their missions to specific problems and to enable a rich cross-sectoral exchange of knowledge to occur. Care should be taken not to create a physics center that is physically distant from the chemistry

The biggest obstacle to cross-sectoral learning is the narrow specialization that characterizes the search and application of knowledge

laboratory. The sciences and technologies emerging from these disciplines grow by interaction. The social sciences are also an integral part of this process, creating a context in which to understand the source, modes of creation, dissemination, and impact of science and technology.

Promoting convergence across many areas of science, engineering, and technology means encouraging organization that enables flows of information across them. This can be done using ICT, as well as by pointing out the success stories of universities and research institutions that have "deinstitutionalized" their departments and encouraged cross-sectoral research. One way of promoting convergence is to develop a style and method of technology assessment such as that of the Netherlands Office of Technology Assessment, where social and economic goals in need of innovation are translated into R&D programs.

The biggest obstacle to cross-sectoral learning is the narrow specialization that characterizes the search and application of knowledge. Organizing research efforts by problems rather than by disciplines is a good way of fostering cross-sectoral learning. The problem is that researchers usually do not know how their knowledge can be utilized to address developmental problems. It is the responsibility of policymakers to devise strategies to help researchers find out how they can contribute to development. This is especially important in the new technologies highlighted in chapter 4 (ICT, biotechnology, nanotechnology, materials science, and spatial information technology).

Conclusion

Economies change over time through processes of social learning that involve the generation, use, and diffusion of new knowledge. New knowledge drives economic systems. While government acts as a facilitator, technological capabilities accumulate in enterprises. This interactive process is incomplete without the inclusion of knowledge-based institutions. Economic transformation no longer occurs in a world in which macroeconomic interventions trigger the process of economic adjustment. Economic transition now involves a mosaic of complex interactions involving a wide range of players. The role of knowledge—expressed in the form of technological change and institutional innovation—lies at the center of this process.

2

Gearing up

Chapter 4

Platform technologies with wide applicability

Most developing country governments acknowledge that science, technology, and innovation are important tools for development. But their policy approaches differ considerably. Most countries still distinguish between science, technology, and innovation policies designed to focus on the generation of new knowledge through support for R&D and industrial policies that emphasize building manufacturing capabilities. Convergence of the two approaches would focus attention on the use of existing technologies while building a foundation for long-term R&D activities.

This approach requires that attention be paid to existing technologies, especially platform (generic) technologies that have broad applications for or impacts on the economy. Until recently, countries relied on investment in specific industries (textiles, automobile manufacturing, chemicals) with broad linkages in the productive sector to stimulate economic growth. Policy attention has now turned to ICT, biotechnology, nanotechnology, and new materials as platform technologies whose combined impacts will have profound implications for long-term economic transformation. Their role in meeting the Goals requires policy attention.

Information and communications technology

ICT has created a new way of viewing the ways in which different industrial, agricultural, and service elements link together so that more than just the economic contribution of these different growth segments can be identified. These technologies challenge us to find new ways in which human efforts can enhance institutional life and sustain technological learning in developing economies so that gains in one area can be translated and multiplied as gains in learning in another (box 4.1).

ICT can be applied to meeting the Goals in at least three areas. First, ICT plays a critical role in governance at various levels. Because of the fundamental

While there are many examples of the transformational impact of ICT, there is still much debate about how and to what extent its application relates to the achievement of social goals and economic growth. There is considerable interest in identifying ways of measuring the socioeconomic impacts of ICT and its potential contributions to the implementation of the Goals. Anecdotal claims about the impact of ICT on development need to be accompanied by strong conceptual and methodological foundations. Toward that end, the United Nations' ICT Task Force is working on defining precisely how ICT can be used to further achievement of basic development objectives. Building on the foundation provided by the Goals and the indicators already developed by the United Nations, the task force is conducting a qualitative and quantitative analysis of the role of ICT in supporting each of the Goals. This exercise will identify a series of ICT-specific targets and suggest possible indicators for measuring progress. The overall objective is to design a progress-tracking tool that could be used to illustrate how ICT can help meet each of the Goals.

The initial results of this work were presented at the World Summit on the Information Society in Geneva in December 2003. Work is continuing, in particular by identifying a group of pilot countries in which the proposed indicators could be used to help governments assess their progress in using ICT to achieve the Goals.

link between technological learning and the ways societies and their industrial transformations evolve, it is important to situate technological innovation and the application of ICT at the center of governance discussions. Second, ICT can have a direct impact on efforts to improve people's lives through better information flows and communications. Third, ICT can enhance economic growth and income by raising productivity, which can in turn improve governance and the quality of life.

The benefits of the new technologies are the result not only of an increase in connectivity or broader access to ICT facilities per se. They accrue from the facilitation of new types of development solutions and economic opportunities that ICT deployment makes possible. When strategically deployed and integrated into the design of development interventions, ICT can stretch development resources farther by facilitating the development of cost-effective and scalable solutions.

Networking technology can be deployed to enable developing countries to benefit from new economic opportunities emerging from the reorganization of production and services taking place in the networked global economy. ICT will become one of the main enablers in the pursuit of poverty alleviation and wealth creation in developed and developing countries alike. At the same time, as a facilitator of knowledge networking and distributed processing of information, ICT can be used to foster increased sharing of knowledge.

ICT differs from other development sectors and technologies—and not simply because of its status as a lucrative source of revenue and taxation for business and government. As accelerator, driver, multiplier and innovator, both established ICTs (radio, television, video, compact disc) and new ICTs (cell

Central to the Goals is ICT's power to store, retrieve, sort, filter, distribute, and share information

phones, the Internet) are powerful if not indispensable tools in the massive scaling up and interlinkage of development interventions and outcomes inherent in the Goals.

ICT is a powerful enabler of development goals because it dramatically improves communication and the exchange of knowledge and information, strengthening and creating new social and economic networks. ICT is pervasive and cross-cutting and can be applied to the full range of human activity, from personal use to business and government uses. It allows people with access to networks to benefit from exponentially increasing returns as network usage increases (network externalities). It fosters the dissemination of information and knowledge by separating content from physical location.

ICT can also radically reduce transactions costs. Central to the Goals is ICT's power to store, retrieve, sort, filter, distribute, and share information, which can lead to substantial efficiency gains in production, distribution, and markets. ICT is also global in nature, transcending cultural and linguistic barriers as it challenges policy, legal, and regulatory structures within and between countries.

Given current rates of progress many countries and regions will be unable to meet the Goals by 2015 (World Bank 2003). To catalyze progress, new models and modalities of operation and implementation are required in key areas, ranging from policy to partnership to resource mobilization. ICT, a fundamentally generic technology, will likely have the greatest impact on achievement of the Goals, because it anticipates and foreshadows many of the critical socioeconomic growth and development models and modalities of the future.

Even within the science, technology, and innovation community itself, the seismic changes continuing to occur in computing and communications are often underestimated. For example, progress in computing is providing the foundation for innovation in industries as far afield as wireless communications and genomics. This "ripple effect" will continue to expand with the exponential growth of processing power, storage capacity, and networking bandwidth. The processing power available at a given price currently doubles every 18 months, storage capacity per unit area doubles every year, and the volume of data that travels across a fiber optic cable doubles every 9 months. The impact of this technological progress has only just begun to be felt. It will be profound.

The ripple effects from the Internet are at an embryonic stage of development. Already the fastest-growing communications medium in history, the Internet marks the beginning of the technological convergence between telephone, television, and computer. Reversing the relations between quality, functionality, and price, it has already turned telecommunications orthodoxy on its head. Today the Internet is being run on top of the telephone network. Tomorrow telephony will run on top of the Internet.

Not only is an almost entirely unregulated network threatening to topple its highly regulated predecessor, but the Internet and other ICTs embody

New network economics and dynamics have combined multiple "positive feedback mechanisms" and "network effects"

many of the elements of the future communications marketplace—the arrival of local-global calls, the onset of freeware, the separation of networks and provision of services, the availability of affordable mass access, and the provision of scalable broadband communications. The implications for developing countries of a global Internet grid—cheap, reliable, and always on—are too compelling to ignore.

Converging fields, common interests

The field of ICT for development is at a turning point. The past decade has witnessed the most dramatic growth in the history of global computing and communications, with the near ubiquitous spread of mobile telephony and the Internet. But the gap between people with access to local and global networks and people without such access is widening.

Narrowing this gap represents an enormous challenge. The means to meet this challenge are already within reach; failure to urgently and meaningfully exploit them may consign many developing countries, particularly least developed countries, to harmful and possibly permanent exclusion from the network revolution.

Within the development community, there is growing awareness that failure to include developing countries in the ICT revolution will have serious consequences for achievement of the Goals. Harnessing the strategic and innovative use of ICT in development policies and programs may enable the world to meet the Goals. Without such technology, doing so by 2015 will be impossible.

In 2000, the same year as the Millennium Summit, two major multistakeholder initiatives were launched, the G8 Digital Opportunity Task Force and the UN ICT Task Force, in an attempt to address the growing digital divide and its repercussions for social and economic development. With the planned comprehensive review of the progress made in the fulfillment of all the commitments in the United Nations Millennium Declaration by the United Nations in 2005 and the second phase of the World Summit on the Information Society in 2005, the global ICT and Goal initiatives are set to converge. A unique opportunity therefore exists to focus on practical initiative and action to use ICT to meet the Goals.

The network revolution

In recent years the network revolution has forced a radical transformation of both developed and developing economies. New network economics and dynamics have combined multiple "positive feedback mechanisms" and "network effects" with disruptive and discontinuous change. This change encompasses rapidly decreasing technology costs with volume and innovation; vastly increased system development costs, risks, and timescales; new competitive market forces; heightened user expectations; uncertain industry restructuring

ICT cuts across all seven Goals targeted at specific objectives and appears as an Goal itself within the eighth

and financial market behavior; and standardization that is often nonproprietary. In addition, additional network benefits, such as electronic commerce, have appeared.

The economics and dynamics of networks are complex and only partially understood; development is also a complicated process. Analyzing the interaction between the two is therefore very difficult. ICT is multidimensional in nature. It is primarily for this reason that the debate over poverty reduction and the broad and systematic use of ICT in development policy and programs has until quite recently been polarized between skeptics and enthusiasts. Given the need to focus on basic development needs and priorities, such as food, clean water, education, and disease eradication, some view ICT as a luxury. Others view it as almost a panacea for development problems. With the shift from anecdotal to empirical evidence of its full development impact, a more balanced perspective has emerged, in which ICT is no longer seen as an end in itself but rather as a critical enabler in the development process, particularly in the context of the Goals.

There is already a strong correlation between ICT and the Goals based on a mutually shared objective: the efficient, scalable, affordable, and pervasive delivery of services to the masses. ICT cuts across all seven Goals targeted at specific objectives and appears as an Goal itself within the eighth goal ("develop global partnerships for development"), which focuses on how to achieve the first seven goals.

Rapid progress to date has been made toward Goal 8, target 18, which is on track. The International Telecommunications Union estimates that access to telephone networks in developing countries tripled in the 10 years between 1993 and 2002, rising from 11.6 subscribers per 100 inhabitants to 36.4. By the end of 2002 there were more mobile cellular subscribers than fixed telephone lines in the world. Growth has been particularly strong in Africa, where an increasing number of countries now have more mobile phones than fixed telephones.

Growth in personal computers and the Internet has been equally impressive. By the end of 2002 there were an estimated 615 million computers in the world, up from only 120 million in 1990. In 1990 just 27 economies had direct connection to the Internet; by the end of 2002, almost every country in the world was connected, and some 600 million people worldwide were using the Internet. Growth has been most rapid in developing countries, where 34 percent of users resided in 2002, up from only 3 percent in 1992 (ITU 2003).

ICT has obvious benefits for economic growth, including pro-poor growth. But it is as a generic technology and development enabler (Goals 1–7) rather than a stand-alone production sector (Goal 8) that it will most affect the Goals: by creating new social and economic opportunities, promoting greater participation in development policies and processes, and increasing the efficiency, accountability, and delivery of public services.

Making the case for the strategic deployment of ICT to support the Goals requires demonstrating the technology's impact

Missing links

Ironically, the great self-sustaining, self-replicating, and multistakeholder enterprise that constitutes the global Internet seems to have acquired the attributes of a global public good almost by accident. The missing links in the Internet value chain not only mirror the missing links in the development value chain, they also impinge on precisely the areas of difficulty and contention faced by the Goals in meeting the 2015 agenda: intellectual property rights, the integration of infrastructure, empowerment of youth and women, and viral growth models for very large-scale projects and initiatives. Most experts concede that the Goals can be attained only if initiatives are promoted at the global level and that these global initiatives must embed growth models based on sustainability, self-replication, and broad partnerships, as evidenced in Internet-based efforts today.

The fact that ICT can act as a powerful development enabler does not mean that it will necessarily do so. In order for ICT to foster development goals, it must be employed where relevant, appropriate, and effective. Perennial cross-sector complexities and issues must be overcome within existing approaches to ICT for development. These include full demonstration of development impact, integration and prioritization within national development and poverty reduction programs, policy realignment on basic infrastructure deployment, improved government and donor coordination and cooperation, increased private sector engagement; and enhanced mechanisms for resource mobilization.

Making the case for the strategic deployment of ICT to support the Goals requires demonstrating the technology's impact. Few studies or strategies outline a strategic programmatic vision with regard to ICT and development in terms of benchmarks, goals, and indicators. It is generally agreed that the indicators proposed by target 18 of the Goals—the number of telephones and personal computers—are inadequate as measures of development impact on poverty, health, education, empowerment, or the environment.

Awareness of the development potential of ICT is often not fully reflected in the formulation of national e-strategies, many of which lay primary emphasis on the development of ICT as a new growth and export sector or focus on ICT as enabler in a piecemeal fashion. National development strategies in general and poverty reduction strategies in particular provide the framework for focusing on core development priorities, but they fail to fully integrate or mainstream ICT. According to the OECD (2003), of the 29 Poverty Reduction Strategy Papers (PRSPs) of Heavily Indebted Poor Countries (HIPC) in 2003, only 12 defined or positioned ICT as a strategic component of poverty reduction and addressed it as an independent item in their PRSPs.

With the trend toward deregulating and privatizing the global telecommunications industry in the 1990s, development banks and national donor agencies effectively withdrew from public infrastructure finance, ceding the way to the private sector. In hindsight, this decision was premature. Market and

Development projects using ICT have had difficulty moving beyond pilots to mass-market deployment

regulatory failures, particularly in Sub-Saharan Africa, have led to privatized state entities that retain monopoly control, limiting competition and reducing network investment. While mobile cellular networks are believed to have brought some 80 percent of the world's population within reach of a telephone, licensing conditions have failed to extend coverage to rural and remote areas. Reappraisal of the role of the private sector in the provision of basic telecommunications infrastructure is urgently needed.

Development projects using ICT have had difficulty moving beyond pilots to mass-market deployment. This has been due partly to lack of coordination and duplication by donor agencies and government initiatives within countries, with competition for volume taking precedence over impact. Local actors and local content have also been underemphasized in many initiatives. Both donors and governments have been slow to foster the requisite private sector participation at the earliest stage of project implementation, which is essential to ensure buy-in and long-term investment. Innovative public-private or broad partnerships between government, business, and civil society, which combine core complementary competencies and share financial risk, are increasingly viewed as essential for large-scale ICT for development projects. But the number of such partnerships remains small.

The private sector has an enormous role to play in ICT for development, in advocating for pro-poor growth strategies; integrating private sector development and poverty reduction strategies; helping create enabling legal and regulatory environments; providing finance and mitigating risk; developing human and social capital and innovation; developing product, commodity markets, and trade; investing in and deploying infrastructure; and interacting with donors and donor organizations. Although the role played by the private sector has significantly increased in the digital era, investment shortfall due to the global technology downturn means that nurturing of their involvement by donors and governments will be required for some time to come.

The most important issue concerning mainstreaming ICT to help achieve the Goals is resource mobilization. The developing countries believe that enough evidence exists to justify a massive billion dollar financial contribution and a special fund aimed at bridging the digital divide. The developed countries remain reticent to commit to this level of contribution and unwilling to establish a new financial mechanism. In this context, the UN Task Force on Financial Mechanisms for ICT for Development will attempt to play a catalytic role.

Applying information and communication technology to specific Goals
ICT and technology "push" projects are generally ill suited to fulfilling the requirements of the Goals. "Pulling" ICT into development projects where appropriate and relevant at an early stage—often with a mix of traditional and new media—to achieve greater efficiency and service delivery will have greater

**Consensus is
building in the
development
community
on the need
to focus
attention
on ICT
interventions
that match
local
needs and
conditions**

impact on poverty reduction. The success of the shift from push to pull will depend on fully integrating ICT into national development plans and PRSPs at an early stage and prioritizing ICT in sectors in which the potential benefits are greatest.

Research has shown that the greatest Goal benefits have accrued to countries that have adopted and implemented bottom-up and holistic e-strategies that are aligned with overall national development strategies. These countries have brought ICT to bear on all of the diverse components of national development agendas, such as governance and institution building; infrastructure and access; and health, education, and capacity building; local content development. They have created enabling policy and regulatory environments that stimulate competition, entrepreneurship, commerce, investment, job creation, and growth. Their success suggests that when a set of interrelated conditions is pursued simultaneously, the interplay among them becomes catalytic, creating a development or Goal dynamic (UNDP 2001).

One of the difficulties of comprehensive acceptance by government and business of the role of ICT in supporting the Goals is the continued lack of hard data on the impact of ICT interventions and of its potential to scale and replicate. What would be the impact on pro-poor growth strategies of blanket, national mobile cellular coverage or broadband in a country? How would Internet access in and between major cities and global connectivity affect the Goals? What is the role of knowledge and information in achieving the first seven Goals? What can ICT do to contribute to empowerment and the PRSP process, to improve the efficiency of public service delivery, and to enhance livelihoods?

Eradicating poverty and hunger. The multidimensional nature of poverty has complex causes. Apart from lack of material wealth and possessions, poor people are often deprived of basic nutritional, educational, and healthcare needs. In addition, they are denied access to knowledge and information, a primary source of economic opportunity and political empowerment, rendering them vulnerable and prey to social exclusion. ICT can be viewed as both an accelerating and driving force as well as an outcome of human development.

Promoting opportunities for the poor is an essential element of poverty reduction. Consensus is building in the development community on the need to focus attention on ICT interventions that match local needs and conditions and concentrate efforts in four principal areas (World Bank 2003):

- Stimulating macroeconomic growth, through the contribution of the ICT sector to the economy and the effect of investment in ICT on economic growth and job creation.
- Increasing the market access, efficiency, and competitiveness of the poor through microlevel and people-oriented interventions (using village payphones, for example, and knowledge centers that improve

Box 4.2

Village phones in Bangladesh are bringing telephone access to 70 million people

Source: OECD 2004.

An impressive example of the development impact of ICT partnership comes from the OECD's updated analysis of Bangladesh's village payphone operator, GrameenPhone. Originally held back by local regulatory constraints and overambitious growth forecasts, the venture has since taken off. Since 1997 GrameenPhone has provided some 45,000 telephones to 39,000 villages in Bangladesh, bringing telephone access to some 70 million people. The village phone model has been successfully replicated in Uganda.

In 2003 GrameenPhone was the largest source of foreign direct investment ($230 million) and the second-largest corporate taxpayer ($280 million) in Bangladesh. The company is now leveraging its market power to lobby the government to ease punitive taxation so that it can boost network investment (as a provider of flood disaster relief, the company provides a public good) and introduce innovations, such as $0.50 prepaid scratch cards.

agricultural practices through access to information on crop selection, irrigation, fertilizers, and fishing and livestock conditions) (box 4.2).

- Increasing interactivity, making ICT continuously available, reducing its cost and global reach, and making social inclusion of poor and disadvantaged groups more feasible.
- Facilitating political empowerment, with improved planning in the PRSP process through inclusive, informed priority setting, increasing accountability, and good governance.

Improving primary education. More than 370 million of the world's 1.3 billion school-age children (28 percent) are not in school. Most live in Sub-Saharan Africa, South Asia, and parts of Latin America, the Caribbean, and the Middle East.

The problem of poor schooling and lack of schooling is unlikely to improve without major interventions. An additional 15–35 million educated and trained teachers will be needed over the next decade if all countries are to achieve the Goal of universal primary education by 2015.

The basic building blocks of a good education system—teachers, infrastructure, curriculum and content, teaching and learning tools, and administration—are missing in many developing countries. ICT can help overcome many of these deficits in an efficient way (Hepp and others 2004). ICT-based distance training can overcome the shortage of well-trained teachers by accelerating their training. Ineffective distribution of content can be tackled through ICT-based delivery of content. Administration can be streamlined through basic ICT applications.

Although pilot projects in the Researching ICT for Education in Africa Program (ICT4E) have shown the potential of ICT in schools, it is essential to move beyond these pilots and create comprehensive, demand-driven, coordinated "end-to-end" systems. Creating such systems will require bringing together coalitions of stakeholders in each country or region to plan and

ICT promotes gender equality by providing online opportunities that are not always available in the off-line world

implement national or regional e-schools initiatives. These initiatives will require technical, financial, and other support from global players, especially donors and relevant private sector companies.

The Global eSchools and Communities Initiative (GeSCI), founded by the United Nations and the governments of Canada, Ireland, Sweden, and Switzerland, will aim to catalyze and support national and regional e-school initiatives that bring together local actors under the leadership of the local ministries of education and ICT. GeSCI will help countries plan and connect to global partners who can provide expertise or financial support. Currently working in Bolivia, Ghana, Namibia, and Andhra Pradesh in India, GeSCI emphasizes the fact that ICT in schools has impact far beyond the classroom, yielding enormous benefits to local communities in the form of employment, adult education, health, business services, communication, and e-government.

The role of ICT in education is limited by the absence of business models that take advantage of the emergence of a wide range of versatile devices that can be adapted to various uses. For example, satellite technology could be combined with memory and audio devices to create libraries of educational materials in rural areas in developing countries. What is missing is not devices but the lack of content development. Partnerships between the ICT, media, and entertainment industries and actors from developing countries could help find ways to put existing technologies to educational uses. In addition to building the foundation for participation in creative industries, such partnerships could also revolutionize education through the use of animation in the design of teaching material (Lowe 2003).

Although the Goals focus on primary education, the role of education at other educational levels is also important (de Ferranti and others 2003). A good example of the use of ICTs to promote tertiary learning is the African Virtual University, created in 1997 as pilot project of the World Bank (box 4.3).

Working toward gender equality. Goal 3 seeks to "eliminate gender disparity in primary and secondary education preferably by 2005 and in all levels of education no later than 2015." ICT can be used to influence public opinion on gender equality, increase economic opportunity, improve women's education and conditions for women as educators, and enhance women's ability to know their rights and participate in decisionmaking.

ICT promotes gender equality by providing online opportunities that are not always available in the off-line world. The Internet allows women to interact with men from remote locations, without face-to-face contact. ICT helps female entrepreneurs reduce transactions costs, increase market coverage, and expand across borders. The Self-Employed Women's Association (SEWA) of India use mobile village phones, the Internet, satellites, and television to promote the artisan handicrafts of the 5,000 women who belong to the network and to provide them with access to market information.

Box 4.3

The African Virtual University is reaching thousands of young Africans— including many who might not have attended a traditional university

Source: http://www.avu.org/.

Headquartered in Nairobi, Kenya, the African Virtual University (AVU) represents an important approach in using ICTs for educational purposes. In its first phase (1997–99), the AVU used the expertise and facilities of the World Bank, with additional support from vice-chancellors from universities in various African countries. In its transitional phase, the AVU established 31 learning centers in 17 African countries. More than 23,000 people were trained in journalism, business studies, computer science, languages, and accounting. Enrollment of women was more than 40 percent, a result of the flexibility offered by distance learning.

Since 2002 the AVU has expanded its activities to all African regions, offering degree and diploma programs. The program is focusing simultaneously on research and development of its technology delivery model. It aims to disseminate the pedagogy model as well as the general technology infrastructure in partner universities.

The AVU has created a network of 33 partner institutions in 18 African countries and registered more than 3,000 students in semester-long courses. It has enrolled a large number of African women in its specialist programs and is affiliated to a global network of leading universities. It is possible that the AVU model could be adopted at the national level, linking national universities and possibly helping universities offer training to neighboring pre-university schools.

Primary responsibility for childcare, cooking, and other household tasks have impeded women's ability to attend school. In some countries social customs make it difficult for women to participate in activities that involve mixing with men. In most developing countries, female school enrollment declines after childbearing age. ICT can help overcome these problems, through distance learning. Women's enrollment for ICT–based teacher training has outnumbered that of men in many countries.

Promoting health. ICT has already had an enormous impact on healthcare in developing countries. It has enabled healthcare workers to conduct remote consultation and diagnosis, access medical information, and coordinate research activities more effectively in the past two decades than in the history of medicine. ICT is an essential component in providing remote health care services, storing and disseminating healthcare information, conducting research, and training and networking health workers. Through both traditional (radio, television, video, CD) and new (wireless, Internet) media, ICT also provides an effective and cost-effective channel for disseminating information on healthcare and disease prevention to the masses.

The role of ICT in achieving health-related Goals is indispensable. ICT is an invaluable tool for both healthcare workers and the international development community in reducing child mortality (Goal 4), improving maternal health (Goal 5), and combating HIV/AIDS, malaria, and other diseases (Goal 6). Childhood diseases prevented 9 percent of the world's children from living to see their third birthday. Healthcare workers can use ICT to establish

ICT plays a key role in environmental management in activities ranging from optimizing clean production methods to decision-making

databases to track vaccination programs, coordinate shipments of antibiotics, and inform communities of medical services that can prevent child mortality.

Maternal death is the leading cause of death for women of reproductive age in the developing world. ICT can critically reduce the incidence of maternal death numbers by facilitating access to information and healthcare services.

In the fight against HIV/AIDS, ICT can strengthen disease monitoring and management, drug distribution systems, disease monitoring and management, drug distribution, training of caregivers, patient education and monitoring, and support networks for people living with HIV/AIDS and the people who care for them. The potential to enhance the response to HIV/AIDS has not yet been fully leveraged in the countries most affected by the crisis. Many of these countries lack the infrastructure and the human capacity (weakened by the toll taken by brain drain and HIV/AIDS) required to implement comprehensive ICT strategies that could improve prevention, treatment, and policy support. The potential of ICT as a cross-cutting tool across the Goals that can add value in addressing the pandemic has not been widely recognized.

Several initiatives to use ICT to prevent and treat HIV/AIDS are currently under way. These initiatives range from networks aimed at enhancing access to knowledge on HIV/AIDS treatments to the use of geographic information systems to map the spread of the disease in relation to socioeconomic variables and treatment (Committee on the Geographic Foundation for Agenda 21 2002). In some cases, clinical information infrastructure systems and simple mechanisms have been used to address the logistics of distribution and monitor the use of essential drugs. Virtual forums and lists have facilitated the discussion of access and treatment, enhanced advocacy, and raised awareness. Evaluations of effectiveness and the identification of good practices and mechanisms to scale up interventions and systems have not yet been conducted. The HIV/AIDS response needs to be cross-sectoral to address the pandemic's multiple dimensions. A more widespread coordination and strategic deployment of ICT that create new synergies and enhance overall response effectiveness are overdue.

Improving environmental management. Goal 7 proposes integrating the principles of sustainable development into country policies and reversing the loss of environmental resources, halving the proportion of people without access to safe drinking water, and achieving significant improvement in the lives of slum dwellers. Managing and protecting the environment improves human health conditions, sustains agriculture and other primary production sectors, and reduces the risks of natural disasters.

The effects of ICT on sustaining the environment are multidimensional. ICT facilitates greater participation by the population in activities to protect the environment through networking and information exchange. It provides researchers with critical tools for observing, simulating, and analyzing environmental processes. It promotes environmentally friendly work habits, by reducing

Molecular diagnostics present a powerful set of methods to address the health-related Goals

paper consumption and facilitating telecommuting; raises awareness of the environment, through knowledge sharing; facilitates environmental monitoring and associated resource management and risk mitigation; enables greater environmental sustainability in other industrial, commercial and agricultural sectors; and improves communication and implementation of policies.

ICT plays a key role in environmental management in activities ranging from optimizing clean production methods to decisionmaking. Spatial information is information related to a particular geographic location or area. It allows analysts to view the distribution of income across a country as a grid in order to target areas for action, understand demographic trends, and monitor progress. Spatial information collected by satellite or airborne remote sensing can be used to understand the capability of the land to support economic activity and water use efficiency. This information can help ensure that natural resources are used efficiently and sustainably.

New technologies are being developed that provide more accurate and timely estimation of risk. Spatial information about fire, rainfall, wind, and salinity may help countries identify and estimate risk more accurately.

A great deal of information is currently available to developing countries for use in making policy decisions. Some of this information (such as that obtained from satellites) is not released. Often the systems or skills needed to manage the data are lacking. Capacity building and information donation or exchange would address this issue.

Biotechnology

Biotechnology has emerged as one of the tools that can be used to address development challenges (Acharya, Daar, and Singer 2003). The realization of this potential, however, depends on a diverse set of policy instruments aimed at translating scientific discoveries into goods and services.[1] A study by the University of Toronto identified 10 biotechnologies as most likely to improve health in developing countries within the next 5–10 years (Daar and others 2002).[2] These biotechnologies included molecular diagnostics, recombinant vaccines, vaccine and drug delivery, bioremediation, sequencing pathogen genomes, female-controlled protection against sexually transmitted infections, bioinformatics, nutritionally enriched genetically modified crops, recombinant therapeutic proteins, and combinatorial chemistry (table 4.1).

Molecular diagnostics

Molecular diagnostics use recent advances in biology to diagnose infectious disease by detecting the presence or absence of pathogen-associated molecules, such as DNA or protein, in a patient's blood or tissue. They present a powerful set of methods to address the health-related Goals.

While improving public health infrastructure to prevent disease is crucial, diagnosis and treatment methods are also essential. Rapid and accurate diagnosis

Table 4.1

Genomics and related biotechnologies that can help countries meet the Goals

Millennium Development Goal	Statistics	Biotechnology to address Goal
Goal 1: Eradicate extreme poverty and hunger	Malnutrition plays a role in more than half of all child deaths.	• Productivity-enhancing biotechnologies • New biotechnology products • Product quality–improving technologies
Goal 3: Promote gender equality and empower women	Women account for 57 percent of HIV cases in Sub-Saharan Africa. Average HIV infection rates in teenage girls are five times higher than rates among teenage boys.	• Female control over sexually transmitted disease protection • Vaccine and drug delivery
Goal 4: Reduce child mortality	About 11 million children die before reaching their fifth birthday (WHO 1998).	• Molecular diagnostics • Vaccine and drug delivery • Recombinant vaccines • Female control over sexually transmitted disease protection • Enriched genetically modified crops • Combinatorial chemistry
Goal 5: Improve maternal health	More than 500,000 maternal deaths occur every year.	• Molecular diagnostics • Vaccine and drug delivery • Recombinant vaccines • Female control over sexually transmitted disease protection • Enriched genetically modified crops • Combinatorial chemistry
Goal 6: Combat HIV, malaria, and other diseases	HIV/AIDS, malaria, and tuberculosis are responsible for about 40 percent (5 million) of all deaths in the developing world. In 2002, 2.8 million people died of AIDS, 1.6 million of tuberculosis, and more than 1.2 million of malaria.	• Molecular diagnostics • Vaccine and drug delivery • Recombinant vaccines • Female control over sexually transmitted disease protection • Bioremediation • Sequencing pathogen genomes • Bioinformatics • Enriched genetically modified crops • Combinatorial chemistry
Goal 7: Ensure environmental sustainability	Waterborne diseases cause 5 million deaths a year.	• Bioremediation

increases the chances of survival, prevents resources from being wasted on inappropriate treatments, and helps contain disease. Many diagnostic tools currently in use in developing countries are cumbersome, time-consuming, and expensive.

Molecular diagnostics can be simple to use and relatively cheap, and produce quick results. These technologies include polymerase chain reaction

Antigens feature in simple handheld test devices capable of providing a diagnosis in minutes

(PCR), monoclonal antibodies, and recombinant antigens. PCR is a quick way of producing millions of copies of a specific sequence of DNA. PCR tests are extremely sensitive and can provide results in a few hours (as opposed to days for culturing methods). They can also be used to detect infectious organisms that are difficult or impossible to grow in culture (such as tuberculosis and malaria) or are dangerous to handle (such as HIV/AIDS).

Antibody-based applications are well suited to the developing world. Antibodies are molecules produced by the immune system in response to infection. They recognize and bind antigens, which are produced by pathogens. The fact that every antibody recognizes and binds to a specific type of antigen makes antibody-based applications excellent tools for diagnosing infectious disease. The recent development of simple antibody-coated dipstick tests, like those used to diagnose malaria and HIV, has increased the relevance of this technology for the developing world, since these tests can be used where clean water and electricity are not accessible and people may have to travel long distances to reach a medical facility.

Recombinant antigens are genetically engineered antigens that are mass-produced by fast-replicating organisms such as bacteria or yeast. Like antibodies, antigens feature in simple handheld test devices capable of providing a diagnosis in minutes. The Oswaldo Cruz Institute in Brazil has developed a commercial diagnostic kit for Chagas disease based on recombinant *Trypanosoma cruzi* antigens.

Recombinant vaccines

Recombinant vaccines can play an important role in achieving Goal 4 (reducing child mortality), Goal 5 (improving maternal health), and Goal 6 (combating HIV/AIDS, malaria, and other diseases). Vaccines stimulate the body to produce a protective immune response against infectious organisms. They are arguably the most important medical advance of the past hundred years. Vaccination has resulted in the eradication of smallpox, the control of polio, and a dramatic reduction in the prevalence of many other infectious diseases.

Until a few decades ago, all vaccines consisted of either killed or inactivated (attenuated) pathogens. Injection of these vaccines stimulated the person's immune system to produce antibodies against the foreign organism, making the person resistant to future infections. Because inactivation is sometimes insufficient, however, the vaccine carries some risk of causing a fatal infection.

Genetic engineering makes it possible to produce single proteins of the pathogen in nonpathogenic microorganisms. This approach produces safer vaccines, since the individual foreign proteins cannot cause the disease. Recombinant vaccines made with only part of the genome of a pathogen are known as *subunit vaccines*.

Recombinant vaccines may also prove cheaper than traditional vaccines, because of innovative production methods and because improved storage characteristics may allow some of them to be maintained without refrigeration.

Scientists are exploring a number of alternatives to needle-based delivery of drugs or vaccines

Much progress is being made in recombinant vaccine development. A major roadblock is the long time it takes to run clinical trials and obtain regulatory approval, which has limited the number of products on the market.

Researchers are working to develop techniques to overcome some of the difficulties with recombinant vaccines, such as the correct presentation of recombinant antigens to the immune system and the limited lifetime of the engineered protein in the body. In 1997 Shantha Biotechnics (www.shantha-biotech.com), an Indian company, launched a recombinant hepatitis B vaccine, which it sells for $0.40 per dose—a fraction of the $8–$10 per cost of the of imported vaccine. The vaccine recently received WHO certification, and UNICEF has ordered 8.5 million doses of it for distribution worldwide.

Viral vector vaccines consist of a benign virus that has been genetically modified to contain genetic material belonging to the pathogen. Upon injection, the virus delivers the genetic material into the cell's nucleus, where the new genes get incorporated into the cell's genome. Naked DNA vaccines, or plasmid DNA vaccines, use a plasmid to introduce the antigen genes into the individual's cells. Plasmids are small circular molecules of DNA normally found in bacteria that can easily enter cells and recruit the cell to translate their genetic information into protein. DNA vaccines are potentially faster, cheaper, and easier to use than other types of vaccines, and because DNA is heat stable these vaccines may be able to bypass refrigerated transport and storage, a major cost barrier to efficient vaccine delivery. Plants such as tomatoes and potatoes can easily be engineered to express foreign proteins. These vaccines can be produced, stored, and transported relatively inexpensively, and they can be grown locally, making them attractive for applications in developing countries.

Vaccine and drug delivery

Closely related to advances in vaccines are improved methods of vaccine and drug delivery, which will help meet Goals 4, 5, and 6. Thousands of children die each year from vaccine-preventable diseases because the logistics of vaccine delivery are prohibitively expensive. Refrigerated transport and storage are a major expense in all vaccine programs. The need to hire trained medical personnel to deliver vaccinations also adds to their cost.

Unsanitary drug and vaccine injections are associated with the spread of bloodborne diseases, particularly HIV and hepatitis. The reuse of needles causes an estimated 80,000–160,000 new cases of HIV/AIDS, 8–16 million new cases of hepatitis B, and 2–4 million new cases of hepatitis C each year (Kane and others 1999). Long and complicated drug regimens are difficult for people to comply with, especially if they involve visits to medical facilities. Partial treatment can lead not only to death but to the emergence of drug-resistant strains of disease.

Injection-free and controlled-release delivery systems could help solve many of these problems. Scientists are exploring a number of alternatives to needle-based delivery of drugs or vaccines. The skin is an attractive route into the

Reduction of pollution in water supplies and the food chain can help reduce mortality and improve health

body because of its easy access. Needle-free injections propel the vaccine or drug through the skin and into the body with a high-speed jet of gas. Solutions, rubbing gels, and skin patches rely on simple diffusion to introduce agents into the body. Another avenue into the body is the mucus membrane, which lines all of the inner cavities of the body, including the intestines and the lungs. Vaccination through nasal sprays and inhalers in the lung membranes generates immunity in the rest of the body's mucus membranes, inducing systemic immunity.

The refrigeration required to store and transport conventional vaccines and drugs is costly. The discovery that some microorganisms can be rejuvenated after complete dehydration has led to the development of powdered vaccines and drugs that are heat stable. These organisms contain a nonreactive sugar (trehalose), which stabilizes them while they are desiccated. With this and other stable sugars, researchers have been able to dehydrate liquid vaccines and drugs and store them at room temperature for up to several months without affecting their potency. Injection devices for dried vaccines have been developed. Some involve the reconstitution of the dried substance into a liquid just before injection, others introduce the substance into the body through the skin as a powder using needles or a high-speed jet of gas.

Improved drug delivery can also help reduce the length and complexity of drug treatment regimens. Controlled-release drugs and vaccines can be introduced into the body in association with a biodegradable polymer that gradually releases its contents as it is broken down by the body. One disease for which this would be very useful is tuberculosis. Sustained-release treatments would lower the number of doses a patient must receive, thereby increasing compliance and limiting the emergence of drug-resistant strains of tuberculosis. Preliminary studies of controlled release antibiotics have been promising. Recently a group has reported the development of temperature-stable, controlled-release formulations using oligosaccharide ester derivatives of trehalose and a synthetic peptide analogue of hepatitis B surface antigen. The ability of these novel delivery systems to induce strong immune responses in mice without the requirement for multiple doses or cold-chain storage is encouraging.

Bioremediation

Bioremediation refers to the use of biological agents like bacteria or plants to clean up the environment (box 4.4). It has direct significance for Goal 7 (ensuring environmental sustainability), but it also has an impact on the health-related goals.

Reduction of pollution in water supplies and the food chain can help reduce mortality and improve health. Two main types of pollution threaten the health and well-being of human populations: organic waste and heavy metals, such as lead, mercury, and cadmium. Bacteria can detoxify both. Plants can break down most forms of organic waste, but, with very few exceptions, they are usually unable to metabolize heavy metals. They can, however, store harmful metals in their tissues, making it easier to collect, harvest, and even recycle metal waste.

Box 4.4

Bangladesh is using bacteria to treat contaminated groundwater

Source: Santini and others 2000.

Naturally occurring contamination of Bangladesh's groundwater is causing what some have called the largest mass poisoning of a population in history. At least 100,000 people have already been affected, and another 50 million people are at risk. A bacterium called NT-26, recently discovered in a gold mine in Australia, may be able to help. NT-26 has the natural ability to transform arsenite, a soluble form of arsenic, into the much less toxic arsenate. The Australian Research Council is supporting research to investigate the potential of NT-26 to reduce the toxicity of arsenic dissolved in water. Knowledge of the genomic sequence of NT-26 could enhance bioremediation tools. Genome Canada plans to sequence the genomes of two arsenic-metabolizing bacteria, including NT-26.

Water contaminated by human waste harbors large amounts of pathogenic organisms and has been implicated in the transmission of cholera, typhoid, hepatitis A, and other waterborne diseases. Sewage treatment can dramatically reduce the incidence of these diseases. Bioremediation techniques can augment conventional chemical sewage treatment.

Several low-cost alternatives to conventional sewage treatment have been developed. One system is in use in southern China. It uses floating rafts, called *restorers,* to supply beneficial microorganisms to a canal contaminated with human waste. This floating ecological treatment engine has been transformed into a garden featuring a dozen species of native Chinese wetland plants.

Bioremediation can also help clean up mosquito-infested water and control the spread of malaria, especially where other control methods have become less effective. The malaria-carrying *Anopheles* mosquito has developed resistance to several chemical insecticides. Many antimalarial prophylactics are losing their efficacy, and they remain too expensive for many people in developing countries.

Canada's International Development Research Centre has supported research at the Instituto de Medicina Tropical Alexander Von Humboldt in Lima to explore the use of bacteria and coconuts in controlling malaria. Researchers at the institute have developed a method of biologically controlling mosquitoes that is a simple, inexpensive, and environmentally safe alternative to insecticides. Coconuts are used to culture bacteria that are toxic to mosquito larvae but harmless to people and other organisms. *Bacillus thuringiensis* var. *israelensis* H-14 *(Bti),* a bacterium that produces a toxin lethal to mosquito larvae, is introduced into the coconut through cotton swabs and allowed to incubate inside the coconut for a few days. The nut is then broken and tossed into ponds where mosquitoes breed. The mosquito larvae eat the bacteria and are killed. A typical pond needs only two or three coconuts for each treatment, usually lasting two months.

Sequencing of pathogen genomes
The sequencing of pathogen genomes has direct relevance to Goal 4 (combating HIV/AIDS, malaria, and other diseases). Pathogen genomics can also contribute to the search for a cure for these diseases.

Genomics and other biotechnologies are enabling the development of new forms of female-controlled protection against sexually transmitted diseases

Sequencing a genome involves discovering and recording the entire sequence of nucleotides in an organism's DNA. DNA codes for proteins, the mainstay of structure and biochemical function in all organisms. Knowledge of the genomic sequence of a pathogen is helpful in unraveling its biology and discovering ways of controlling its relationship with humans.

Most sequencing strategies are based on a technique known as the dideoxy, or Sanger, method. Small-scale sequencing projects can be conducted manually, but large-scale projects (such as the sequencing of an entire genome) require high-throughput automated DNA sequencing machines. Major sequencing projects use many automated sequencing machines simultaneously, yielding millions of bases of sequence data per day. These data must be stored, managed, and analyzed by computers. (This requirement has given rise to an entirely new field in biology, bioinformatics, discussed below.)

Knowing the sequence of a pathogen's genome can accelerate the process of drug discovery. Comparative genomics compares the genomes of different organisms in order to apply information known about one organism to another. In a comparison of disease-causing and benign strains of the same organism, genes unique to the pathogenic strain are likely to play an important role in pathogenesis, and the proteins for which they code may make excellent drug targets. Analysis of pathogen genomes could also identify genes that play a role in helping pathogens develop drug resistance and point researchers toward treatments that can prevent these genes from functioning. Scientists can compare the genomes of resistant and nonresistant strains or analyze the genes at work in the drug-resistant stage of an organism's lifecycle.

Genomics and bioinformatics helped resurrect the little-used antibiotic fosmidomycin as a novel antimalarial drug. Scientists successfully searched the *Plasmodium falciparum* genome for the gene of an enzyme targeted by fosmidomycin (Jomaa and others 1999). Fosmidomycin inhibits the growth of multiresistant strains of *P. falciparum*. It was found to be safe and effective when administered to adults in Gabon with malaria.

Recently, scientists in Brazil and China sequenced two species of the parasite that causes schistosomiasis, *Schistosoma mansoni*, found in Africa and South and Central America, and *Schistosoma japonicum*, prevalent in Asia. The genomic sequences point to potential therapeutic and vaccine targets to manage the disease, which affects more than 200 million people in 74 countries (Hu and others 2003; Verjovski-Almeida and others 2003).

Female-controlled protection against sexually transmitted infections
Genomics and other biotechnologies are enabling the development of a number of new forms of female-controlled protection against sexually transmitted diseases. These biotechnologies include recombinant vaccines, monoclonal antibodies, and new approaches to the development of vaginal microbicides. These technologies can help meet Goal 6 (combating HIV/AIDS, malaria,

Bioinformatics can be used to identify drug targets and vaccine candidates

and other diseases) and Goal 3 (promoting gender equality and empowering women).

The global burden of sexually transmitted diseases is borne most heavily by women. Despite the urgent need to protect themselves against these diseases, women have few options. The condom requires male consent, which many women living in patriarchal societies find hard to negotiate. The female condom's indiscreetness makes it a less than ideal option. Vaginal microbicides are an attractive alternative. These gel or cream formulations of chemical compounds block the transmission of infection across the vaginal wall. Six first-generation vaginal microbicides are now in safety and efficacy trials.[3]

Bioinformatics

Bioinformatics is the use of computer hardware and software to store, retrieve, and analyze large quantities of biological data (box 4.5). High-throughput technologies (DNA sequencers, DNA and RNA microarrays, combinatorial chemistry, two-dimensional gel electrophoresis, and mass spectrometry) have resulted in an explosion in the volume of biological data available. Bioinformatics organizes this sea of data into meaningful databases and conducts sophisticated computer analyses (data mining) to generate answers to research questions.

Bioinformatics applies computer algorithms to transform large-scale biological data sets into useful information. For example, an algorithm could be applied to quickly identify potential drug targets in pathogen genomes. Without bioinformatics, this task would be extremely laborious and prone to error, and it would take scientists years to realize the potential of genomic sequencing.

Many bioinformatics algorithms are available free over the Internet, along with basic tutorials. Many can be found on Web sites with public bioinformatics databases. Their accessibility to scientists helps promote R&D. To help meet the worldwide demand for skilled bioinformaticians, a consortium of six universities is offering a free accredited Web-based course in bioinformatics.

Bioinformatics can be used to identify drug targets and vaccine candidates. The genes that encode most antigens have characteristic sequences. In their

Box 4.5

Researchers can access biological databases over the Internet free of charge

Several biological databases have been established as public resources available to all over the Internet. GenBank is a massive online database of all publicly available gene sequencing. The database, which is maintained by the National Center for Biotechnology Information of the U.S. National Institutes of Health, can be accessed free of charge over the Internet. GenBank exchanges data daily with the DNA DataBank of Japan and the European Molecular Biology Laboratory. SWISS-PROT is a protein sequence database developed by the Swiss Institute of Bioinformatics and the European Bioinformatics Institute. The Molecular Modeling Database, maintained by the National Center for Biotechnology Information, contains three-dimensional biomolecular structures, including information on biological function and the evolutionary history of large molecules.

Vitamin A–enriched golden rice is a well known example of a nutritionally enhanced genetically modified crop

analysis of *Chlamydia pneumoniae* (a cause of respiratory infections), researchers identified 147 cell surface proteins, 58 of which produced an immune response when injected into mice. Bioinformatics techniques helped researchers tackle an organism that had been a challenge to study using conventional laboratory techniques (Grandi 2001).

Nutritionally enriched genetically modified crops

Nutritionally enriched genetically modified crops can help meet the three health-related Goals (reducing child mortality, improving maternal health, and combating HIV/AIDS, malaria, and other diseases). This potential, however, must be viewed against a background of concerns related to environmental, human health, and socioeconomic risks associated with new and existing technologies (J. López, Friends of the Earth International, personal communication, 2004). More than half of all infant deaths in developing countries are associated with a lack of essential vitamins and nutrients. Malnutrition also impairs cognitive and physical development and is associated with multiple illnesses attributed to specific nutrient deficiencies. These include blindness due to Vitamin A deficiency, which affects an estimated 500,000 children in developing countries. Anemia, caused by iron deficiency, is one of the leading causes of maternal mortality. Pregnant women with anemia are more likely to give birth to low birthweight infants and are at increased risk of death during childbirth. Malnutrition, which affects about one in five people in developing countries, amplifies the effects of infectious diseases. Lack of essential vitamins and minerals impairs the immune system, increasing the likelihood that infection will develop into disease and impairing the ability of the body to recover.

Genetically modified crops are crops whose composition has been altered by genetic recombination. The crops are altered by inserting a gene—with a gene gun or a carrier organism, such as a benign virus—into a plant very early during its development so that all of the plant's cells acquire the gene. Various traits can be introduced into crops through genetic modification. One application of genetic modification in crops is to enhance their nutritional value. This type of modification might involve insertion of genes that encode for enzymes that synthesize vitamins.

Vitamin A–enriched golden rice is a well known example of a nutritionally enhanced genetically modified crop, although its future benefits continue to be disputed. Researchers in India have developed a potato rich in all essential amino acids (Chakraborty, Chakroborty, and Datta 2000). The potato contains the gene AmA1, which codes for the protein albumin, which contains high levels of all of the amino acids the body is incapable of making on its own.[5] The gene gives potatoes a third more protein than normal. This enriched potato is particularly important in India, where a large percentage of the population is vegetarian. Scientists believe the protein-rich genetically modified "protato" could help combat malnutrition among India's poorest children.

Some
recombinant
therapeutic
proteins
would be
useful for
developing
country
diseases

Both genetic modification and traditional breeding change the characteristics of an organism. Both forms of breeding can cause unexpected results. In traditional breeding the introduction of a gene into an organism by cross-breeding different strains of the same species is a trial and error process that takes a long time. Genetic recombination makes it possible to complete the process more rapidly and more precisely, and it enables the introduction of new genes from different species. One disadvantage is that that the introduced foreign genes may cause unknown gene-gene or gene-environment interactions. Ecological concerns include risks to human and animal health, food safety, and unforeseen consequences of the spreading of foreign genes into the natural environment. Gene-flow, the natural spread of genetic traits when a plant variety is introduced into the environment, is in itself not alarming, but the potential introduction of cross-species genes and the spread of genes that produce novel traits in related weeds or crops could be. Some scientists believe that extensive testing and careful monitoring are necessary for the world to reap the benefits of this technology while avoiding any potential risks.

Recombinant therapeutic proteins

Therapeutic proteins, such as insulin, are used to treat many noncommunicable diseases. The technology to make recombinant therapeutic proteins is therefore significant for meeting Goal 6. As poorer countries develop, they face a double burden of disease: the burden of infectious diseases as well as the burden of noncommunicable diseases more commonly associated with the developed world. Affordable and sustainable sources of therapeutic proteins for treating these diseases are therefore critical.

Using recombinant technology, researchers can insert a gene or genes for a therapeutic protein into an organism. As the organism grows, it reads and translates the foreign gene with its own genes and produces the therapeutic protein, which can be harvested for use. Bacteria, particularly *Escherichia coli*, were the first organisms to be drafted for the production of therapeutic proteins. Under the right conditions, the bacteria grow and divide rapidly, accumulating the recombinant protein in their interior fluids. Protein purification processes harvest the protein from the bacterial culture.

Bacteria have one main disadvantage: they are extremely simple organisms and lack the ability to make specific chemical modifications to the proteins after the proteins have been formed. Most human therapeutic proteins require these modifications to function normally. As more complex organisms, yeasts can carry out many forms of protein modification, and, like bacteria, they reproduce quickly and easily. Because of its safety and familiarity, *S. cerevisiae* is the most popular yeast for making recombinant proteins. Mammalian cells are still a more attractive source of recombinant therapeutic proteins, since they are capable of almost all posttranslational modifications. Mammalian cell cultures are difficult to maintain, however, and they have a relatively low protein yield. One way

Combinatorial chemistry has a bearing on the health-related Goals, particularly combating HIV/AIDS, malaria, and other diseases

around these limitations is to use transgenic animals that are engineered to secrete the protein in an easily harvested body fluid, such as milk, urine, or semen.

Some recombinant therapeutic proteins that would be useful for developing country diseases include erythropoietin for the treatment of anemia, alpha interferon for the treatment of viral infections and leukemia, and insulin for the treatment of type I diabetes. Insulin from the pancreas of pigs and cattle varies slightly from human insulin, so it may induce an allergic reaction in some diabetics. Recombinant technology has made nonallergenic human insulin available in abundance. Wockhardt, an Indian company, recently became the first firm outside the United States or Europe to develop the technology to produce recombinant human insulin, which it is now selling for less than imported insulin. The patent on recombinant human insulin expired in January 2003, allowing developing countries to manufacture the product locally and at more affordable prices.

Combinatorial chemistry

Combinatorial chemistry has a bearing on the health-related Goals, particularly combating HIV/AIDS, malaria, and other diseases. There are many diseases prevalent in the developing world for which effective and affordable treatments are lacking. And some pathogens, such as those that cause malaria and tuberculosis, are acquiring resistance to the only treatments available. Child mortality is caused in large part by pneumonia, diarrhea, and malaria, three diseases that are acquiring drug resistance. Combinatorial chemistry can be used to provide new or more effective medications for these diseases. It may also help industries in developing countries become competitive and economically viable in the global market. The increase in efficiency also potentially decreases costs, wastes less material, and creates fewer by-products, all of which help protect the environment.

Combinatorial methods are easily automated techniques for making many different kinds of chemical compounds. The resulting collection of compounds, known as a library, is biologically screened to select the compounds with the most therapeutic promise. First developed in the early 1980s, combinatorial chemistry has become a mainstay of drug discovery and development in industrial countries. In many cases, it has replaced the much more costly and time-consuming one-compound-at-a-time method.

Two features make combinatorial chemistry exceptionally efficient for drug discovery and development. First, robots can be used to do most of the preparation and screening of compounds. Second, many unique compounds can be produced from fewer experiments.

Nanotechnology

Nanotechnology is the study, design, creation, synthesis, manipulation, and application of functional materials, devices, and systems through control of

Cost-effective agricultural applications of nanotechnology could decrease hunger, malnutrition, and childhood mortality

matter at the atomic and molecular levels and the exploitation of novel phenomena and properties of matter at that scale.[6] At this scale, matter is affected by quantum effects. Matter at the nanoscale can be more chemically reactive than other matter; sometimes materials that are inert at the macroscale become reactive at the nano-level. Quantum effects at the nano-level can also affect the strength and the optical, electrical, and magnetic properties of materials.

The use of nanotechnology applications for water treatment and remediation; energy storage, production, and conversion; disease diagnosis and screening; drug delivery systems; health monitoring; air pollution and remediation; food processing and storage; vector and pest detection and control; and agricultural productivity enhancement will help developing countries meet five of the Goals. The convergence of nanotechnology with other emerging technologies, such as biotechnology, genomics and information technology, will help implement the Goals.

Nanotechnology may have a significant impact on all areas of human endeavor. According to Richard Smalley, a nanotechnology pioneer who was awarded the Nobel Prize in chemistry in 1996 for his discovery of fullerenes, "the impact of nanotechnology on health, wealth, and the standard of living for people will be at least the equivalent of the combined influences of microelectronics, medical imaging, computer-aided engineering, and man-made polymers in this century" (Smalley 1999). Nanotechnology is likely to be particularly important in the developing world, because it involves little labor, land, or maintenance; it is highly productive and inexpensive; and it requires only modest amounts of materials and energy. Nanotechnology products will be extremely productive, as energy producers, as materials collectors, and as manufacturing equipment.

Nanotechnology can contribute new tools with which to address sustainable development problems, and it can strengthen the technologies already available and make them more efficient. It will coexist with rather than replace established technologies. Its impact will be felt in multiple ways, depending on how other technologies converge and align themselves around it.

Advances in nanotechnology tend to be geared toward the interests of industrial countries. Applications for cosmetics, sports apparel, and various digital gadgets do not address the pressing needs of the more than 5 billion people in developing countries.

Significant nanotechnology activity is already occurring in developing countries (table 4.2). This activity may be derailed by a debate that fails to take account of the perspective of developing countries. The evolution of nanotechnology can benefit from the lessons learned from previous technologies. The aim should be to encourage public discourse and consider potential benefits for the developing world.

Reducing hunger

Cost-effective agricultural applications of nanotechnology could decrease malnutrition, and childhood mortality, in part by increasing soil fertility

Table 4.2

Research and development on nanotechnology in selected developing countries

Nanotechnology status	Countries	Nanotechnology activity	Example
Frontrunner	China, India, Republic of Korea	• National government-funded nanotechnology program • Nanotechnology-related patents • Commercial products on the market or in development	*China* • National Center for Nanoscience and Nanotechnology • Clinical trials of nanotechnology bone scaffold *India* • Nanomaterials Science and Technology Initiative • Commercialization of nanoparticle drug delivery *Republic of Korea* • Nanotechnology Development Program • World's first carbon nanotube field emission display
Middle ground	Brazil, Chile, the Philippines, South Africa, Thailand	• Development of national government-funded nanotechnology program • Some government support (research grants) • Limited industry involvement • Numerous research institutions	*Brazil* • Institute of Nanoscience, Federal University of Minas Gerais *Chile* • Nanotechnology Group, Pontificia Universidad Católica de Chile *Philippines* • University of the Philippines/Intel Technology Philippines optoelectronics project *South Africa* • South African Nanotechnology Initiative *Thailand* • Center of Nanoscience and Nanotechnology, Mahidol University
Up and comer	Argentina, Mexico	• Organized government funding not yet established • Industry not yet involved • Research groups funded through various science, technology, and innovation institutions	*Argentina* • Nanoscience research group, Centro Atómico Bariloche and Instituto Balseiro *Mexico* • Department of Advanced Materials, Instituto Potosino de Investigación Científica y Tecnológica

and crop productivity. Crop health can be monitored using nanosensor arrays. Nanosensors can raise the efficiency of crop monitoring activities. Sensors applied to the skin of livestock or sprayed on crops can help detect the presence of pathogens. Nanoporous materials such as zeolites, which can form well-controlled stable suspensions with absorbed or adsorbed substances, can be

Nanotech-nology can enable rapid, accurate, timely, and affordable methods of diagnosis and prevention

employed for the slow release and efficient dosage of fertilizers for plants and of nutrients and drugs for livestock.

Promoting health

Applications of nanotechnologies addressing health in developing countries are especially promising, particularly for diagnostic tools, drug and vaccine delivery, surgical devices, and prosthetics. Nanotechnology can enable rapid, accurate, timely, and affordable methods of diagnosis and prevention, which can allow more effective treatment with existing drugs. It can help detect pathogens, such as mycobacteria and HIV.

Nanotechnology-based solutions in developing countries will depend on cost, supply, and ease of use, especially where a wide range of screening can occur with relatively inexpensive sensors in local clinics using diagnostic kits. Microfluidic devices (lab-on-a-chip), carbon nanotube-based biosensor arrays, fluorescent semiconductor nanoparticles, magnetic nanoparticles, and quantum dots offer significant diagnostic advantages over conventional fluorescent dyes. Dendrimers, in conjunction with antibodies, have been designed to detect HIV and cancer. Atomic wires and nanobelts can be used to detect cancer, since these nanomaterials are capable of revealing specific malignant agents through changes in their electronic transport characteristics.

Nanotechnology can also be applied to synthesize and target the delivery of drugs. It provides encapsulation systems that can protect drugs while slowly delivering and releasing them. This capability can be very valuable in countries without adequate drug storage capabilities and distribution networks. Long-term delivery obviates the need for patients to take pills daily at well-defined times. Polymers for the slow release of drugs can be especially useful for drug regimens that are long and complex, such as those used to treat tuberculosis. Nanotechnology can also reduce transportation costs and even required dosages by improving the shelf-life, thermo-stability and resistance to changes in humidity of existing medications. A more specific and selective delivery of drugs and vaccines can be obtained by the use of nanocapsules, liposomes, dendrimers, and buckyballs. Other areas of bio-nanotechnology that are being actively researched include regenerative medicine and nanoscale surgery. Nanoceramics can be used to produce more durable medical prosthetics.

Improving water and sanitation

More than 2 million children die each year from water-related diseases, such as diarrhea, cholera, typhoid, and schistosomiasis, which result from a lack of adequate water and sanitation services. Arsenic, fluoride, and nitrates threaten water supplies in many regions. In some cities in the developing world, only 10 percent of sewage is treated. Conventional bacterial and viral filters trap pathogens inside granular carbon or porous ceramic or polymer materials. These filters are often difficult to clean and must be changed frequently.

Harnessing renewable energy sources through cleaner, more affordable, and more reliable technologies can prevent the dependency of developing countries on fossil fuels

Nanomembranes and nanoclays are cheap, easily transportable, and cleanable systems that can purify, detoxify, and desalinate water. Filters made of carbon nanotubes have been developed by researchers at Banaras Hindu University in Varanasi, India, in collaboration with researchers at the Rensselaer Polytechnic Institute, in the United States. Nanosensors for the detection of contaminants and pathogens can improve health, maintain a safe food and water supply, and allow for the use of otherwise unusable water sources. Nano-electrocatalysts for anodic decomposition of organic pollutants and for the removal of salts and heavy metals from liquids will permit the use of heavily polluted and heavily salinated water for drinking, sanitation, and irrigation.

Other applications of nanotechnology for water recycling and remediation include the use of zeolites and nanoporous polymers to purify water and absorb toxic metals; attapulgite clays to remove heavy metals, oils, organic pollutants, and bacteria from water; engineered membrane technology with biochemical modifications to purify and filter water; magnetic nanoparticles to adsorb metals and organic compounds; and titanium dioxide and iron nanoparticles to catalytically degrade pollutants. By-products of remediation, such as toxic metal ions, can be transformed into useful inorganic nanomaterials.

Developing renewable energy sources

Harnessing renewable energy sources through cleaner, more affordable, and more reliable technologies can prevent the dependency of developing countries on fossil fuels and avert potential energy crises and environmental degradation brought about by the depletion of oil and coal. Improved access to clean energy could play a role in improving health (by reducing indoor air pollution, for example) and increase the efficiency of agricultural production. Applications of nanotechnology such as solar cells, fuels cells, and novel hydrogen storage systems based on nanostructured materials promise to deliver clean energy solutions. Nanophotovoltaic devices, such as those based on quantum dots or ultrathin films of semiconducting polymers, can significantly reduce the costs associated with conventional solar cells. Carbon nanotubes can be used in composite film coatings for flexible solar cells.

A major expense associated with hydrogen as a source of energy is its generation from water, a process that requires energy. Photo- and thermo-chemical nanocatalysts can be used to generate hydrogen from water at low costs. Electricity can also be cheaply produced using green technology from artificial systems that incorporates energy transduction proteins into an engineered matrix. Organic light-emitting devices based on semiconducting nanospheres can be developed to improve rural lighting. Carbon nanotubes used in hydrogen storage systems can provide lightweight materials for pressure tanks and liquid hydrogen vessels. Carbon nanotubes could provide strong, flexible conduits for electricity distribution networks. Ideally, all of these applications will be robust and easily maintained and serviced.

Nanobiotech-
nology, the
convergence
of nanotech-
nology and
biotechnol-
ogy, can be
harnessed
to enrich
biodiversity

Improving environmental management

Many developing countries rely on fossil fuels for most of their energy. Waste products resulting from the use of these fuels have a deleterious effect on both human health and the environment. Almost 800,000 deaths are caused by urban air pollution every year, nearly two-thirds of them in developing countries.

Nanocatalysts can reduce air pollution, especially from waste products of nonrenewable energy sources, decreasing the dependence of developing countries on these sources and preventing health and environmental problems. Metal oxide nanocatalysts, especially TiO_2 nanoparticles in self-cleaning coatings, can be used to photocatalyze air pollutants and reduce fossil fuel emissions. Intense research is being conducted on nanodevices that can absorb and separate toxic gases and on nanosensors that can be used to detect toxic materials and leaks.

Nanobiotechnology, the convergence of nanotechnology and biotechnology, can be harnessed to enrich biodiversity. Researchers at Chiang Mai University, in Thailand, are using nanotechnology to develop a strain of rice that has shorter stems and that is not sensitive to sunlight, thereby reducing vulnerability to wind damage and decreasing storage related costs. The National Aeronautics and Space Administration's Nanopore Project is developing a device that can sequence single molecules of nucleic acid at a rate of 1 million bases per second by using nanopore technology. The device will allow for faster sequencing of the DNA of all living organisms, creating a database of information underlying the biodiversity of the planet and enabling sensible ecosystem management.

Nanotechnology should be used responsibly to avoid compromising environmental integrity. Desirable properties of nanomaterials, such as high surface reactivity and the ability to cross cell membranes, could potentially have negative consequences if these technologies were used inappropriately. Measures must be taken to ensure that nanomaterials are contained and disposed of appropriately. This calls for careful research into the potential hazards of nanotechnology and for the design of appropriate regulatory systems to manage the benefits and risks of this new technology.

New materials

Materials are playing an increasingly important role in technological innovation. Research on materials is of vital importance for technological change and particularly important for developing countries in achieving the Goals. The development of low-cost building materials could boost construction of schools and shelter in developing countries and help meet the Goal of universal primary education. By providing better living environments, low-cost building materials could reduce child mortality, improve maternal health, and improve environmental sustainability. Making the benefits of new technologies available

Devices using solid-state ionic materials could contribute to economic development in developing countries

to developing countries requires formulating a strategy that ensures that they have access to new technologies such as materials science.

Knowledge of the mechanical, electronic, ionic, and nuclear properties of metals, semiconductors, polymers, ceramics and composites, and magnetic and radioactive materials is necessary to use these materials effectively in industry. Investment in higher education and research in materials science should form part of developing countries' strategies for industrial development. Materials—both natural and man-made—are rich with properties that can be harnessed for modern technological needs. Understanding the principles underlying the properties of materials is essential for developing new materials with properties suitable for new technologies.

Most developing countries are in the tropics. The development of cells created from new materials and photo-electrochemical cells could help formulate strategies that could help them exploit renewable sources of energy. Semiconductor research can lead to the development of new generations of integrated circuits and the solid-state memories used in ICT, semiconductor lasers, light-emitting diodes, and light-detecting devices, and technologies like photolithography.

Newer ceramic materials, such as piezoelectric ceramics, bioceramics, and electronic and electro-optic ceramics, provide technologically important alternatives to traditional ceramic materials. Ceramic composites, ceramic coatings, ceramic films, and glass materials (including glass ceramics, glass-ceramic composites, and conducting glasses) are important materials for industry. Special purpose polymers could be used in applications such as artificial muscles and light-emitting devices. Devices using solid-state ionic materials (such as solid electrolytes and electrode materials) form the basis for new types of batteries, fuel cells, and sensors. All these materials could contribute to economic development in developing countries.

Influence of platform technologies beyond 2015

The Goal timeline of 2015 is but the first step in the long march to sustainability in this century. Beyond 2015 the impacts of these platform technologies will be even more marked. The field of energy and vehicle transportation shows just how.

About 80 percent of all climate warming is caused by emissions of carbon dioxide. The installation of large and conventional fossil-fuelled power generating units cannot be continued unabated. The concomitant power grids channel power in one direction from massive power generators through extra-high-voltage transmission systems and then lower voltage distribution networks to consumers. This infrastructure system is very capital-intensive, with a typical 1,000 MW fossil fuel power plant costing about $1 billion. China currently faces acute electric power shortage and needs an additional 30,000 MW of electric power generating plants, which will cost about $30 billion.

Energy experts have suggested that hydrogen fuel cell will be the most positive development for energy and transportation in sustainable development

One promising solution will be to develop small power plants, units, and systems that are environmentally benign. The medium-term prospects are promising. Nanotechnology and new materials can develop small and environmentally benign power-generating devices like hydrogen fuel cells, which will allow electricity to be supplied to rural, remote, and poor urban communities using localized and flexible bidirectional power networks.

Increasing wealth in the developing world could lead to massive increases in car ownership—and thus to much higher levels of local, regional, and global pollution. The developing world, not unreasonably, is reluctant to accept advice that it needs to adopt the pollution-free methods of transportation that the developed world has found it difficult to implement. Transportation is a massive consumer of energy and it has a profound environmental impact, yet modern lifestyles depend on modern transport systems. Cars produce pollutants, which contribute to the greenhouse effect, acid rain, health problems, and a range of issues associated with "quality of life"—including noise, physical division of communities, and visual intrusion. The conflict between economic development and protecting the environment pervades the transportation debate.

Energy experts have suggested that hydrogen fuel cell will be the most positive development for energy and transportation in sustainable development (box 4.6). Millions of hydrogen fuel cell vehicles will be able to feed electricity to the local flexible power networks while they are parked. The huge capital savings in massive power generating plants and transmission systems throughout the world could be better used for development.

Conclusion

Technology presents a vast array of opportunities for improving the human condition. But many challenges lie ahead in harnessing its power. The infrastructure for development in general and technological innovation in particular

---

Box 4.6

What will automobiles look like in 2050?

Source: www.racfoundation.org/index2.html.

Britain's Royal Automobile Club (RAC) Foundation recently carried out a major study on the future of motoring. It concludes that "the 2050 car will look relatively familiar from outside. The average European car of 2050 will be much the same size as today's car and will weigh about the same. It will, however, embody many features that will make it more versatile. It will have a fuel cell power-train, almost certainly using compressed hydrogen gas as its fuel. Thus its on-road emissions will be zero, except for a small amount of water vapor. Its energy consumption will be substantially less than half that of current cars, and it will be exceptionally quiet, which will highlight the need to extend the adoption of 'quiet' road surfaces to urban areas."

What is even more promising is the active participation of all automobile manufacturers, demonstrating in no uncertain way that fuel cells for cars will be a commercial reality. DaimlerChrysler expects to have fuel-cell cars on the market by 2004. Honda, Toyota, and General Motors also say their fuel cell cars will be ready by then. BMW has recently unveiled a prototype version of its 7-Series car with a hydrogen-powered internal combustion engine.

must be developed. Competence in technical fields needs to be increased. The environment needs to be improved so that it fosters entrepreneurship and the commercialization and wider diffusion of technologies. The capacity to participate effectively in the global trading as well as in the global knowledge system needs to be increased. And the overall policy environment needed to promote the application of science, technology, and innovation to the Goals needs to be improved. The rest of this report addresses these issues.

Chapter 5

Adequate infrastructure services as a foundation for technology

One of the problems that hinders the reduction of poverty in the developing world—and the achievement of other Goals—is the lack of adequate infrastructure services.[1] Infrastructure affects economic development in various ways. It affects the production and consumption of firms and individuals by generating substantial positive and negative externalities. Because infrastructure services are intermediate inputs into production, their costs directly affect firms' profitability and competitiveness. Infrastructure services also affect the productivity of other production factors. Electric power allows firms to shift from manual to electrical machinery. Extensive transport networks reduce workers' commuting time. Telecommunications networks facilitate flows of information. As an "unpaid factor of production," infrastructure increases the returns to labor and other capital. The availability of infrastructure may also attract firms to certain locations, which create agglomeration economies and reduce factor and transactions costs (Fan and Zhang 2004).

The challenge of infrastructure for the science, technology, and innovation community is to identify and implement the infrastructure services needed to achieve the Goals. The challenge for policymakers is to undertake infrastructure development in a manner that not only promotes equity, efficiency, participatory decisionmaking, sustainability, and accountability but develops domestic capabilities in science, technology, and innovation as well (DFID 2002).

Infrastructure and technological innovation

Infrastructure development provides a foundation for technological learning, because infrastructure uses a wide range of technologies and complex institutional arrangements. Governments traditionally view infrastructure projects from a static perspective. Although they recognize the fundamental role of infrastructure, they seldom consider infrastructure projects as part of a technological

The development of new innovations and technology also contribute to infrastructure development

learning process. Governments need to recognize the dynamic role of infrastructure development and take a more active role in acquiring knowledge about infrastructure development, through collaboration between indigenous and foreign construction and engineering firms. Building railways, airports, roads, and telecommunications networks, for example, could be structured to promote technological, organizational, and institutional learning.

Infrastructure contributes to technological development in almost all sectors of the economy. It serves as the foundation of technological development; its establishment represents, in effect, technological and institutional investment. The infrastructure development process also provides an opportunity for technological learning.

The creation and diffusion of technology relies on the availability of infrastructure. Without adequate infrastructure, technology cannot be harnessed. The advancement of information technology and its rapid diffusion in recent years could not have happened without basic telecommunications infrastructure. Many high-tech firms, such as those in the semiconductor industry, require reliable electric power and efficient logistical networks. In the manufacturing and retail sectors, efficient transportation and logistical networks allow firms to adopt process and organizational innovations, such as the just-in-time approach to supply chain management.

The concepts of innovation systems and interactive relationships stress the links between firms, educational and research institutes, and governments. These concepts cannot be implemented without the infrastructure that supports and facilitates the connections. Particularly in the era of globalization and knowledge-based economies, the quality and functionality of ICT infrastructure, as well as logistical infrastructure, is essential for the development of academic and research institutions (box 5.1).

While efforts to expand the use of technology in development depend on the existence of infrastructure, the development of new innovations and technology also contribute to infrastructure development. For example, the advancement in communications and data-processing technologies has fostered the development of intelligent transportation systems for more efficient traffic management. The use of geographic information systems and remote-sensing technologies enables engineers to identify groundwater resources in urban and rural areas. Infrastructure and technological innovation for development thus reinforce each other. For these reasons the construction and maintenance of infrastructure represents a technological and institutional investment. Infrastructure is a fundamental element of a comprehensive and effective science, technology, and innovation policy.

Infrastructure and technological learning processes

Infrastructure contributes to technological development by providing opportunities for technological learning associated with the acquisition of technology

Box 5.1

Malaysia's Multimedia Super-Corridor has helped attract high-tech businesses

Source: Ramasamy, Chakrabarty, and Cheah 2004.

As part of its efforts to enhance its technological base in the ICT sector, the Malaysian government initiated the Multimedia Super-Corridor Project in 1995. Located in the corridor between Kuala Lumpur and Putrajaya, the new administrative capital of Malaysia, the Multimedia Super-Corridor accommodated a cluster of firms in the information technology sector.

The key element of the project is the provision of high-quality infrastructure. To attract high-tech multinational corporations—from small and medium-size high-tech firms to large corporations, such as Microsoft and Oracle—the government invested heavily in developing physical and communications infrastructure in Cyberjaya and other "cybercities" in the Multimedia Super-Corridor. This infrastructure includes a fiber-optic backbone with an estimated 2.5–10 gigabits per second capacity that has links to international centers, open standards, high-speed switching, and multiple protocols.

The project is complemented by other large infrastructure projects, such as transportation routes that link it with Kuala Lumpur and the new international airport. Recognizing that human resources are key to technological development, the project provides other infrastructure services and amenities that aim to improve the quality of life. It is clear that the Malaysian government considers infrastructure development to be a key component of its science, technology, and innovation policy.

(Putranto, Stewart, and Moore 2003). Because of the fundamental role of infrastructure in the economy, the learning process in infrastructure development is a crucial element of a country's overall technological learning process (box 5.2). This dynamic aspect of infrastructure is often overlooked in the development and infrastructure literature.

Every stage of an infrastructure project, from planning and design through construction and operation, involves the application of a wide range of technologies and institutional and management arrangements. Because infrastructure facilities and services are complex physical, organizational, and institutional systems, deep understanding and adequate capabilities are required on the part of engineers, managers, government officials, and others involved in these projects.

Infrastructure plays another crucial role in science, technology, and innovation efforts in developing countries: it is one of the most important factors in attracting foreign direct investment, in addition to being itself an investment target whose future economic sustainability is expected to stabilize (Ramamurti and Doh 2004). Infrastructure is one of the key factors that multinational corporations consider in determining the location, scope, and scale of their investments.

Foreign direct investment in infrastructure increased substantially in the 1990s, for several reasons, including favorable foreign direct investment policies, the reduced risk of expropriation in developing countries, and the development of innovative financing strategies, such as nonrecourse project financing and securitization. Increased foreign participation in infrastructure projects,

Box 5.2

Learning from a foreign consortium helped the Republic of Korea build a high-speed train network

Source: Rouach and Saperstein 2004.

In 1993 the Korea High-Speed Rail Construction Authority announced that it had selected a French consortium to build a high-speed train network linking Seoul with Pusan and Mokpo. Its experience with the French consortium has already helped Korea develop its own bullet train system. The Korean experience shows that in many respects an infrastructure project is a technological and institutional investment. It shows that a government can structure an infrastructure project in a way that allows domestic industries to benefit from technology transfer and organizational and institutional arrangements.

Korea expects the industrial and technological effects of the project to be enormous, because high-speed rail spurs the development of advanced aerodynamics, civil engineering, and mechanical and electronics technologies. Such technologies can also be applied to materials, automation, information, aerodynamics, and other industries. The project enhanced Korea's overall design capability for mass transportation, and the automatic computer control and self-diagnosis technologies it mastered can be applied to the automation of industrial robots.

particularly in the form of foreign direct investment, means that there are now more opportunities for developing countries to use infrastructure development as part of their technological and institutional learning process.

Governments need to design and implement the rules and regulations that govern private networks that are no longer under public control. They also have the option of building up the infrastructure that replaces private networks. Given that the global economy relies increasingly on information and knowledge flows, governments are faced with strategic options that could have significant implications for their science, technology, and innovation policies.

Innovation in energy: the sustainability challenge

The linkages between infrastructure development and technological innovation are illustrated by global trends to adapt to changing energy needs and new environmental standards. The emergence of alternative energy technologies and the challenges they pose to conventional sources illustrate the degree to which improvements in energy technologies have become central to long-term energy security and environmental management (Holdren and others 1999).

After the 1970s fuel crisis, the Brazilian government initiated a large program to encourage the design and manufacture of ethanol-only cars, as well as to cultivate sugarcane and refine it into ethanol as a way to reduce country's dependence on imported oil. By the end of the 1980s, ethanol engines powered almost 80 percent of cars produced in Brazil. The industry faced occasional shortages of ethanol fuel, however, and during the 1990s the price advantage of ethanol declined as gasoline prices fell. As a consequence, by 2002 ethanol-only cars represented a mere 3.5 percent of new car sales in Brazil.

Some auto-parts producers came up with the idea of building flex-fuel engines as a way out of the difficulties faced by ethanol vehicles (box 5.3). Some multinational auto-parts producers that located their world research centers

Box 5.3

Sales of flex-fuel cars are booming in Brazil

Source: Viotti 2004.

Flex-fuel was introduced in the Brazilian market in September 2003. By the end of the year, about 50,000 flex-fuel cars had been sold. By September 2004 sales of flex-fuel cars reached 150,000 and represented nearly 20 percent of new car sales in Brazil.

Almost all the large multinational carmakers established in the Brazilian market are in a race to launch more flex-fuel models. By the end of August 2004, one of them introduced the first car in the world to that can run on gasoline, ethanol, or natural gas (a fuel that is available at the pumps in Brazilian largest cities). The fuel efficiency of the engine, however, is lower than regular models.

The flexibility of the new engines could help overcome one of the most serious obstacles to liberating the transportation system from its dependence on gasoline: the lack of a distribution infrastructure for alternative fuels. Since flex-fuel engines can run on alternative as well as conventional fuels, the risk of running out of fuel due to the lack of alternative fuel pump stations is not a problem. The lack of a large distribution infrastructure does not prevent the introduction of the new fuel; the network of pumps of alternative fuel could be built progressively.

Flex-fuel engines can be built very inexpensively, because they use regular internal combustion engines with some adaptations and new electronic sensors, devices, and software to automatically adjust the engine operation to different fuels and blends of fuels. The new technology has transformed the conventional gasoline engine into an "intelligent" engine.

One of the main difficulties in using ethanol is that it is more corrosive than gasoline. Consequently, fuel pumps, gaskets, and piston rings need to be made less vulnerable to corrosion. Overcoming this and some other hurdles are feasible for the Brazilian industry, because of the large technological experience it accumulated with ethanol engines.

A preferential tax system is facilitating the rapid introduction of the car into the marketplace. In addition to the domestic market, car manufacturers and auto-part producers have high expectations about exporting flex-fuel cars and technologies. Several delegations from around the world have already visited Brazil to gather information about flex-fuel technologies.

in Brazil on related technologies built on Brazil's technological capabilities in ethanol engines to develop flex-fuel technologies. Flex-fuel technologies can give customers and nations the flexibility to respond to volatile changes of fuel prices. These technologies also reduce urban pollution and the production of greenhouse gases. Flex-fuel engines also increase agricultural employment and income generation in developing countries.

Research facilities as infrastructure

Defining infrastructure to include technological innovation requires rethinking the strategic importance of research facilities (Nightingale 2004). Indeed, infrastructure projects can serve as research facilities themselves while maintaining strong links with other research institutions (Conceição and others 2003). The management of geothermal energy facilities, for example, require continuous in situ research as well linkages with external research facilities.

Infrastructure should include direct links to human resource development, enterprise creation, and R&D

But much of the research associated with infrastructure projects in developing countries is usually implicit.

Support to strategic technology development should be considered part of the national infrastructure, in the same category as energy, transportation networks, and water and sanitation. A number of developing countries, such as South Africa, are starting to work toward creating networked research facilities that are accessed in a managed way. Other countries have consolidated research entities to create single research institutions designed to maximize synergies in human resources.

The best-known research facility of this kind is the Industrial Technology Research Institute (ITRI) in Taiwan (China). ITRI was created in 1973 by the Ministry of Economic Affairs as a nonprofit R&D organization focused on applied research and technical service. Its original aim was to address the technological needs of Taiwan's industrial development. By 2003 it had more than 6,000 people in 11 laboratories. It acts as a locus of technical support to industry and an unofficial arm of the government's industrial policies. ITRI operations have become global.

ITRI's main task has been identifying the latest technology available globally, adapting it to local needs, and then diffusing it into Taiwan's industrial sector. Most of the major semiconductor foundries in Taiwan (China) have their roots in the Institute. ITRI also undertakes contract research for the private sector, provides technical training, carries out long-term research projects for the state, and provides incubation facilities to help entrepreneurs establish high-tech firms.

Planning for infrastructure development

An essential aspect of economic planning in developing countries is fostering the development and maintenance of infrastructure in a way that is appropriate to local conditions and consistent with ecological and other principles. Planning for infrastructure development should be placed on par with other planning processes.

Infrastructure serves as a strategic foundation for the application of technology to development. As an essential element of a country's long-term development efforts, it should include direct links to human resource development, enterprise creation, and R&D.

Developing countries need to prioritize infrastructure investment according to the degree of needs and the potential impact of particular investments on the economy and the society as a whole. Doing so does not mean that they should focus only on basic infrastructure, however, and forgo investment in infrastructure that is of strategic importance. To the contrary, developing countries need to upgrade strategically important infrastructure in order to tap into the opportunities that may arise from rapid technological change and the increasingly integrated global economy.[2]

Infrastructure services may be provided through combinations of public and private enterprises, while taking into account the needs of the poor

Developing countries also need to enhance their own ability to develop, operate, and maintain infrastructure services. Foreign construction and engineering firms will continue to be the main sources of technological, organizational, and institutional knowledge for infrastructure development. But governments in developing countries should devise policies to encourage technology transfer and build local capabilities in infrastructure projects (box 5.4). Research and development activities for the development, operation, and maintenance of infrastructure should also be promoted, and linkages should be established with both domestic and overseas research networks.

Infrastructure services may be provided through combinations of public and private enterprises, while taking into account the needs of the poor. Governments may reduce their role as producers of infrastructure but retain their roles as regulators, financiers, suppliers, and even competitors of private providers. Whatever roles they play, governments need to recognize that different types of infrastructure require different policies and approaches.

Although infrastructure services have several common characteristics, they also have important differences. Telecommunications is less essential than water, energy, and transportation. Its pricing is therefore less politically sensitive and reflects its true financial, if not economic, costs. This could mean that the payback periods for investments in telecommunications are shorter than other types of infrastructure. Different types of infrastructure have different technologies and organizational arrangements. Governments may need to assume a direct role

---

Box 5.4

Learning-by-doing in Algerian infrastructure development

Since the 1970s Algerian policymakers have considered the construction industry one of the "industrializing industries" that generates a large share of employment and GDP. To spur the industry, the government encouraged the purchase of complex, advanced, and costly technologies from foreign firms. Sophisticated and highly integrated contracts, such as turnkey and product-in-hand contracts, were used to assemble and coordinate all project operations—from conception through implementation and installation—into one package. The aim was to transfer all responsibility to the foreign technology supplier.

These types of contracts did not lead to as much technology transfer as the Algerian government had hoped. The turnkey contracts required that the foreign supplier take full responsibility for the project, but they did not include the sourcing or training of local people. This meant continuous reliance on external assistance, the inefficient operation by local management due to a lack of understanding and skill, or both.

Having learned from its failures, the government later encouraged "decomposed" or "design and installation supervised" contracts, under which infrastructure projects are more fragmented and involve more local firms. Local firms now take charge of the preinstallation phases (exploration and planning). With the technical assistance and supervision of foreign suppliers, local managers carry out the projects. This new approach not only reduces uncertainty in implementation, it also facilitates the process of learning-by-doing in local firms, enhancing their technological capability. The approach has also contributed to the development of investment and managerial capabilities of local managers.

Successful development of infrastructure services to meet the Goals requires mobilizing the energies of the engineering profession

in certain infrastructure projects if they see strategic importance in fostering the transfer and building up of the local capability of the required technologies.

In-country studies need to be carried out to identify the essential infrastructure services necessary to support achievement of the Goals.[3] The location of the poor and their critical infrastructure service needs should be pinpointed, and the cost and cost-effectiveness of infrastructure interventions to meet these needs should be calculated. Another fundamental task will be to highlight and address problems of implementation.

Such calculations should take into account the implications of infrastructure projects for technological learning. For example, linkages between the projects and research institutions should be considered as an investment whose returns will be reflected in the overall enhancement of technological competence.

Mobilizing the engineering profession and young professionals

Successful development of infrastructure services to meet the Goals requires mobilizing the energies of the engineering profession. Most national institutions of engineers have worldwide memberships. Members in developing countries include both expatriate and local engineers. Their nonprofit organizations include Engineers Against Poverty and Registered Engineers for Disaster Relief in the United Kingdom and Engineers without Borders in the United States and Canada. Many young and women engineers are the movers and shakers in these organizations. Much more could be done to spread these voluntary service organizations worldwide. The United Nations and its

Box 5.5

Young professionals have much to offer developing countries

A number of programs tap into the energy of young professionals. The United Nations Educational, Scientific and Cultural Organization (UNESCO) formed the International Forum on Young Scientists during the World Conference on Science in Budapest in 1999. The UN Program on Space Applications formed the Space Generation Advisory Council (open to professionals between 20 and 35). The World Bank, the Organisation for Economic Cooperation and Development (OECD), the Food and Agriculture Organization (FAO), and the International Labour Organization (ILO) all have young professional programs, designed to both develop and learn from young professionals around the world. Regionally, groups from the Asian Coalition for Housing Rights and the London Business School have young professionals, and many of the main organizers of NGOs are young professionals.

There are also a large number of young professional networks around the world that can be engaged, such as the Waikato Young Professionals in New Zealand, the Thai American Young Professionals Network, and the International Young Professionals Foundation. While the main focus of many of these groups is networking, many also understand that professional development can be achieved through sustainable development. With the right assistance from the United Nations, international development agencies, governments, and corporations, and with young professionals driving their own networks and organizations, these young professionals will be the most potent force in achieving the Goals.

Without adequate infrastructure, developing countries will not be able to harness the power of science, technology, and innovation to meet the Goals

specialized agencies should consider how they might capitalize on and reinforce these networks, particularly through their global organization, the World Federation of Engineering Organisations. In planning and implementing any Goal project, including infrastructure projects, efforts should be made to harness the enthusiasm and drive of young professionals, many of whom are looking for an opportunity to serve the developing world (box 5.5).

In the current knowledge economy, a large number of young professionals in both the developed and developing world have become captains of cutting-edge industries in ICT and other emerging technologies. Solidarity has always been strong among young people: knowledgeable young people, in developed and developing countries alike can surely be mobilized in an orderly way to provide help for development, following the leading example of Médicins san Frontières. Such a group could become a major force harnessing science, technology, and innovation for development.

The International Development Initiative at the Massachusetts Institute of Technology (MIT) is responding to the needs of partners in developing countries by bringing the resources of MIT to the task of technology development, education, and capacity building in their communities. Design that Matters (DtM) provides MIT students with the opportunities and resources to work on projects for underserved communities in developing countries as independent projects (DelHagen, MIT, personal communication, 2004). Students have developed numerous innovative strategies for solving problems in health, water testing and treatment, and rural education, among others. One student group designed a novel IV clamp to make treatment of cholera and other diseases more accessible in areas with few trained health workers. Another project brought down the cost of testing water for bacterial contamination by two orders of magnitude and made it accessible in off-grid communities, where it is most needed. A basic principle of fluid dynamics was applied by a DtM team to create a water chlorination system that passively adapts to large changes in the water flow rate that occur throughout the changing seasons. A project to deploy student-designed low-cost microfilm projectors for rural education initiatives has recently received funding from USAID for a field test in Mali.

Establishing standards

The design, manufacture, supply, and delivery of infrastructure hardware, software, and systems are now global. This globalization would not have been possible without internationally agreed on standards. In order for infrastructure services in developing countries to become more effective and extensible, countries need to create and enforce national standards that conform to international benchmarks. Efforts should be made to facilitate the coordination, skills development, and use of standards to promote the interoperability of infrastructure systems from the early design stages (Andrew and Petkov 2003).

Box 5.6

Government policymakers have a catalyzing role to play in licensing the radio spectrum

Licensing the radio spectrum can spur technology transfer, entrepreneurship, and foreign investment. Aligning their spectra with those of Western countries would allow developing countries to take advantage of existing wireless device economies of scale and expertise. Unlicensed spectra lead to the innovation of wireless standards like WiFi and WiMax and could provide a friendly environment for entrepreneurship, reducing barriers to entry and the risk of regulatory failure and ultimately providing a low-cost solution in low-income countries with poor telecommunications infrastructures (A. Raghunathan, Harvard Business School, personal communication, 2004). Significant heterogeneity in the regulation of 2.4 and 5.7 GHz bands across Africa hinders growth of telecommunications and the Internet by reducing potential economies of scale. The associated confusion, uncertainty, and poor policy enforcement have negative impacts on new entrants and small players. Significant heterogeneity of policy in developing countries will deter foreign direct investment and inhibit economies of scale (Neto, Best, and Gillett 2004).

The interoperability challenges are often associated with heterogeneity in legislation, which can hamper technological innovation (box 5.6).

Conclusion

Without adequate infrastructure, developing countries will not be able to harness the power of science, technology, and innovation to meet the Goals. Because infrastructure uses a wide range of technologies and complex institutional arrangements, its development provides a foundation for technological learning. Infrastructure is also critical in attracting foreign direct investment. Developing countries need to strengthen their infrastructure and enhance their ability to develop, operate, and maintain infrastructure services.

Chapter 6

Investing in education in science and technology

Investment in science, technology, and innovation education has been one of the most critical sources of economic transformation in the newly industrial countries. Such investment should be part of a larger framework to build capacities worldwide. The one common element of the East Asian success stories is the high level of commitment to education and economic integration within the countries. This strategy was a precursor to what have come to be known as *knowledge societies* (World Bank 2002).

The commitment of the Republic of Korea to higher education suggests that spectacular results can be achieved in a few decades. These experiences are not limited to this region. The impact of education on local economies is also being recorded in less developed countries. Policy approaches to education, however, continue to generate considerable controversy in international development circles.

Primary and secondary school education in science

The growth of higher education needs to be accompanied by an increase in opportunities for graduates to apply what they learn. Developing countries need to devote resources to allowing more young people to obtain higher education, paying special attention to the barriers that appear at the secondary-school level. To increase job opportunities for graduates, they need to give incentives to private enterprises, particularly small and medium-size firms, to hire young university graduates, a strategy that helps create a virtuous circle of technological upgrading.

It is becoming evident that science education should be strengthened at the earliest level in educational systems. This will require greater emphasis on science education in primary schools (box 6.1). The importance of introducing science education in early childhood is illustrated by the failure in many parts

Today's economic circumstances make higher education a more compelling need in developing countries than it has ever been

of the world, especially in Africa, to understand the scientific basis of disease. This failure not only makes it difficult to implement public health programs, it has been a major factor in the spread of infectious diseases, especially HIV/AIDS. Providing an early foundation in science education is therefore critical to human development.

Although the education Goal is limited to achieving universal primary education, science, technology, and innovation education at the secondary and tertiary levels are critical to creating an innovative society.

Developing countries should be encouraged to adopt curricula that ensure that all students completing secondary school in any field will have been exposed to at least one area of science. They should also be encouraged to invest in science education at the secondary and tertiary levels in order to increase the number of scientists, engineers, and technologists.

Changes are also needed at the high school level. High school curricula need to be modified to prepare students for the materials introduced at universities. Teaching methods should also be changed to reflect the spirit of scientific inquiry by encouraging independent projects, inviting experts to speak as guest lectures, and taking students on field trips.

Higher education in science, technology, and innovation

Higher education is increasingly being recognized as a critical aspect of the development process, especially with the growing awareness of the role of science, technology, and innovation in economic renewal. While primary and secondary education have been at the focus of donor-community attention for decades, higher education has been viewed as essential to development only in more recent years. Today's economic circumstances make higher education a more compelling need in developing countries than it has ever been. Key factors in this change include increased demand for higher education due to improved access to schooling, pressing local and national concerns that require advanced knowledge to address, and a global economy that favors participants with high-technological expertise.

Box 6.1

The La Main à la Pâte program is shaping young minds through primary science education

Source: www.inrp.fr/lamap.

The most widely adopted primary science education program being promoted by the Inter-Academy Panel and the International Council for Science is the La Main à la Pâte (LAMAP) program of the French Academy of Sciences. Brazil, China, Colombia, Egypt, France, Hungary, Morocco, Senegal, Viet Nam, and soon Malaysia have adopted the program. The hands-on, discovery-based methodology makes imaginative use of ICT. Its well-designed Web site is the most popular resource used by French primary school teachers.

LAMAP is also an active teachers forum. Its Web site allows teachers to communicate directly with scientists and engineers. Scientists and university science students act as advisors to classroom teachers. In order not to undermine the authority of the teacher, they are not encouraged to interact directly with students.

The scientific, technological, and engineering community and the associated institutions are among the most critical resources for economic transformation

Universities have immense potential to promote technological development. But most universities in developing countries are ill equipped to meet the challenge. Outdated curricula, undermotivated faculty, poor management, and a continuous struggle for funds have undermined the capacity of universities to play their roles as engines of community or regional development.

Vocational and polytechnic institutes in developing countries are very important. Technologists, technicians, and craftspeople are the bedrock on which small and medium-size enterprises are founded, especially in operations and maintenance. Many developing countries have made the mistake of neglecting the training of technicians and technologists.

During the 1970s many engineering graduates left India to seek employment abroad. Others were underemployed as draftsmen. This underutilization of highly trained human resources took place at a time when India suffered from a critical shortage of skilled craftspeople, such as pattern makers and instrument technicians. This experience highlights both the importance of training technicians and technologists and the need to foster internal demand for engineers.

Science and engineering courses continue to be unattractive to women even though the role of women in economic development is being recognized (box 6.2). Equipping women with the necessary scientific knowledge and technical skills needed for full employment is a critical aspect of the ability of developing countries to participate in the global economy. Developing countries are starting to explore ways to expand higher education opportunities for women. This could be a critical starting point for receiving support to higher education from developing international development agencies, such as the World Bank.

The need for training and capability building of technicians and technologists in developing countries has become even more acute with the advent of computer-aided design and drafting in engineering and construction industries. The proliferation of sophisticated computer-controlled machineries and instruments for manufacturing has also increased demand for technicians and technologists. These people are also needed in healthcare and banking.

Developing countries should invest in and promote institutions that provide recognition and continuing professional development of technologists and technicians, institutions such as the Institution of Incorporated Engineers and the Institution of Technician Engineers in the United Kingdom.

Scientists and engineers in the global economy

The scientific, technological, and engineering community and the associated institutions (universities, technical institutes, professional associations) are among the most critical resources for economic transformation. They deserve special policy attention. A disturbing global trend is the decline in enrollment in engineering courses in universities and institutions of higher learning, especially in developed countries, where some engineering departments have closed.

Box 6.2

Improving gender equality will enhance development

Women are central to economic and social development, through their productive, reproductive, and community management responsibilities. They make a major contribution to the production of food and the provision of energy, water, health care, and family income in developing countries. In addition, in many communities in developing countries, women are the primary holders of indigenous knowledge and know-how on sustainable use and management of the environment. Development would benefit from greater involvement of women in the decisionmaking process for development policies. Girls and women should receive scientific and technical education, so that they can apply what they learn in the performance of these tasks and roles.

A good example of how women are contributing to economic growth and development is found in many developing countries' efforts to increase exports. Most developing countries, especially the least developed among them, are dependent on one to three commodities for export revenues. This dependency on commodities has kept countries poor, because the prices of most commodities have been falling for several decades. The outlook is not encouraging. As a result, most developing country governments are trying to diversify their economies away from commodities. Several countries are succeeding, with production of nontraditional exports in rural areas. A World Bank study (Dolan and Sorby 2003) on the production of cut flowers, poultry, fruit, and vegetables in several countries in Africa and South America shows that many of these successful industries employ mostly women. Despite the central role of women in these industries, men are given more access to training opportunities. Getting rid of these obstacles would open the way for further growth and development.

Many technologies could improve the lives of women. Simple technologies such as treatment of water with chlorine in homes can improve the safety of water and sanitation. Improved technologies can help women produce more food and manage natural resources. They can reduce the burden of their work and improve the well-being of communities. ICT can create educational, economic, and employment opportunities for women and enhance their participation in political decisionmaking.

To meet the shortage of engineers and scientists, developed countries recruit from developing countries. Ironically, developing countries are putting their scarce resources into education and training that benefits the developed world.

Developing countries' ability to absorb scientists and engineers is limited due to their early stage of development. But highly educated human resources can attract foreign firms interested in investing in science, technology, and innovation in the developing country. Expatriates have helped establish small and medium-size enterprises by investing in their country of origin, often using technology acquired abroad, and they are involved in establishing joint enterprises between their home countries and adopted countries.[1] Public policy and a dynamic business community facilitate these processes.

Nevertheless, "brain drain" remains one of the most hotly debated international issues. The home country's loss of skills—and educational investment—needs to be set against the experience gained abroad by scientists and professionals, which may be available for use upon their return if adequate measures toward that end are implemented (see chapter 8 for further discussion on the diaspora).

Arrangements like the Colombo Plan can effectively support low-income countries that lack sufficient institutions of higher learning in rapidly building technological and scientific expertise

The international mobility of skilled people is one of the key mechanisms for the transition of technological capability across countries. To use this mechanism effectively, countries need to design institutions that enable them to use the skills of their nationals wherever they live. Such institutional arrangements need to rely on a commitment to international cooperation and partnerships.

A new Colombo Plan for Sub-Saharan Africa

Since 1951 donor countries have offered scholarships and fellowships to developing countries in the Asia Pacific region under the Colombo Plan for Cooperative Economic Development in Asia and the Pacific. During its first three decades, the Colombo Plan played an important role in supporting the development of technological and scientific expertise in Indonesia, the Philippines, Malaysia, Singapore, and Thailand. The Colombo Plan also contributed significantly to the stable administrative transition from colonial rule in Southeast Asia. It had an important impact on donor countries, especially Australia, where the presence of Colombo Plan students from Asia triggered a flow of students from Southeast Asia.

The Colombo Plan Scholarship and Fellowship Program is a collection of bilateral programs between donor and recipient countries that is largely devoid of multilateral bureaucracy and politics. As a result, program implementation is very focused on the needs of the recipient and the capabilities of the donor.

Arrangements like the Colombo Plan can effectively support low-income countries that lack sufficient institutions of higher learning in rapidly building technological and scientific expertise. Donor countries should establish a second Colombo Plan for Sub-Saharan Africa. The program could build on the existing expertise and structures of the first Colombo Plan. Such an arrangement would permit the rapid scaling up of investments in professional manpower across Sub-Saharan Africa.

The beneficiaries of such a plan could help lay the foundations for stronger institutions of higher education across the continent as part of the emergence of systems of innovation (Muchie, Gammeltoft, and Lundvall 2003). Toward that end, provisions could be made in the scholarships and fellowships that ensure that recipients return to their home countries after completing their studies abroad.

Having knowledgeable people is not enough, however. If investments in science and technology are inadequate, scientists and engineers will have few opportunities to apply what they have learned. The acquisition of knowledge and opportunities to apply it creatively are two inseparable parts of the learning process.

Learning is an endless process. Lifelong learning is based on being able to participate in activities in which explicit and tacit knowledge is shared, exchanged, and created.

Learning societies can be defined as places where a sizable proportion of the population and of the social and economic organizations permanently perform

Universities can contribute to economic revival and high-tech growth in their surrounding regions

knowledge-demanding activities in which many actors need to, and are able to, systematically upgrade their individual and collective skills, as well as their awareness of scientific and technological changes. In other words, learning societies are "interactive learning spaces" (Arocena and Sutz 2003). Fostering the development of and strengthening interactive leaning spaces can be seen as a fundamental developmental task. If it is achieved, the use of new knowledge in a socially valuable way will follow, as will better possibilities to face the challenges posed by scientific and technological changes. In this respect, international development agencies and their African counterparts could launch a new Colombo Plan with a focus on the sciences. Such a program could also be launched as a partnership between African and Asian countries that have previously benefited from the Colombo Plan and are willing to their share experiences.

New roles for universities and technical institutes

A new view that places universities at the center for the development process is starting to emerge. This concept is also being applied at other levels of learning, such as colleges, research and technical institutes, and polytechnic schools. Universities and research institutes (including polytechnics) are now deeply integrated into the productive sector as well as society at large. Universities are starting to be viewed as a valuable resource for business and industry; universities can undertake entrepreneurial activities with the objective of improving regional or national economic and social performance.[2] Others are charged with explicit reconstruction mandates (box 6.3).

In facilitating the development of business and industrial firms, universities can contribute to economic revival and high-tech growth in their surrounding regions. There are many ways in which a university can get integrated into the productive sector and into society at large. It can conduct R&D for industry; it can create its own spin-off firms; it can be involved in capital formation projects, such as technology parks and business incubator facilities; it can introduce entrepreneurial training into its curricula and encourage students to take research from the university to firms. It can also ensure that students become acquainted with problems faced by firms—through internships, for example. Universities should also ensure that students also study the relationships between science, technology, innovation, and development, so that they are sensitive to societal needs. This approach is based on the strong interdependence of academia, industry, and government.[3]

Industry in the developed world has benefited from the activities of research universities, particularly from their state-of-the-art laboratories, which conduct cutting-edge research for them. Universities benefit from the research funds provided by industry.

Many universities in developing countries serve merely as degree- or certificate-awarding institutions, providing the necessary documentation for

Box 6.3

**Rwanda is using
knowledge to
foster national
reconstruction**

Source: www.kist.ac.rw/.

Reconstruction efforts following the genocide in Rwanda have been associated with an emphasis on the role of science, technology, and engineering in economic transformation. This is illustrated by the decision by the Rwandan government to convert military barracks into a home for a new university, the Kigali Institute of Science, Technology and Management (KIST), the first public technological institute of higher learning in Rwanda.

KIST aims to contribute to Rwanda's economic renewal through the creation of highly skilled manpower. It seeks to become a regional center offering courses in science, technology, and management; carrying out extensive research activities and knowledge dissemination; and providing technical assistance and services to all sections of the community.

KIST was created as a project of UNDP in 1997. It was established with the help of the government of Rwanda as the main stakeholder, UNDP (Rwanda) as the executor of the project, and the German Agency for Technical Cooperation (GTZ) as the implementing agency. Initial funding came from UNDP core funding and a UNDP Trust Fund obtained from generous contributions by the governments of Japan and the Netherlands.

KIST was officially inaugurated in April 1998. In July 2002 it held its first graduation, awarding 403 diplomas and 62 degrees to its 465 proud pioneers in management and computer science disciplines.

Despite many challenges, KIST today boasts a highly motivated and trilingual student population of 3,247, enrolled in both regular and part-time undergraduate programs. Students choose from a wide variety of engineering and management courses. KIST recently introduced a postgraduate diploma in demography and statistics.

thousands of young people to apply for jobs. Marginalized in the development process, these universities seek only to churn out graduates. Universities need to be re-envisioned as potentially powerful partners in the development process.

This adjustment can be implemented in a top-down manner by changing existing norms and procedures. It can be done for all academic departments of the university or certain select ones deemed to be of more importance with regard to national development goals. Imposing new standards on only certain departments would imply widely different standards for students and faculty and would likely require a separate administrative setup for the departments with higher standards. Moreover, the university's location would have to be appropriate for the selected disciplines. A benefit of this approach would be working with an established institution. Such an institution already has libraries, staff, and very likely some links with other research institutes.

Technical institutes are created to serve industry. By nature they are disposed to work with firms. Without neglecting their essential and primary roles in capability building for technologists and technicians, some of these institutes could be upgraded to university status.

New universities may also be created, particularly if a new field of knowledge in which existing universities have inadequate capability has been made a national priority or if student demand has outstripped university capacity. These universities could be entirely new institutes or expansions of industry-based training institutes.

Universities that are expected to boost technology-based industry need to be located near high-tech firm clusters and research institutes

For universities to be able to contribute to science and technology–based regional development, appropriate supporting institutions will be necessary. These include both enabling policies and organizations that can increase the pathways of interaction between academia, government, and industry. Specific measures include tax breaks, venture capital funding, low-interest loans, changes in intellectual property rights, higher returns on inventions, heavy investment in ICT, business incubation, and technology parks and centers within or near universities.

Partnerships with other institutions, at the national or regional level, could be of great benefit. Many developing country academics are benefiting from institutional partnerships with universities and R&D institutes abroad. Research partnerships across academic, industry, and government institutions help reduce knowledge gaps, especially in small and medium-size enterprises, which often lack adequate R&D facilities.

Reshaping universities to perform development functions will include modifying their curricula, changing schemes of service, modifying pedagogy, shifting the location of universities, and creating a wider institutional ecology that includes other parts of the development process. To help universities adopt a key development role, national development plans will need to incorporate new links between universities, industry, and government (box 6.4). This is likely to affect the entire national innovation system, including firms, R&D institutes, and government organizations. Developing countries will not be able to exploit the might of new technologies unless they become seriously involved in high-technology fields.

For this reason, university curricula are vitally important. The science, technology, and innovation curricula in many developing country universities are outdated or lack a cross-disciplinary approach. In certain departments, the research emphasis needs to be shifted toward issues of local and national relevance.

University faculties in many developing countries are poorly rewarded and thus undermotivated. Faculty are not always conversant with the latest developments in their fields. Their teaching methods tend to be old-fashioned, with little use of audio-visual equipment during lectures or of advanced apparatus during laboratory sessions, for example. Some of these problems are caused by inadequate funds. Faculty need to be aware of developments at the frontiers of their research.

Research ability will need to be considered when assessing applications for graduate study. Incentives such as scholarships and low-interest loans should be made available for the most promising students.

Universities that are expected to boost technology-based industry need to be located near high-tech firm clusters and research institutes, most likely in urban areas. If firm formation is expected to take off after the university is established, the university needs to be located in an area that is conducive to further development.

Universities and technical institutes that are expected to play an important role with regard to community development are likely to be more effective in

Box 6.4

University research partnerships are being forged in Campinas, Brazil

Source: UNCTAD 2004.

Since the mid-1990s, research partnerships between universities and the private sector, including foreign investors, have been established in Brazil. The University of Campinas (UNICAMP), in the State of São Paulo, has been involved in several partnership projects. One of these is the CPqD–FITEC (Centro de Pesquisa e Desenvolvimento–Fundação para Inovações Tecnológicas), the main technological center in Brazil, where university experts connect a company's needs for research with the expertise of UNICAMP's institutes, professors, and researchers.

More than 250 partnership agreements with private companies and 60 agreements with public companies have been established at UNICAMP. The companies include major global corporations with significant foreign direct investment in Brazil, such as Aventis, Bayer, Bristol, Compaq, Ericsson, Glaxo, HP, IBM, Monsanto, Motorola, Novartis, Roche, Syngentha, and Tetra Pak.

The partnership contracts include the details of the project and spell out the conditions of intellectual property rights. Patent ownership is determined on the basis of the technology disclosure and the innovative contribution given to the invention. If the private company provides most of the knowledge, it holds the patent. If the discovery is linked mainly to the university's work, UNICAMP holds the patent. UNICAMP holds about 300 patents, 3 of which have been licensed. UNICAMP expects to obtain 3 percent over the net profit of the licensee.

The success of R&D partnerships has been such that UNICAMP is now launching a bolder initiative: the creation of the UNICAMP Innovation Agency and the development of a technological park. The park will occupy 7 million square meters and provide human and physical resources, as well as facilities and services for R&D. The initiative will require about $1.5 billion, to be provided by the Ministry of Science and Technology, the Secretary of Science and Technology of the State of São Paulo, and the Municipality of Campinas. Private investors will also be called to participate in development of the park.

rural areas. Institutions that are involved in research that is very site specific will need to locate themselves, or some of their laboratories, accordingly. (Universities interested in marine research, for example, should be located near the coast.)

Universities throughout the world are undergoing reform and seeking new models to address challenges of sustainable development (box 6.5). Latin American, African, and Asian countries are exploring new approaches that can guide the creation of new universities and reform existing ones. The search is focusing on identifying appropriate curricula and pedagogy and integrating these institutions into the communities in which they are located. The new models emphasize educating graduates who serve as agents of socioeconomic change rather than mere holders of degree certificates.

Broadly speaking, there are three possible categories of action: reforming existing universities, upgrading existing institutes, or starting new universities. In all cases, supportive policies and regulations will need to be made and links created between universities, industry, and government.

For universities and technical institutes to adopt their new role as development partners, a new set of management procedures will be required. The

Box 6.5

Costa Rica's EARTH University is creating agents of change

The potential for adapting universities to social needs is illustrated by the case of Costa Rica's EARTH University, a private, nonprofit, international university designed to contribute to the sustainable development of the humid tropics (J. Zaglul, EARTH University, personal communication, 2004).

Created in 1990, the university currently has about 400 undergraduate students from more than 20 countries. Most of the students come from Latin America. EARTH University is focused on training leaders who will help promote sustainable development in their countries of origin. To foster the creation of agents of change, EARTH University has developed a distinctive and novel curriculum that emphasizes agriculture as a human activity, holistic integration of many academic disciplines, understanding today's changing and globalizing world, and a philosophy of learning by doing. The curriculum is characterized by practical learning, entrepreneurial capabilities, ethics and values, teamwork, group problem-solving, communication skills, vertical and horizontal integration of the curriculum, and fostering of social sensitivity through the acquisition of community development skills (L. Aylward, Harvard University, personal communication, 2004).

Over a four-year period, the EARTH program includes work experience, community experience, entrepreneurial projects, and an internship. Work experience, taking place on EARTH's teaching farms, gives students the opportunity to understand what happens day to day on a farm. Students work with members of the community to plan, organize, and execute projects for the benefit of the community and local rural farmers. This program is designed to promote an understanding of everyday rural family life.

Arguably the most distinguishing aspect of EARTH University's curriculum is the entrepreneurial project program. Provided with a loan from the University, students design a project, carry out feasibility and market studies, and develop and run their own business during the first three years of study.

In their third trimester of their third year, students leave campus and take part in a 15-month internship program with a host organization, such as a business, nonprofit organization, or farm. Using knowledge and skills acquired in their first three years at EARTH University, students obtain real-world practical experience upon which they can reflect during their fourth academic year. Instead of writing a dissertation or thesis, they prepare the equivalent of a business plan, which they use to start their own business upon graduation.

recommended changes—in many cases requiring drastic revisions in student and faculty selection procedures, new incentives and transparency mechanisms, and revised curricula and teaching methods—are likely to cause upheaval and resentment in various circles of the university. These organizational transformations must be effected, taking into account of the different systems of governance of universities, which differ across countries.

In some cases strong management can be recommended to ensure that the new schemes are put and remain in place. In other cases this recommendation makes no sense. In Latin America public universities are autonomous bodies ruled by processes in which faculty and students go through democratic procedures to elect rectors, vice-chancellors, and deans. Systemic tuning is needed to help the three actors—universities, government and industry—interact in a productive and respectful manner.

Science, technology, and innovation education can be enriched through partnerships with NGOs

Universities and technical institutes will very likely work closely with industry as well as government in the pursuit of national objectives. Therefore, it is important that the university have mechanisms in place through which it can retain its autonomy.

Forging partnerships with nongovernmental organizations

Science, technology, and innovation education can be enriched through partnerships with NGOs. The case of the Foundation for the Application and Teaching of the Sciences (FUNDAEC) in Colombia illustrates the importance of creating such partnerships (G. Correa, FUNDAEC, personal communication, 2004). The organization was created 30 years ago in the Valle del Cauca region of Colombia by a small group of physicists, mathematicians, agronomists, and professors in the social sciences who saw the need to extend high-quality education beyond the walls of the traditional university. The founders developed a common perspective that the right of the masses to have access to information and to fully participate in the generation and application of knowledge are fundamental to social and economic development.

This fundamental principle led to the creation of the University for Integral Development. The university has brought together a large number of organizations from across the world, working together to learn about how to involve populations in the processes of knowledge generation in pursuit of greater well-being (C. Honeyman, FUNDAEC, personal communication, 2004).

FUNDAEC has pursued a variety of lines of action toward this central goal, including systematic investigations with rural families in the area of agricultural and livestock production, helping to form cooperative community groups, developing appropriate agro-industrial technologies, developing the capacities of rural youth, and working with rural economies and small-scale businesses. As FUNDAEC has engaged in each of these areas, it has codified what it has learned in a series of educational materials written for secondary school and university levels. Some of these materials are available through FUNDAEC's University Center for Rural Well-Being, reaching more than 550 undergraduate and graduate students since its foundation. A further 75 interactive texts make up the curricular material for the Tutorial Learning System (*Sistema de Aprendizaje Tutorial* or SAT), an innovative secondary-school education and community development program. Some 70,000 students in Colombia have graduated from this program and another 30,000 are currently enrolled. The program has also been implemented on a small in several other countries in Latin America.

SAT was originally created to contribute to the process of development within a defined microregion near the city of Cali. Over the past few decades, however, as the reputation of the program has grown, it has become recognized as a formal secondary school system. More than 40 NGOs now offer its educational materials within an expanding number of regions, with FUNDAEC

**It is more
important
than ever for
developing
countries
to move
ahead in
scientific and
technological
development
at an
advanced
level**

continuing to provide training and curricular development. Often funded directly by local and municipal governments, the SAT program exemplifies a successful collaboration between the public and private sectors, carried out in pursuit of a common goal. Carrying forward FUNDAEC's central principle, SAT students are involved from the very beginning of their studies in the processes of generating knowledge, as they carry out investigations in their own communities and develop projects and initiatives to meet the particular needs they identify.

In its willingness to engage with others in such a far-reaching and ongoing process of learning, FUNDAEC provides an important example of the ways in which educational innovations can succeed in involving populations that have, for too long, been excluded from worldwide processes of knowledge generation and application.

Conclusion

It is more important than ever for developing countries to move ahead in scientific and technological development at an advanced level. Doing so will enable them to build local capacity that can help solve the many science and engineering–related problems they face. It will also position them to take an active part in the global knowledge economy.

Universities are vastly underutilized and potentially powerful vehicles for development in developing countries, particularly with respect to science and technology. If both universities and industry are encouraged to work actively together, universities will be able to assume new roles that could accelerate local and national development. Rendering these institutions more effective as key development partners will require changes at several levels of university administration. It will also require deep changes in enterprises, private as well as public, so that they can become strong demanders of the universities' capabilities, helping transform these capabilities into capacities. Government will need to act as a careful facilitator of interactions between these two actors. If this is achieved, the "loneliness syndrome" that for so long affected universities in developing countries will be redressed, allowing them to contribute to economic growth and social development.

Chapter 7

Promoting technology-based business activities

Policymakers in developing countries can do much to promote business activities in science, technology, and innovation. They can foster the creation and growth of small and medium-size enterprises, improve access to financial capital, establish industry extension services and help firms establish international partnerships and linkages, and use government procurement and selective industrial policies for technological development. Developing countries must also ensure that their enterprises comply with international agreements and meet international standards, including those governing intellectual property rights and phytosanitary and other standards.

Fostering the creation and growth of small and medium-size enterprises

Small to medium-size enterprises should be encouraged to take a leading role in exploiting new opportunities. There is a need to develop, apply, and emphasize the important role of engineering, technology, and small enterprise development in poverty reduction and in sustainable social and economic development. Initiatives are needed that build capacity, establish appropriate financial systems, increase public awareness, craft and implement policy, and ensure that engineering and technology are included in Poverty Reduction Strategy Papers (PRSPs). Governments, universities, NGOs, and international agencies all need to play roles in developing and implementing strategy.

In advanced industrial economies, small and medium-size enterprises have developed much of the innovative and cutting-edge technology (Andreassi 2003). In many developing economies these enterprises have been the foundation of industrialization. In Taiwan (China), for example, small and medium-size enterprises were the engines behind the postwar industrial upgrading of the economy. By serving as suppliers to multinational corporations and foreign

Incubators play major roles in the creation and facilitation of small and medium-size businesses

buyers, small and medium-size enterprises in Taiwan (China) gradually acquired both the process and product technologies that enabled the economy to upgrade its technology. Similar evidence on the role of small and medium-size enterprises is emerging from mainland China (Gibb and Li 2003; Jun 2003).

Despite the importance of small and medium-size enterprises, investments and incentives to grow them have been minimal or nonexistent in most developing countries. The focus of governments and foreign investment in developing countries has been on large infrastructure and industrial projects.

Supporting these enterprises is critical, but doing so is fraught with financial, administrative, legal, and market-related difficulties. Developing countries therefore can help foster the growth of small and medium-size enterprises by creating business and technology incubators, supporting clusters, and establishing export-processing zones. Each institution has benefits and drawbacks.

Business incubators

Incubators play major roles in the creation and facilitation of small and medium-size businesses (Scaramuzzi 2002; Vedovello and Godinho 2003).[1] Their role ranges from providing affordable space to providing core enterprise support functions, such as enterprise development, financing, marketing, and legal services. Governments in developing countries are encouraged to support business incubators (Lalkaka 2003).

Incubation comes in many forms, ranging from government-funded initiatives to public-private partnerships. Governments are encouraged to provide grants, low interest rate loans, and tax incentives to private companies that provide incubation resources for small and medium-size enterprises. They should also consider funding university-based incubators focused on a particular area of science, technology, or innovation area, as well as not-for-profit–based incubators.

Technology parks provide environments in which small and medium-size enterprises tend to flourish. Governments should designate areas throughout the country as technology zones and offer incentives to companies willing to relocate to these zones. Governments should also focus on making it simple for new businesses to obtain the necessary legal documents, facilities, and ICT.

Business incubation catalyzes the process of starting and growing companies, providing entrepreneurs with the expertise, networks, and tools they need to make their ventures successful (Grimaldi and Grandi 2003). Incubation programs diversify economies, commercialize technologies, create jobs, and build wealth. They promote the development of new and qualified small and medium-size enterprises by providing them with the resources (premises, infrastructure, and services) they need to improve their chances of success.

Many business incubators have strong links with real estate business development. Many receive significant public funding and are located near research institutes and technical universities.

The best results occur when start-up and existing companies are mixed, to encourage mutual learning and stimulation

The past 20 years of experience with business incubators has revealed three critical factors that are important to their success. The first is the creation of the incubator itself and its management. The second is the incubation process. The third is performance assessment.

Successful business incubator creation depends on careful planning and preparation based on thorough and objective analysis. The preparation and implementation of a business incubator may take one to two years. During this period a management team of up to 10 people defines the objectives of its activities and establishes selection criteria. It also gathers information about local or regional conditions to assess the feasibility of the incubator (von Zedtwitz 2003). Four aspects are important for assessing feasibility: profiles of local entrepreneurs and their needs, identification of the potential for mobilizing support, identification of suitable locations, and projection of investment requirements.

Designing the incubator organization and management structure, selecting staff members (especially experienced entrepreneurial managers and board members), and defining resources are also critical during this period.

Initial funds of $500,000–$1.5 million may be required to launch a business incubator. Securing these funds is a major obstacle in this early phase. Business incubators often require three to five years to become self-sustaining. The best results occur when start-up and existing companies are mixed, to encourage mutual learning and stimulation.

A successful incubation process consists of three steps. The first is entrance of entrepreneurs into the incubator based on clear admission criteria and procedures. Survival rates of the graduates from incubators strongly depend on admission policies.

The second—development of enterprises in the incubator—is done by creating a nurturing environment and providing various services, including physical infrastructure; business planning, assistance, and counseling services; advertising and marketing services; financial advisory services; management training services; know-how services; management advisory services; networking services; industrial infrastructure (roads, water, electricity, ICT, buildings, and industrial machines); secretarial services; security services (especially for intellectual property protection); and postincubation support. The objectives of the incubator define the services offered.

The third step, graduation of businesses from the incubator, needs to be based on policies that determine clear time frames and an agreement on the type, amount, and value of services provided during the incubation process. The success of the incubation process depends on the effective policies and management of the incubator itself.

Performance assessment needs to be carried out to evaluate the outcome of incubation, management policies and their effectiveness, and services and their value-added. Two types of information are needed. One is measurement based on incubator effectiveness versus alternative policy approaches. The other is

Technology incubators are a special type of business incubator that focuses on new ventures that employ advanced technologies

the measurement of the enabling factors for private sector development and the main institutional and structural gaps at the country level.

Business incubators increase the likelihood that small and medium-size enterprises survive, encourage information exchange and mutual benefits, overcome small business isolation and powerlessness by clustering small and medium-size enterprises, and become role models. In OECD countries survival rates of new ventures nurtured in business incubators are about 80–85 percent—much higher than the 30–50 percent rate of success of other firms. Survival rates among new ventures that emerge from incubators are as high as 85 percent in some developing countries, such as Brazil and China, where strong support from government and tight links with the university system are available.

Business incubators do have some downsides, including limited scope for job creation and short-run benefits, limited outreach and "picking winners" problems, the possibility of creating dependency on government support, the need to provide focused assistance and subsidies until incubators become self-sustainable. They also depend on having good business infrastructure in a good location. Business incubators are not a development panacea. They can address some important development issues but not all of them.

Technology incubators

Technology incubators are a special type of business incubator that focuses on new ventures that employ advanced technologies (box 7.1). Although technology incubators share the same general goals as business incubators, they focus more on the commercialization and diffusion of technology by new firms, both of which are often impeded by market and institutional failures and the high level of uncertainty associated with technology development. Commercialization and diffusion of technology increases the return from public investment.

Technology incubators help create high-tech companies. Unlike basic business incubators, they have the mission of turning innovative ideas into successful business. They provide an environment for prototyping and test-marketing knowledge on how an idea can be turned into a business.

Most technology-focused incubators come in the form of private companies. They often consist of a combination of venture capital resources and business support functionality.

Commercialization of technology has been a main focus of business and technology incubation activities in both developed and developing countries. In newly industrial and transition economies, technology incubators emerged from central government schemes rather than from local public-private initiatives. They aim mainly to build bridges between academia and industry, promote innovation in small and medium-size enterprises, and encourage investment in technology-based start-up firms. One important feature of technology incubators is that they are usually not stand-alone ventures but have a strong tendency

Box 7.1

**Good practices
can help
technology
incubators
succeed**

Source: Nolan 2003.

Both technology incubators and general business incubators require clear definition of objectives at the outset and recruitment of experienced entrepreneurial managers. Sharing experiences on what works is also important for both types of incubators.

Some good practices are particularly important for technology incubators. One is the emphasis on particular cluster-focused technologies, which helps the incubator achieve a critical mass, focus on specific needs arising from technology incubation, and enhance synergies among firms.

Selection criteria of technology incubators are also different from those of general incubators: they should not depend entirely on business plans but focus on factors such as marketability of products, entrepreneur experience, and the overall fit with other incubator tenants (in order to foster synergies).

Another good practice for technology incubators is tailoring and leveraging existing services. Since technology incubators are often too small to provide the entire range of services, tailoring services to clients' needs and providing access to existing outside resources through brokering and networking can be helpful.

Diversification of financial sources for entrepreneurs is also important for technology incubators, because it helps match entrepreneurs to particular types of capital that support technology activities.

Another very important factor is the effort to integrate technology incubators with the surrounding infrastructure for innovation and the broader national innovation system. Many previous experiences show that real estate management should not be the primary goal for technology incubators.

Services provided by technology incubators are similar to those provided by general business incubators. But since their main objective is accelerating the transfer and diffusion of technological know-how and industrialization, several services hold particular importance. In OECD countries technology incubators tend to provide more assistance than general incubators in technology consulting and support services that connect enterprises with technology transfer programs providing access to external technical facilities and resources. These resources include university faculty and students; linked to manufacturing extension services; financing assistance for equity financing, including venture capital funds, mutually guaranteed loans and royalty financing; legal assistance for incorporation, drafting license agreements, and protecting intellectual property rights; and marketing (OECD 1997).

to affiliate with public and private sources of research knowledge, including universities, public research institutions, and large technology-based firms.

Technology parks have been the most popular kind of technology incubators. They have proliferated not only in developed economies but also more recently in Southeast Asia and Latin America. Technology parks have strong R&D components in their organizational structure. They are based on the possession of property and usually include university and research institutions, which ensure access to research facilities, simplify technology transfer operations, and allow the incubation of spin-off enterprises that can be launched by faculty or researchers from research institutions.

Silicon Valley is located near Stanford University and the Stanford Research Park; the industrial cluster along Route 128 is located near MIT. The

The clustering of university and research institutions and enterprises is expected to yield more efficient use of innovation resources

Hsinchu Science-Based Industrial Park is located near the National Tsing-Hua and the National Chiao Tung universities, in Taiwan (China). The Hsinchu Science-Based Industrial Park has helped reverse the brain drain in Taiwan (China), and it has exerted positive spillover effects on the surrounding area. The congregation of high-tech firms has enhanced competition between traditional and high-tech industry. These parks contribute to reindustrialization, regional development, and the creation of synergies. Within technology parks, there are numerous variations according to the services offered based on their objectives, which define types and levels of R&D and other technological capabilities required to create and sustain them.

Technology parks facilitate networking. By encouraging interactions, feedback, and awareness by bringing people from different institutions together physically, technology parks facilitate the transfer of technology from university and research institutions to enterprises. They also stimulate innovation through the cross-fertilization of ideas between researchers and entrepreneurs. In terms of stimulation of innovation activities, the clustering of university and research institutions and enterprises is expected to yield more efficient use of innovation resources and link basic research to commercialization through applied research (Link and Scott 2003).

Incubators without walls

Costs are an important determinant of services offered by incubators. Costs are especially high for technology incubators, which are usually facilities based. To avoid these costs, so-called "incubators without walls," or virtual incubators, are sometimes created. Most of them are technology incubators, often created by a university or research institution. These incubators are non–property-based ventures that require lower fixed investment. They serve small and medium-size enterprises in areas where a sufficient critical mass of tenants is lacking. The important characteristic of these incubators is their ability to operate both within and outside of walls, by linking them through computer and telecommunications networks.

Production networks and clusters

Networking is very important, because it allows small and medium-size enterprises to access skills, highly educated labor, and pooled business services. In the rapidly changing technological and global business environment, more attention is paid to groups of firms, teams, and interfirm networks than to individual firms (Chen, Liu, and Shih 2003). This makes networking more important than ever before.

Networking within the incubator is critical. Industrial clustering is effective tool for networking, because it brings actors into close proximity. This has been an important assumption behind property-based incubation activities. But effective networks do not occur just by bringing actors together. They are

Foreign direct investment can lead to an increase in productivity in the host country through technology diffusion to participating domestic firms

formed on the basis of mutual needs: cooperation happens when one entity has a need for goods or services that another can deliver. Connecting needs, rather than just bringing actors together in close proximity, is the most important role that incubators play.

Networking can also extend to existing and established firms outside the incubator facilities. Incubators can provide their services to outside firms (known as *affiliate clients*) and large or established firms (known as *anchor firms*). These firms can increase incubator revenue, help market products, and bring experience to tenant firms.

Export processing zones

Export processing zones (EPZs) are areas in developing countries that permit participating firms to acquire their imported inputs duty free as long as they export 100 percent of their products. This scheme works when selling manufactured goods at world prices is profitable given a country's low wages. The concept has been most widely used in Asia.

EPZs are an important mechanism for acquiring technology and diffusing it in the local economy. But strategies to promote the establishment of such zones must be designed with long-term technological development in mind.

EPZs can be used as business incubators, and they can be very useful for developing enterprises with export and foreign trade potential. But EPZs' linkages are generally with the international community; they have little potential to strengthen the local economy, due to their limited backward linkages or technological spillovers. This is because the focus of EPZs is attracting foreign direct investment by facilitating business services and providing access to infrastructure and tax incentives.

Foreign direct investment can lead to an increase in productivity in the host country through technology diffusion to participating domestic firms as well as backward and forward linkages. But forming such linkage formations is difficult, because most foreign direct investment to developing economies is vertical investment that has a much lower level of technology transfer than market-seeking horizontal investment. In vertical foreign direct investment, the investing firms fragment their production chain into stages, matching factor intensities of their activities with factor endorsements of host countries. EPZs can match demand and supply between foreign firms and local factories and help incubate new ventures within the zones.

The Republic of Korea and Taiwan (China) have been the most successful users of EPZs. Most of their rapid growth was the result of their export orientation. EPZs were the starting point of export-oriented performance standards. EPZs and exports by participating firms were tied to subsidies. In the Republic of Korea large exporters were given access to cheaper and longer term investment capital and tariff protection for their sales in the domestic market.

Taiwan (China) granted large exporters permission to sell products in several industries in the highly protected domestic market.

Improving access to financial capital

The main sources of finance for technological innovation are banks and financial institutions, individual private investors ("angels"), and public funds.

Banks and financial institutions

Banks and financial institutions can play an important role in fostering technological innovation. However, their record in this field in developing countries has been poor. There is a need to reform some of the banking and financial institutions in these countries so that they can play a role in promoting technological innovation. Such reforms should be part of a larger set of policies, incentives, and strategies aimed at funding innovation (box 7.2).

Box 7.2

Governments can take a variety of steps to increase access to financing for science, technology, and innovation

Governments can facilitate access to financing for science, technology, and innovation in many ways.

Create sound monetary and financial policies. Measures could include reducing cost inhibitors, allowing loans to be secured with intellectual property, and providing insurance and indemnity protection on loans to small and medium-size enterprises.

Provide additional capital incentives for specific technologies. This could be geared toward venture capitalists and lending institutions through specific policies that support small and medium-size enterprises engaged in developing technologies of particular interest. Incentives could include differential interest rates, access to domain experts, or preferential access to new R&D from local or foreign government or university research institutions.

Establish a government-funded venture type investment strategy. Capital markets do not automatically exist for all sectors or technologies. Indeed, part of the process of development is creating institutions to stimulate interest in a particular type of technology that the government or public deems a priority for development but for which private sector funding is not forthcoming.

Help capital to become professionally managed. In India the government funds R&D, but managers of these funds often find it difficult to assess new technologies, because they lack the expertise or for other reasons. The "graduation" of such traditional investors to more professional and technological management requires not only government support but ideally exposure to international learning as well.

Support microfinance. Microfinance schemes are emerging as a key way to help poor entrepreneurs help themselves. The technological components of such enterprises can be substantial, ranging from food processing to auto repair to solar energy and other initiatives. Microfinance also provides an opportunity for very small firms to build links and scale up, and it facilitates simple technology transfer and the consideration of export opportunities.

Many semi-industrial countries provide non-reimbursable loans to small and medium-size enterprises for technological innovation projects

Venture capitalists and angel investors

Attracting venture capital and encouraging the emergence of "angel" (private) investors can increase finance for technological innovation.[2] Small and medium-size enterprises have flourished in most developed countries because of the critical role that capital markets, especially venture capitalist markets, have played (Branscomb and Auerswald 2001; Bruton, Ahlstrom, and Yeh 2004). Venture capitalists do not just bring money to the table; they help groom start-ups into multinational institutions. Bringing venture capital markets into developing countries could help ensure the sustainability of the companies in which they invest (Chocce 2003). This realization is forcing developing countries to start reforming their venture capital systems (Dossani 2003).

Public sources of finance

In the absence of well-functioning capital markets and market-based mechanisms such as venture capital, most developing countries rely on publicly funded trust funds or specialized financial agencies to upgrade technology and promote innovation. These specialized technological financing agencies provide loans to firms or consortia of firms, particularly small and medium-size and research institutions, to undertake research and technological development, develop new products and production techniques, improve existing products and processes, and upgrade product quality and strengthen innovative capacity. In addition, many semi-industrial countries, such as Brazil and Mexico, provide nonreimbursable loans to small and medium-size enterprises for technological innovation projects.

The Inter-American Development Bank began financing science, technology, and innovation in 1962. It has made loans to Argentina, Chile, Mexico, Peru, and Venezuela. Brazil and Mexico have a number of special credit programs to encourage technological innovation by private enterprises.

In Brazil the Ministry of Science and Technology's Program to Support Scientific and Technological Development, funded by the World Bank, and the federal innovation-financing agency, FINEP, provide credit for innovation. The Bank-sponsored program includes two subprojects, a support program, which finances technological sector entities, such as QSTM (quality, standards, testing, and metrology) institutes, and a technology management and competitiveness program, which supports pilot partnerships between firms and research institutes. FINEP offers integral support credit for all stages of a technological innovation business plan, from design to licensing or purchase of technology, training, technical assistance, and initial working capital. It even offers pre-investment credit for engineering consultancy or quality management plans for environmental, technological, and product quality (IADB 2001). Provision of this support, especially to small and medium-size enterprises, has been instrumental in leveling the playing field for companies that lack the size and financial capability to venture into financially risky areas.

Establishing a virtual center is an exciting prospect that could bring knowledge to places that badly need it

This experience is of great interest and relevance for developing countries. It strongly suggests the need to develop differentiated institutions and facilities to support domestic technological development as one of the building blocks of genuine systemic gains in competitiveness. Microfinance is particularly important in the innovation and transfer of technology to small and microenterprises in developing countries. Many small loans are taken out for the purchase of technology, particularly by women. It is important to match microfinance models to local social and economic situations, as the transfer or innovation of inappropriate microfinance models frequently fail.

Establishing industry extension services

"Food production in developing countries relies heavily on technical support through agricultural extension services. Such support, however, is not widely provided. The Japanese government is starting to incorporate such support in its development assistance to Indonesia as part of a joint effort to strengthen the country's industrial clusters (KRI International Corporation 2004).

Knowledge extension can be applied to help meet the Goals using science, engineering, and technology in many ways. ICT can be used to match people with knowledge with people who need that knowledge. However, it must not be forgotten that tacit knowledge is a fundamental part of the ability to solve problems, and this type of knowledge can be deployed only face to face. Industry extension services will need to ensure that people can interact both physically and virtually.

Establishing a virtual center—one that ties into the many existing extension and engineering centers around the world—is an exciting prospect that could bring knowledge to places that badly need it. Compiling knowledge of best practices into freely accessible databases would be another way to use ICT to diffuse technology and encourage its appropriate adoption in developing countries.

The loss of skills may come about through many different processes. These include allowing universities to languish, allowing lack of funds or a track record of innovation to erode the confidence of local individuals to participate in global innovation, introducing new technologies too rapidly, and letting the infrastructure necessary to sustain previously made gains erode and importing technologies that require foreign technicians to service them without creating a local technical capability.

Establishing international partnerships and linkages

International partnerships and linkages are an important aspect of technological development in developing countries. Incentives should be provided that encourage such partnerships. These include the diffusion of hardware technologies from centers such as Silicon Valley and Route 128 through diaspora channels to countries like Israel, India, and Ireland. In addition, the potential exists for establishing private-public partnerships to invest in new technolo-

Public technology procurement can be instrumental in developing technical specifications and improving standards in cooperation with manufacturers and buyers

gies. An often neglected development is the link between the private sector and the open source material from public sector institutes all over the world.

Building local, regional, and international linkages can provide relevant services, and it can integrate local infrastructure with national and international sources of technologies and markets. In Germany, for example, networks of technology and innovation centers connect not only throughout Germany but also with those in Central and Eastern Europe.

Using government procurement

Government technology procurement can be an important tool in low-income countries, which have weak productive sectors and a weak technological demand (box 7.3). There is a debate over the role of public support for procurement as a tool for technological development. But many countries have created and nurtured new industries or lagging old ones on this basis. Firms have gradually acquired technological capability in this way and become globally competitive over time. The question is not whether public procurement is a legitimate mechanism appropriate but when it should end and how it can help firms compete on their own.

Government technology procurement is currently used most in building public health infrastructure and increasing access to medicine. This experience can be used to develop government technology procurement with strict guidelines for selection of firms and evaluation of products and services delivered. The process must all ensure that participation is inclusive.

Public technology procurement can be instrumental in developing technical specifications and improving standards in cooperation with manufacturers

Box 7.3 **Public procurement can spur the development of domestic firms**	In the drive to make nationally owned firms globally competitive, the Chinese government promotes domestic computer hardware firms through both direct and indirect support, including favored treatment in government procurement of technologies developed in state R&D institutions. The Indian government gives similar support to the country's pharmaceutical industry to produce "essential" drugs. The Nordic countries have successfully used public procurement to promote industrial development, particularly in the telecommunications sector. The lessons these countries learned from these industrial development processes are now being extended to other fields, such as environmental management.
	In Scandinavia government technology procurement has helped solve national problems while helping local firms grow and become international. Projects on a large scale (in Sweden) and a small scale (in Denmark) have fostered innovation and global competitiveness among domestic enterprises. Working on public projects (the civil use of nuclear technology, railroads, telecommunications) helped Swedish firms like ASEA and Ericsson become global players. Public technology procurement in areas related to health, such as electronic medical devices, and other areas, such as wind energy, were key to allowing small and medium-size Danish enterprises to become global players in niche markets.

**Some of
the new
international
trade rules
limit the
application of
some policies
previously
critical to
fostering
domestic
industrial
development**

and buyers and hence promoting higher efficiency and increased returns arising from the adoption of new technologies (Nelson, Peterhansl, and Sampat 2004). For example, by supporting the prototype development or issuing competitive bids for products that match or exceed certain technical specifications, public sector agencies can directly support learning and innovation in domestic firms.

Using selective industrial policies

International trade is one of the most important sources of impetus for rapid technological innovation. In the past, countries were able to use various trade and industrial policy instruments to build up domestic technological capabilities. Many of these instruments are now prohibited under the new trade rules, especially those of the WTO. Some of the new international trade rules limit the application of some policies previously critical to fostering domestic industrial development. These policies include infant industry protection, export subsidies and targeting, local content rules and other performance requirements on foreign investors, directed credit, copying and reverse engineering, and restrictions on foreign entry, ownership and treatment.

The theoretical underpinning of the new rules is the efficiency of free markets. The issue is not whether markets fail but the extent to which governments can improve upon them and promote faster industrial and technological development. History shows that it is possible for governments to do this, but it also shows that they can also go very wrong. Given the risk of government failures, the policy issue is then how to improve government capabilities, not to presume that governments can do no right.

The main forms of selective policies permitted under the new rules pertain to skill formation, technology support and financing of innovation, promotion and targeting of foreign direct investment, infrastructure development for information technology, and general subsidies that do not affect trade performance. The advanced industrial countries and most semi-industrial countries use all of these tools—and some that are not in conformance with the spirit of the rules. The least developed countries tend not to use them.[3]

It is imperative that all countries maximize their deployment of available instruments to build industrial capabilities. It clearly requires advanced administrative competence, information and flexibility—capabilities not found in many countries (Amsden 2001; Amsden and Chu 2003). The first challenge of new industrial policy must be to strengthen these capabilities.

Until recently, the trading system, dominated by the WTO, addressed development only in a piecemeal fashion. Debates on trade at the WTO were conducted with little reference to a broader vision of how trade fits into development. Concerns over the agreement on Trade-Related Aspects of Intellectual Property Rights (TRIPS) have taken center stage. Patent law changes have occupied much of the WTO's time and created excessive pressures on developing countries to harmonize their systems with those of the advanced industrial countries.

It is imperative that all countries maximize their deployment of available instruments to build industrial capabilities

There has been relatively little appreciation of the amount of time institutional reform may take, even when developing countries learn from the histories of the industrial countries.

The 2000 WTO Ministerial Meeting recognized that the links between trade and technological development needed to be better understood. Decision-makers at the meeting agreed to set up a Working Group on Trade and Transfer of Technology to examine these links and make recommendations on how to accelerate technology flows to developing countries (WTO 2002). The WTO also agreed to put development at the heart of the WTO Work Program. This agreement, together with the establishment of the Working Group on Trade and Transfer of Technology, has opened a window of opportunity to make the multilateral trading system more technology oriented. Doing so will be very difficult. Subsequent WTO negotiations under the Doha Ministerial Declaration have shifted attention to other issues such as agriculture, and technology is no longer a major subject on the agenda.

Complying with intellectual property rights regulations

Protecting intellectual property rights is a critical aspect of technological innovation. But overly protective systems could have a negative impact on creativity. It is therefore important to design intellectual property protections systems that take the special needs of developing countries into account. Provisions in international intellectual property agreements that provide for technology cooperation with developing countries need to be identified and implemented immediately.

To encourage innovation and unlock local capital, individuals and corporations need to feel that their research is protected; where intellectual property rights have been violated, compensation must be provided. However, most countries developed without these protections being structured across the economy in any clear way. Indeed, institutional development of patent regimes usually occurred after a country's firms achieved a significant level of innovation capability and then desired to protect their investments. This line of thinking would lead to a global intellectual property regime that acknowledges the co-evolutionary nature of technological innovation and enforcement of intellectual property rights.

One way of adjusting intellectual property rights based on a country's level of development would be to create a three-tier system. Tier A countries would be required to comply with all provisions of TRIPS, including the legal framework and "effective enforcement," as required under Article 41. Developing countries with per capita GDP of, say, more than $5,000 would fall into this category (alternatively, an export criterion could be used). Tier B could apply to countries with per capita GDP of $1,000–$5,000. These countries would adopt the full legal framework required under TRIPS, perhaps with some minimal level of enforcement. Countries with per capita GDP of less than $1,000 (Tier C countries) would establish the legal framework required

Protecting intellectual property rights is a critical aspect of technological innovation

under TRIPS, perhaps with the exception of patent laws and protections for integrated circuits.

If one of the applicants or the assignee is from a developed country, the initial application would need to be made in a country with A-level protection. If all the applicants were from a least developed country, they could apply for protection in their own country, where the laws may provide C-level protection. If these applicants wanted to extend their rights to cover a developed country, they would be able to obtain only C-level protection for their invention, even in the country that has A-level protection.

The recent recognition by the TRIPS Council of the right of developing countries to obtain generic drugs to fill their domestic needs should be built upon to help countries develop the ability to manufacture pharmaceuticals for local (and perhaps ultimately export) consumption. Less developed countries could be permitted to use process patents to make drugs for their own markets and for markets in other countries that lack domestic manufacturing facilities or competence, but they would not be able to compete in markets with A-level protection. Compulsory licensing procedures for such uses could be simplified, at least for C-level countries.

Successful developing countries with C-level protection may become industrial and in time meet the GDP criteria to reach the intermediate level. They would then have to amend their laws to afford B-level protection. This might facilitate the eventual adoption of patent regimes desirable to both advanced industrial and developing countries, while still allowing developing countries to frame their own laws.

The TRIPS agreement represents an important step in establishing minimum standards for national laws governing intellectual property protection. Most of the key elements of the intellectual property systems of the United States, the European Union, and Japan were similar and could be harmonized. These regions are the largest sources of inventions. Areas of divergence between their systems include first-to-invent systems, the scope of patentable subject matter, the treatment of plants and animals, geographical indications, and the degree to which moral values should influence the granting of intellectual property rights.[4]

The need to strike a balance between enforcing intellectual property rights and meeting the technological needs of developing countries became a key theme in the Uruguay Round of negotiations. Article 8 of TRIPS states that countries "may, in formulating or amending their laws and regulations, adopt measures necessary to protect public health and nutrition, and to promote the public interest in sectors of vital importance to their socioeconomic and technological development, provided that such measures are consistent with the provisions of this Agreement." Article 8.2 provides countries with the freedom to adopt measures that "may be needed to prevent the abuse of intellectual property rights by rights holders or the resort to practices which unreasonably restrain trade

Developing countries are increasingly recognizing that traditional knowledge associated with biological diversity forms part of product development

or adversely affect the international transfer of technology." This prevention of abuse clause deals primarily with measures that undermine competition.

This flexibility suggests that developing countries need to formulate their interests through national policy and legislation. The successful use of the flexibility granted in the TRIPS agreement will depend on the relationship between a country and its major trading partners in the industrial world, since most of the inventions that are likely to be affected by national laws belong to rights holders in the industrial world.[5] Trading partners are the primary focus for TRIPS protection issues, because only trading partners have the incentive to pursue trade remedies against a country for violating their intellectual property treaty obligations (D.S. Long, John Marshall Law School, personal communication, 2004).

Article 66.2 of the TRIPS agreement states that "developed country Members shall provide incentives to enterprises and institutions in their territories for the purpose of promoting and encouraging technology transfer to least-developed country Members in order to enable them to create a sound and viable technological base." This provision has received little attention, despite a 2003 decision of the TRIPS Council that called for annual reports on its implementation. The reports required by the decision will include information on the type of incentive and the government agency or other entity providing it, as well as information on the practical functioning of the incentives.

Developing countries are increasingly recognizing that traditional knowledge associated with biological diversity that is held by local and indigenous communities forms part of product development (box 7.4) (Dutfield 2004).

Box 7.4

Building on local knowledge

Source: www.nifindia.org.

The role of traditional knowledge in economic transformation is emerging as an important foundation for community development. For example, in 2000 the Indian Department of Science and Technology helped establish the National Innovation Foundation, which focuses on scouting, spawning, sustaining, and scaling up grassroots innovations of relevance to sustainable development. The foundation's work builds on long-standing efforts by the Honey Bee Network and the Society for Research and Initiatives for Sustainable Technologies and Institutions to document local innovations. They have more than 10,000 documented innovations (A.K. Gupta, Honey Bee Network, personal communication, 2004).

The National Innovation Foundation began its first national campaign in 2000 to scout innovations and outstanding traditional knowledge. It has since completed four national campaigns. By 2003 the foundation had documented more than 37,000 innovations in 350 districts of India. In addition, the National Innovation Foundation has access to another 6,000 traditional knowledge examples in the Honey Bee database managed by the Society for Research and Initiatives for Sustainable Technologies and Institutions. The main challenge facing the initiative is how to transform the innovations into products for wider commercial application. To make this possible the National Innovation Foundation is helping to obtain intellectual property protection for qualifying ideas. By 2004 more than 70 patent, trademark, and industrial design applications had been filed in India and abroad.

Open access to sequence data is an important tool for promoting innovation and should therefore be encouraged

They are seeking to enhance their capacity to use such knowledge as part of their efforts to implement the relevant provisions of the United Nations Convention on Biological Diversity, especially those provisions dealing with traditional knowledge and access to genetic resources. Developing countries are seeking intellectual property registration systems that identify and document the sources of genetic material and indigenous knowledge used in product development. Such a system would allow for the sharing of benefits arising from the use of such genetic material and knowledge in accordance with the Convention on Biological Diversity.

One of the most controversial areas of intellectual property protection relates to ownership of genetic information derived from the sequencing of the human genome and other organisms. The private sector would like to extend intellectual property protection to the data using a variety of means. While such a measure would provide the incentives needed by the private sector to invest in product development, there is concern that such measures could undermine long-term research. Open access to sequence data is an important tool for promoting innovation and should therefore be encouraged as part of the large pursuit to balance "open science" and proprietary incentives embodied in intellectual property rights (David 2004).

Meeting international standards and technical regulations

Standards and technical regulations are a set of technical specifications that describe the characteristics of a product, a service, a process, or a material (Lall and Pietrobelli 2003). The use of standards reduces transactions costs, information asymmetries, and uncertainty between buyers and sellers with respect to quality and technical characteristics. Standards and technical regulations provide many benefits to producers and consumers, not the least of which is their information value. In order to protect human health, for example, foodstuffs are required to meet sanitary and phytosanitary standards. Other benefits from standards and technical regulations include those that can be attributed to enhanced competition and economies of scale. When production can be standardized, components can be produced more efficiently around the world. These standards also accelerate the spread of best practice and innovation, especially to small and medium-size enterprises.

Products have to comply with a large number of standards and technical regulations in order to access importing markets. These standards and regulations can sometimes lead to discretional enforcement, effectively restricting market entry despite the absence of tariffs or quotas. Even when applied properly, they require significant technological infrastructure in the exporting country, as it is the seller who must demonstrate that its products satisfy applicable requirements. The Technical Barriers to Trade Agreement and the Agreement on the Application of Sanitary and Phyto-Sanitary Standards, negotiated

The use of standards reduces transactions costs, information asymmetries, and uncertainty between buyers and sellers with respect to quality and technical characteristics

during the Uruguay Round, were meant to ensure that standards and technical regulations do not create unnecessary obstacles to trade.

Metrology provides the measurement accuracy and compatibility without which standards cannot be applied; it is a necessary requisite for the advancement of scientific and technical knowledge. The application of standards and the certification of products necessarily imply testing and quality control services. Quality, standards, testing, and metrology (QSTM) are thus a critical component of the technological infrastructure.

Developing countries' ability to meet their international commitments and participate more meaningfully in global trade depends on having adequate physical, institutional, and technological infrastructure as well as scientific and technological skills and capabilities to comply with current and future standards (UNIDO 2003). Such capacities are often lacking in developing countries, particularly in the least developed countries. Enterprises in developing countries have very little knowledge of or information about the standards and technical regulations required to enter advanced country markets, and they are unable to rely on the domestic technological infrastructure to trace and prevent problems. In addition, for a large and growing number of products, importing countries require independent evidence that their manufacture complies with quality management (ISO 9000) and environmental management (ISO 14000) systems.

Asymmetric information on standards and technical regulations places developing countries at a disadvantage because of the higher costs associated with duplicative testing requirements performed by importers in order to assess conformity with sanitary and phytosanitary standards. This duplication of tests is often associated with lack of international credibility of developing countries' standard organizations, which is partly attributable to underinvestment in these areas. This lack of credibility prevents these countries from participating in what is considered to be an important instrument in liberalizing technical barriers to trade, namely, mutual recognition agreements.[6]

The investments required to meet standards and technical regulations often entail discrepancies between private and social costs and benefits, which therefore often warrant the supply of public goods.[7] Furthermore, while international technical assistance has been increasingly available to train trade negotiators in least developed countries, it has failed to put enough emphasis on the technical infrastructure needs of developing countries in the area of trade capacity building. Overall, the development challenge for the developing countries is not only negotiating better market access but ensuring that the productive capacities are in place to respond to demands and requirements.

While the WTO agreements require developing countries to develop national capacity to implement the agreements on standards and technical regulations, little technical assistance has been provided for them to do so. The

To ensure that international (and national) standards are set in a balanced manner, developing countries need to participate in their development

recent Doha Ministerial Declaration on Implementation Issues indicates serious problems for developing countries in implementing some of the standards.

For many developing countries, minimum levels of investments in technical and human infrastructure needed to comply with standards and technical regulations may exceed their annual health and development budgets (Finger and Schuler 2000). But underinvestment in these standards and regulations reduces the potential growth of exports and GDP, creating a vicious cycle. There is, therefore, a case for providing subsidies to these countries to enable them to create the infrastructure needed to meet the standards and technical regulations.

Meeting the proliferation of standards and technical regulations requires a scientific and technological base that is located largely in industrial countries. It is not surprising that these are the countries that report the highest number of new standard notifications to the WTO.[8]

Currently, although some developing countries have parts of the requirements to deal with international standards in place, in most cases, especially in the least developed countries, major parts are missing. Even if services exist, they are usually not recognized internationally and do not therefore fully assist potential exporters. Because of these missing domestic capabilities, developing countries are not able to technically analyze and challenge importing countries' claims about exported products or participate in international standard setting bodies in a meaningful way.

To ensure that international (and national) standards are set in a balanced manner, developing countries need to participate in their development. This requires establishing and strengthening national and regional standards bodies. These standardization institutions need to be equipped with the technical and human capacity to develop and adopt standards through subsectoral technical analysis. In addition, they can help establish national and regional databases of relevant standards and regulations, providing essential services to inform the private sector. Regional cooperation, especially among African countries, has the added benefit of harmonizing standards and achieving regional economies of scale in information gathering and dissemination.

Other supporting technological infrastructure is required to complement the work of standardization bodies. A national and regional system of metrology ensures that the measurements and tests required for all production, quality, and certification activities are consistent and correct. This includes operational laboratories for primary and secondary physical standards and certified reference materials for chemical and microbiological purposes, laboratory capacities for legal and industrial metrology, and a framework and system for calibration and materials testing.

Certifying that products, management, and production processes comply with applicable requirements and standards requires a certification and conformity assessment system, including internationally recognized testing facilities. Certification for ISO 9000 (evidence of a functional quality management

Creating links between knowledge generation and enterprise development is one of the most important challenges developing countries face

system), ISO 14000 (evidence of a functioning environmental management system), and Hazard Analysis of Critical Control Points (HACCP) are increasingly important prerequisites for international trade. Because sending samples abroad is not feasible, testing facilities must be established domestically.

In order for these facilities to be accepted by international markets, an accreditation system is necessary to evaluate the calibration and testing laboratories and other bodies involved in certification of products, systems, and processes. The regional and national accreditation bodies have to be recognized by the International Accreditation Forum and the International Laboratory Accreditation Cooperation.

Given the many and complex requirements and the quality demands on producers, technical support and information services are essential. Support services provide information on applicable standards and product requirements, including product specifications, quality standards, packaging, and labelling, and they help producers improve their process and product quality.

The production-oriented scientific and technical infrastructure is a source of important externalities, which justifies the provision of public goods. The international community has a responsibility to ensure that products exported from developing countries meet legitimate health, safety, and environmental concerns. But it must also ensure that the export development and economic prospects of developing countries, especially the least developed countries, are not unduly harmed by resource constraints and implementation problems in the standards area.

Building export-related technological capabilities creates further demand for technological learning and product/process upgrading, thus prompting further exports and growth. For this reason, the technological capability development needs of developing countries need to be assessed and addressed. Quantifying capability development is not easy. But it is still possible to undertake national needs assessments of technological capabilities, especially as they relate to trade capacity.

Conclusion

If a developing country is to unlock the potential to turn science, technology, and innovation into business opportunities, it needs to undertake a number of core activities. These include providing broader incentive structures to all firms while creating an institutional environment that encourages entrepreneurship, rewards innovation, fosters start-ups, and sustains existing firms with injections of capital.

Creating links between knowledge generation and enterprise development is one of the most important challenges developing countries face. A range of structures can be used to create and sustain enterprises, from taxation regimes and market-based instruments to consumption policies and sources of change within the innovation system.

3

Forging ahead

Chapter 8

Acquiring knowledge in a globalizing world

The process of technological innovation has become intricately linked to the globalization of the world economic system. The shift from largely domestic activities to more complex international relationships demands a fresh look at policies that integrate science, technology, and innovation into economic strategies.

Despite the increasing globalization of technology, the involvement of developing countries in producing new technologies and innovations is almost negligible. The production of technological knowledge is concentrated in industrial countries. There are major differences in the generation of knowledge not only between developed and developing countries but also among developing countries. The challenge facing the global community is to create conditions that will enable developing countries to make full use of the global fund of knowledge to address development challenges.

Enhancing the capacity to use available technologies

Much of the international debate over technology has focused on new technologies and ignored the global context in which such inventions are applied. Globalization of technology falls into three categories: the international exploitation of nationally produced technology, the global generation of innovation, and global technological collaborations (Archibugi and Pietrobelli 2003).

The first category, international exploitation, includes innovators' attempts to gain economic advantages by exploiting their technological assets in foreign markets. Multinational corporations, as the agent of this type of technological globalization, often maintain their national identity, even when their technologies are sold in more than one country. They exploit their technological assets in overseas markets by selling their innovative products, selling their technological knowledge (through licenses and patents), and establishing local production facilities (through foreign direct investment).

Networking technology can be deployed to enable developing countries to benefit from new economic opportunities

The second category, global generation, refers to the production of technologies by single proprietors (largely multinational corporations) on a global scale. Multinational corporations use international but intrafirm networks of R&D laboratories and technical centers and one of three main approaches. In the center-for-global approach, the core strategic resources—top management, planning, and technological expertise—are located at a company's headquarters. In the local-for-local approach, the firm's subsidiaries develop their own technological knowledge and know-how to serve local demand and preferences. The interactions among subsidiaries are limited in terms of the development of technological innovations. In the local-for-global approach, multinational corporations conduct their R&D activities in multiple locations.

The third category, global technological collaborations, has grown in importance in recent years. Technological collaborations occur when two companies establish joint ventures or formally agree to develop technical knowledge and products, while maintaining their respective ownership. Many partnerships are between firms located in different countries, thus contributing to technological globalization.

ICT has created a new way of viewing how different industrial, agricultural, and service elements link together in ways that distinguish more than just the economic contribution of these different growth segments. These technologies challenge us to find new ways in which human efforts can enhance institutional life and sustain technological learning in developing economies so that gains in one area can be automatically translated and multiplied as gains in learning in another.

ICT can be applied to meeting the Goals in at least three areas. First, ICT plays a critical role in governance at various levels. Because of the fundamental link between technological learning and the ways societies and their industrial transformations evolve, it is important to situate technological innovation and the application of ICT at the center of governance discussions. Second, ICT can have a direct impact on efforts to improve people's quality of life through better information flows and communications. Third, ICT can enhance economic growth and income by raising productivity, which can in turn improve governance and the quality of life.

The benefits of the new technologies are the result not only of an increase in connectivity or broader access to ICT facilities per se. They accrue from the facilitation of new types of development solutions and economic opportunities that ICT deployment makes possible. When strategically deployed and integrated into the design of development interventions, ICT can stretch development resources farther by facilitating the development of cost-effective and scalable solutions.

Networking technology can be deployed to enable developing countries to benefit from new economic opportunities emerging from the reorganization of production and services taking place in the networked global economy. ICT will become one of the main enablers in the pursuit of poverty alleviation and

One way of creating incentives to work on development needs is to rethink the academic reward system

wealth creation in developed and developing countries alike. At the same time, as a facilitator of knowledge networking and distributed processing of information, ICT can be used to foster increased sharing of knowledge.

A distorted academic reward system is preventing researchers in developing countries from enhancing their nations' scientific and technological capabilities. Academics are rewarded for working on problems of interest to international science, not local problems. Researchers who work on important problems for their country or region risk not being able to publish their findings in mainstream journals or not being invited into intellectual circles of international standing. Changing this system could encourage researchers to work on development problems (box 8.1).

One way of creating incentives to work on development needs is to rethink and "endogenize" the academic reward system. A faster way to create incentives is to organize calls for research proposals directed to solve developmental problems, particularly those affecting the poor (box 8.2). This does not mean that scholars should concentrate exclusively on applied research: often a mixture of basic and applied knowledge is necessary to solve the complex issues that affect poor people.

Another significant problem in developing countries is the absence of demand for value-added and more sophisticated technological activity. One of these technological activities is R&D as it relates to enterprises' collective learning functions—that is, their organizational path to assimilating and innovating new technologies. If this important function is left unattended, enterprises will remain dependent on imported technologies, which are expensive and not adapted for local conditions. If demand for future high-level technological activity is not transmitted to enterprises through appropriate policies, countries run the risk of importing equipment without the complementary generation of domestic innovations. One element of successful interventions in East Asia has been precisely this type of demand-side boost to create incentives for enterprises to invest in R&D and raise levels of R&D spending significantly.

Yet another problem for developing countries is the isolation of their research institutes and laboratories. Commercialization of R&D faces problems

Box 8.1

Venezuela is solving development problems while developing long-term capacity

Source: Avalos and Rengifo 2003.

The Venezuelan National Science and Technology Council developed a new strategy to foster long-term research capacity related to development goals. The strategy consisted of selecting a few large complex problems and funding competitive proposals around them. These proposals encouraged interdisciplinary teams, including firms, to address different aspects of each issue. The problems included those associated with the oil industry, urban violence, and a virus that had attacked the cacao crop. The importance of this initiative goes beyond the results obtained: it points to shifting the academic reward system away from an emphasis on publication to prizing the ability to work on problems related to the nation's wealth and people's well-being.

Box 8.2

**Bill Gates' "Grand
Challenges in
Global Health"
is spurring
research on
health problems
affecting the
developing world**

Source:
www.gatesfoundation.org/.

A recent initiative that aims to leverage basic science and engage the world's best scientific minds for health is the Grand Challenges in Global Health, sponsored by the Bill & Melinda Gates Foundation and administered by the Foundation for the National Institutes of Health (Varmus and others 2003). Bill Gates announced the $200 million initiative in January 2003. He described the grand challenge as a call for specific scientific or technological innovations that have the potential to remove a critical barrier to solving an important health problem in the developing world with a high likelihood of global impact and feasibility. The initiative is designed to direct investigators to a specific scientific or technical breakthrough that would be expected to overcome one or more bottlenecks in an imagined path toward a solution to one or preferably several significant health problems.

The Gates Foundation identified the following specific grand challenges:

1. Create effective single-dose vaccines that can be used soon after birth.
2. Prepare vaccines that do not require refrigeration.
3. Develop needle-free delivery systems for vaccines.
4. Devise reliable tests in model systems to evaluate live attenuated vaccines.
5. Design antigens for effective, protective immunity.
6. Learn which immunological responses provide protective immunity.
7. Develop a genetic strategy to deplete or incapacitate a disease-transmitting insect population.
8. Develop a chemical strategy to deplete or incapacitate a disease-transmitting insect population.
9. Create a full range of optimal bio-available nutrients in a single staple plant species.
10. Discover drugs and delivery systems that minimize the likelihood of drug-resistant microorganisms.
11. Create therapies that can cure latent infections.
12. Create immunological methods that can cure chronic infections.
13. Develop technologies that permit quantitative assessment of population health status.
14. Develop technologies that allow assessment of individuals for multiple conditions or pathogens at point-of-care.

Following the announcement of the grand challenges, the Foundation of the National Institutes of Health issued a request for proposals for each of the challenges, with grants totaling $20 million over five years.

of scaling up from laboratory findings to industrial output. There is no easy solution to this problem, except to create opportunities for R&D laboratories in the public domain to work with private industry. In Taiwan (China) R&D consortia are formed to foster cooperation between various laboratories in the government-funded Industrial Technology Research Institute (ITRI) and local small and medium-size enterprises to transfer technologies and develop innovative processes and products (Madsen and Chug 2003) (box 8.3).

Industry associations such as the Taiwan Electrical and Electronics Manufacturers' Association (TEEMA) were involved in identifying enterprises to join R&D consortia and in performing administrative work for the consortia that were established. These R&D consortia are formed to overcome the

Box 8.3

**Taiwan (China)
has created
research consortia
and spin-offs**

Source: Poon 2002;
Hsu and others 2003.

Taiwan (China) has adopted a strategy to blend private and public sources of knowledge with the view to commercialization through group R&D efforts. More than 30 R&D consortia have been formed in Taiwan since the 1980s. These efforts have led to the production of laptop computers, high-definition televisions, videophones, laser faxes, broadband communications, digital switching devices, satellite receiving stations, and smart cards.

The Taiwan New PC Consortium (TNPC) was created in 1994, with the assistance of the computer and communication research laboratories of ITRI. The consortium's members (local manufacturers of personal computers and related computer products) transferred technology from leading information technology firms, including Apple, IBM, and Motorola, in order to make PowerPC microprocessors and products. These products competed with Intel chip–based products.

Private ICT enterprises have spun off from government-sponsored research institutions. United Microelectronics Corporation was the first of a series of spin-off ventures from the government-funded Industrial and Technology Research Institute (ITRI), which created private-sector semiconductor capability. Established in 1980, UMC was a spin-off from the pilot fabrication operations of Electronics Research Service Organization, one of Uteri's laboratories. One of the world's first silicon foundries, Taiwan Semiconductor Manufacturing Company, was created by ITRI in 1986 as a joint venture with the Dutch multinational Philips and a group of Taiwanese firms, with the support of the Taiwan Development Fund. These spin-offs have created a new breed of world-class enterprises that are playing an important role in facilitating technology learning and transfer.

In 2000 the Information Appliances Alliance was formed, with the assistance of the Office of Committee for Information Industry Development and the Market Intelligence Center, which is under the auspices of the Ministry of Economic Affairs. Its aim is to transfer from foreign leading companies the component, hardware, and software technologies required by local manufacturers in the production of information appliances sold in international markets. IAA was established to strengthen the links between Taiwanese manufacturers and overseas organizations competing to define the architectural standards of these new products.

size limitations of small and medium-size enterprises and develop the kind of economies of scale for innovation that are usually enjoyed only by larger firms. Consortium members research and develop products, process technologies, and even technical standards.

Through public-private collaboration of joint R&D, some developing countries have been able to enter a product market right at the beginning of the high-growth stage. Their innovation strategy changed from one of "catching-up" to one of being a "fast follower," able to stay at the leading edge of technology and remain responsive to shifting market trends. Even the "fast-follower innovation strategy" is ineffective as a strategy to upgrade technologically in the face of the changing nature of more dynamic industries, which are essentially an integration of selected industrial sectors. A good example is the ICT industry, which integrates information technology, consumer electronics, and the telecommunications sectors. To overcome such a problem, the government of Taiwan (China) helped local firms form new product consortia and alliances

The ability of developing countries to use existing technologies depends largely on their ability to successfully conduct technology prospecting

to ensure that Taiwanese manufacturers were not left out in the initial stages of developing novel products or new architectural standards considered to have the potential to become popular.

Engaging in technology prospecting

The ability of developing countries to use existing technologies depends largely on their ability to successfully conduct technology prospecting. Technology prospecting entails the searching for, identifying, adapting, and diffusing imported technology. It uses technologies that are readily available, adapting them to the local economy. This process entails both research and enterprise development. It usually involves creating institutions designed to undertake global searches for technology and find ways of adapting them to local and international markets.

One of the best examples of successful technology prospecting is the Fundación Chile, established in 1974 by engineer Raúl Sáez, then Minister of Economic Coordination. Sáez approached the International Telephone and Telegraph Corporation with a proposal to create an institution for research and technology transfer jointly with the government. The private, nonprofit organization was created in 1976 and later authorized by a decree law of the Chilean government.

The aim of Fundación Chile is to undertake "scientific and technological research, its development, and the application to the economy of any advances made…to detect business opportunities, select, transfer, and later disseminate production and marketing technologies that contribute to the country's sustainable development."[1] It implements projects that involve technology transfer, institutional design, and added value based on renewable natural resources. It also promotes the development of human resources. Most of its work has focused on introducing new but proven technologies to the economy.

Fundación Chile creates innovative enterprises, almost always in association with companies or individuals; develops, adapts, and sells technologies to clients in the productive and public sectors, in Chile and abroad; fosters institutional innovations and incorporates new transfer mechanisms; and captures and disseminates technologies to multiple users (as a technological antenna) through seminars, specialized magazines, and project assistance. It has promoted the development of new enterprises in agribusiness, marine resources, forestry, the environment, and chemistry. It created two salmon farming companies that pioneered the industry's boom in the country; developed the technological concept of vacuum-packed beef, introducing centralized slaughtering and later sale of the boxed meat; established quality control and certification of export fruit; and introduced berry crops into Chile.

Fundación Chile creates pilot firms to demonstrate the technical and commercial feasibility of some new technologies, which are then transferred to the economy. Once feasibility is proven and economic profitability established, the

Under the right conditions, foreign companies can contribute to local industrial development by providing capital, markets, and technological and business skills

institution transfers the firm to the private sector. Examples of such transfers include Salmones Antártica, Salmones Huillinco, Salmotec, Finamar, Cultivos Achao, Procarne, Granjanova-Punto Verde, Berries La Unión, Geosig, Tecnoplant, and Auprin. It has sold about 30 of the 40 firms it created to recover the foundation's initial investment and fund new projects.

Attracting foreign direct investment

The global rules for foreign direct investment have changed, as have the modes in which they are most useful. Global production systems have changed the ways in which investment flows and how funds can be made available in certain parts of the world for long-term growth instead of rapid flight to new, cheaper locales. Foreign direct investment needs to be used as a vehicle for carrying tacit knowledge as well as assisting enterprises at the frontiers of world technological learning (Liu and Wang 2003).

Under the right conditions, foreign companies can contribute to local industrial development by providing capital, markets, and technological and business skills (Shi 2001). However, there are many other cases in which foreign direct investment has not contributed much to local technological development (Okejiri 2000). Foreign companies can also increase the local content of their products through subcontracts with local small and medium-size enterprises. Foreign direct investment leads to subcontracting, original equipment manufacturer arrangements, and even own design and manufacture arrangements, creating opportunities for local firms to imitate and learn from the parent companies or contractors.

Governments should promote foreign direct investment. Countries with robust infrastructure, highly trained workforces, and large domestic markets are better able to extract maximum value from foreign companies, particularly multinational corporations. A strategy for promoting foreign direct investment that will contribute to development should target specific sectors and activities. For less developed countries, a good target is commodity diversification and complementary reforms in global trading systems to reform tariff rules that impose an economic penalty on countries that add value to their local material for export.

Upgrading technological capabilities and systems

To move from fast followers to technological leaders, some East Asian developing countries have pursued a "technological diversification" innovation strategy. This approach builds on the strength of their process and prototype development capabilities, adaptive engineering, and detailed design (Lall 2000). Through technological diversification, the late developing firms recombine (mostly known) technologies to create new products or services and expand the company technology base into a broader range of technology areas. This is an attempt to reap technology-related economies of scope (Ernst 2003).

Developing countries can join global value chains by identifying market opportunities and niches

Multinational corporations are now outsourcing some of their R&D activities to developing countries with technological expertise and a good stock of R&D personnel. These are more established channels for local firms in developing countries to learn and upgrade technologically. China, the Republic of Korea, Singapore, and Taiwan (China) are primary locations in which such R&D centers are set up. Specialized R&D clusters have been set up with foreign capital in Indonesia, Malaysia, the Philippines, Thailand, and Viet Nam (Ernst 2003; Chen, Liu, and Shih 2003).

Investing in long-term research capacity in the public sector is most successful when it is tied to specific missions. These can respond to local issues, such as health or environment, or build local capabilities or resources, such as earthquake monitoring. Particularly when it is tied to a threat (such as an earthquake), a mission focus can help generate and maintain critical political support when funding is needed to renew budgets or help disseminate knowledge to users. The challenge is to sustain political support and public interest for more "normal" development problems, which have no short-term fixes.

Private sector capacity can be built in a number of ways, some of which depend on the nature of the industry. In general, however, financial incentives to invest in research equipment or training can help build long-term research capacity. Easing legal restrictions on cooperation among companies can help build networks for shared research. Changing intellectual property laws can help encourage firms to participate in international collaborations that may provide needed information and access to skills. Direct funding for a specific line of research, along with promises of procurement of final products, can also be an excellent way to promote long-term investments in private research capacity.

Joining global value chains

Developing countries can join global value chains by identifying market opportunities and niches. These opportunities will expand as production becomes more globalized. The global economy is now characterized by the integration of trade but the fragmentation of production of goods and services across national boundaries. The global economy consists of many product value chains, which encompass the full range of activities—R&D, design, production, logistics, marketing, distribution, support services—required to bring a product from its conception to its end use and beyond.

These activities are carried out in an unprecedented number of developing and developed countries. Some activities command a higher proportion of value-added than others. To have a chance to climb up the technological development ladder, local firms in developing countries had to first enter the chain and then gradually move up it to engage in higher value-added activities.

An analysis of value chain linkages provides insights into how these linkages facilitate or impede technological and industrial upgrading in developing countries. Policymakers in developing countries need to understand how and

Investing in research on underfunded issues of relevance to developing countries is particularly important in agricultural production, environmental management, and public health

why existing global value chains are structured and function the way they are and how these chains will change over time.

Three variables influence how global value chains are governed: the complexity of transactions, the codification of transactions, and the competence of suppliers. The more complex the transaction, the greater the possibility for global value chains to be organized in one of the three network governance patterns: modular, relational, and captive value chains. Global value chains will be organized as modular supply chains if explicit codification schemes exist to allow easy exchange of complex information between buyers and suppliers and suppliers are competent enough to receive and act on such codified information. If suppliers are not sufficiently competent, buyers may have to keep the activities in-house, leading to more vertical integration, or outsource such activities to a supplier in the captive value chains that have to be tightly controlled and monitored. If a codification scheme in the form of known standards or protocols does not exist, buyers may have to rely on highly idiosyncratic methods based on intensive interaction to work with the suppliers in relational value chains.

Value chain governance patterns will change if any of these factors changes. For example, if a new technology renders an established codification scheme lowering the competence level in the supply base, one might expect modular value chains to become more relational. If there are difficulties finding competent suppliers, captive networks or vertical integration would then become more prevalent. Conversely, rising supplier competence might foster a move of captive networks toward the relational type, and better codification schemes might give rise to more modular networks.

One should not expect such chains to spread automatically or that the East Asian strategy of plugging into such chains can be adopted by other countries. The value chains that drove the East Asian growth, particularly the electronics value chains, may not be accessible to new entrants. The global high-tech production system is now well established in Asia, and China's entry is strengthening its regional cost, productivity, and technology base. Future policy should not be based on the assumption that countries in Africa, the Middle East and North Africa, or most of Latin America and the Caribbean will be to enter these chains. Most developing countries will have to identify niches and opportunities in other value chains.

Conducting research to generate new technologies

Investing in research on underfunded issues of relevance to developing countries is particularly important in fields such as agricultural production, environmental management, and public health. For example, small island states face major sustainability challenges, which require technological responses (box 8.4). There are a variety of ways to channel resources toward pressing development problems that are currently underfunded. First, bilateral donors

Box 8.4

**Technological
responses to
sustainability
challenges
in Jamaica**

Source: P. Paulwell,
Ministry of Commerce,
Science, and Technology,
personal communication,
2004; A. Barnett, Scientific
Research Council, personal
communication, 2004.

Small island states face a variety of ecological challenges that force them to develop technologies that advance human welfare while protecting the environment. Waste treatment is one of those challenges. Jamaica's Scientific Research Council—a research and development arm of the Ministry of Commerce, Science, and Technology—offers practical domestic solutions to the increasing challenges relating to disposal of wastes and wastewater using environmentally sound technologies. The council has adapted anaerobic technologies, deploying three systems that include biogas reactors, biodigester septic tanks, and upflow anaerobic sludge blanket reactors. So far the Scientific Research Council has commissioned 150 biogas reactors and 13 biodigester septic tanks, and it operates two prototype sludge blanket reactors. These technologies are designed to produce biogas for production activities while reducing municipal and agricultural waste. Unlike in regular septic tanks that discharge into sewage systems, bioseptic reactors release nutrient-rich waste that can used for irrigation after tertiary treatment.

Building on such successes, the country is exploring ways by which it could focus on developing technologies of relevance to small island economies and developing countries in general. This vision is reflected in the focus of the Scientific Research Council, which works closely with other government bodies and academic institutions. In addition to the functions of the ministry, the National Commission on Science and Technology in the Office of the Prime Minister provides overall policy coordination. Other organs of the government that contribute to technological innovation include the Bureau of Standards, Jamaica and the Jamaica Intellectual Property Office. The government has designated November as Science and Technology Month. The government convenes a series of events aimed at popularizing science, technology, and innovation, culminating in the granting of the prestigious awards for efforts in these areas.

could increase their official development assistance to fund research that meets both local and widespread needs and that pass the scrutiny of peer review. Second, bilateral and multilateral donors could join forces, as many have in the past, to sponsor international research centers, individually or through consortia such as the Consultative Group on International Agricultural Research (CGIAR), which have their own science, technology, and innovation advisory bodies and work closely with developing countries. Third, donor support for research could be funded as an international cooperative project in which funds are provided to teams proposing to conduct world-class research that focuses on local or underrepresented research activities.[2]

Agricultural production is an area in which global research efforts make eminent sense. Research on food crops for domestic consumption was long neglected in developing countries, where the emphasis of colonial powers was on export crops. But research conducted in one country can often be of value to other countries. This spillover process can often be accelerated and made more efficient by the presence of a multinational research group that can take a broader and longer term outlook and provide global public goods (Dalrymple 2004).

This concept was first put into practice with the establishment of the International Rice Research Institute (IRRI) in the Philippines in 1960, followed

Donor support for research could be funded as an international cooperative project

by the International Maize and Wheat Improvement Center (CIMMYT) in 1967. Other centers followed. All of these centers were supported by the Ford and Rockefeller Foundations.

In 1972 the CGIAR was established to coordinate and manage the emerging system. The CGIAR was established by the World Bank, with the support of UNDP and national development agencies, such as the U.S. Agency for International Development. It includes a Technical Advisory Committee (recently renamed the Science Council).

The CGIAR initially focused on food production, playing a key role in the Green Revolution. The Green Revolution entailed adapting some semidwarf wheat varieties partially developed in the industrial countries (principally Japan and the United States) to local conditions in developing countries. The process involved not merely relocating seed from one place to another but extensive investment in international and local research. Collaboration with local researchers was very important because of the need to adapt the varieties to local conditions.

The area of pharmaceutical research is particularly affected by the low level of investment in problems that occur in tropical countries (Mrazek and Mossialos 2003). Several proposals have been advanced on how to increase research investment in this area. The proposals range from networks of existing institutions to new technology development alliances, many of which focus on vaccine development. Some have suggested the equivalent of the CGIAR for the health sector. Much of the discussion on addressing this issue has focused on levels of funding and choice of research priorities. But the real challenge lies in designing research systems that take into account interactions between social and technical developments.

Private companies already committed to being good corporate citizens for development could be further engaged in this regard. The first step would be to identify the companies and group them by the sector and region in which they operate. Membership lists of gatherings like the UN Global Compact and the U.S. Council for International Business could be used for this purpose. Targeted messages could be developed for each group. A forum could be provided for discussion among companies, governments, and others to identify specific areas of involvement. The UN Global Compact could be engaged to promote public-private sector partnerships for development among its members worldwide.

Countries can also impose cross-subsidies. Malaysia imposes a cess on the turnover of corporate electricity generators to fund rural electrification and renewable energy development throughout the country (box 8.5). Thirty percent of housing units are required to be low cost; these units are subsidized by the sale of medium- and high-priced units. This policy has enhanced social cohesion in urban centers and helped slow the spread of slums.

Cesses on imports could also spur innovation, although the WTO may object to them. To encourage stock markets to contribute to sustainable development in developing countries, a cess of 0.05 or 0.1 percent of the turnover

One way to target sector-specific technological needs is to introduce an industrywide cess. Malaysia has imposed cesses on rubber, palm oil, and timber to fund the Rubber Research Institute, the Palm Oil Research Institute, and the Forestry Research Institute. A cess on tea helps fund research on and marketing of tea in Sri Lanka. Hong Kong (China), Malaysia, and Singapore have all established construction industry development boards. Funding for the boards comes from a compulsory cess on all construction contracts. The revenue is used to build capacity and promote innovations in construction materials and techniques.

A Malaysian project involving government, academia, and industry is the Housing Research Centre at the University Putra Malaysia. Using locally developed building systems and local materials, the center has built experimental houses that are in the process of commercialization. The center's Putra Block, an industrial building system, is patented in the United Kingdom. Malaysia won a gold medal for the system at the International Innovation Expo in Geneva.

of stock markets could be imposed and used to establish a global fund for sustainable development.

Much of the R&D capacity in developing countries is scattered across a wide range of independent research institutions that are not organized around specific technology missions or research programs. As a result, resources are not effectively utilized. One way to address this challenge is to pool resources to pursue research in priority areas identified by national governments.

The Israel Academy of Sciences and Humanities operates a high-level, voluntary, ad hoc Forum for National R&D Infrastructure (TELEM), made up of heads of major national research and funding organizations. Members pool their budgetary resources and catalyze the participation of others to undertake major joint research initiatives in fields of national interest. The members of TELEM include the president of the Israel Academy of Sciences and Humanities (chair); the chief scientist of the Ministry of Industry and Trade; the chief scientist of the Ministry of Science; the head of the R&D Division of the Ministry of Defense; the assistant head of the Budget Department of the Treasury; and the chair of the Planning and Budgeting Committee of the Israel Council for Higher Education. Israel also uses research funds to support and commercialize research (box 8.6).

Given the limited resources in most developing countries, such pooling mechanisms, especially if supported by statutory instruments, could play an important role in advancing local R&D priorities. One important opportunity for such pooling could be through the growing number of regional integration organizations. The East African Community (Kenya, Tanzania, and Uganda) is set to expand to include other countries in the region. The statutory instruments setting up the community as well as its various subsidiary organs offer an ideal opportunity for pooling R&D infrastructure in the region to address pressing challenges in areas such as food security, health, education, and environmental management. Other regional integration organizations in Africa could pursue

Box 8.6

**Incremental
funding for
research in Israel**

Source: www.academy.ac.il

The establishment of research funds is emerging as an important mechanism for promoting basic research and commercializing research results. Such funds often start with modest levels and grow over time. The Israel Science Foundation, for example, is now the country's largest and most comprehensive basic research grants program. It began in 1972, with an allocation from the government to the Israel Academy of Sciences and Humanities to promote basic science. The Academy used the funds to set up a modest Basic Research Fund, which, even after a decade of operation, had an annual budget of only about $400,000 (J. Ziv, Israel Academy of Sciences and Humanities, personal communication, 2004).

In 1986 the Israel Academy of Sciences and Humanities issued a report outlining the imminent crisis in Israeli basic research and setting out a master plan that called for substantial increases in national funding. The Israel Academy of Sciences and Humanities enlisted the help of the Israeli government (through the Planning and Budgeting Committee) and the international philanthropic community. With the support of the C.H. Revson Foundation (which contributed $5 million) and other private and governmental donors, it established an endowment fund for basic research. It also convinced the Planning and Budgeting Committee to vastly increase its annual allocation to the Basic Research Fund. Within a decade these Academy-backed initiatives raised the Basic Research Fund's budget by a factor of 10.

In 1992 the Basic Research Fund reconstituted itself as the Israel Science Foundation, now a legally independent nonprofit organization. The Israel Science Foundation's annual budget for 2003 exceeded $53 million (almost all Planning and Budgeting Committee funds); and it is expected to reach $80 million over the next five years. The core of the Israel Science Foundation is still its highly successful competitive grants program for individual researchers. Of the 989 such projects funded in 2003, some 343 were new projects.

The Israel Science Foundation also supports a variety of newer programs designed to help keep Israel internationally competitive in forefront areas of modern science. Equipment grants contribute up to half the total cost of expensive (up to $1.5 million) state-of-the-art equipment systems. Centers of Excellence grants of up to $1.5 million, spread over four years, support multi-institutional, multidisciplinary initiatives in fields of Israeli research strength.

similar strategies. Such collaborative measures could help countries broaden their cooperation through fields that are more pragmatic and less political in character. The example of the Arab Science and Technology Foundation illustrates the potential for such regional cooperation arrangements (box 8.7).

Other ways of generating funds for research include changing the tax laws to give incentives to private individuals and corporations to contribute to research funds and other technology-related charitable activities.[3] This instrument for supporting public welfare activities is now widely used in developing countries. This is partly because of the lack of experience in managing charitable organizations and partly because of the reluctance on the part of finance ministries to grant tax exemptions in fear that it would erode their revenue base. However, it can be argued that areas such as education, health, and environmental management could benefit from the local generation of revenue where specific exemptions are provided by law to encourage the establishment of charitable trusts.

Box 8.7

**Promoting
regional science
and technology
cooperation in
the Arab world**

Source: www.astf.net/;
A. Alnajjar, ASTF, personal
communication, 2004.

The Arab Science and Technology Foundation was created in 2002 in the United Arab Emirates to promote international cooperation on science and technology among Arab and other members of the international community. It was set up as an independent, non-profit NGO that seeks to bring together Arab scientists at home and in the diaspora. It is a model of regional cooperation that is likely to be emulated by other parts of the world. The foundation is located in Sharjah and plans to set up branches and networks in the Arab world as well as other regions that are willing to enter into collaboration arrangements.

The Arab Science and Technology Foundation enjoys high-level support from his Highness Sheikh Dr. Sultan Bin Mohammed Al-Qassimi, Member of the Supreme Council of the United Arab Emirates, Ruler of Sharjah. The foundation is focusing its research support on such activities of relevance to the region as water resource management, solar energy, and overall environmental management. Its activities are envisaged to expand considerably given its pioneering role. One of its long-term benefits might be to serve as a source of inspiration for the establishment of similar organizations with narrower mandates in the region and other parts of the world.

Forging international technology partnerships

One of the most significant developments in the structure of the globalized economy is a network involving partnering activities. These networks are products of complex interlinkages among a wide range of enterprises, links that are designed to reduce the risks associated with the development of new products and facilitate the exchange of information. These partnering arrangements help provide sources of financing through licensing and upfront fees for R&D expenses, reimbursement of expenses for partnered products and services, royalties, profits, and other "success fees" associated with the achievement of certain milestones. Such arrangements are particularly important in areas with limited access to other forms of financing, such as venture capital. Even where venture capital is available, these arrangements still serve an important risk-reducing function.

Partnering activities are naturally more concentrated in the industrial countries, but these arrangements are being extended to developing countries, especially in agricultural biotechnology. Similar arrangements could be considered in industrial biotechnology. In addition to reducing risk, partnering arrangements can also play a key role in developing technological capabilities in firms and institutions in developing countries. Such capacity would be specialized and related to specific products and services. Such partnering would also be useful in promoting the adoption of good management as industrial production standards in developing countries. It is therefore recommended that partnering models that are relevant to developing countries be identified and promoted as part of the expansion of the new bioeconomy.

One important goal of strengthening the scientific and technological base and improving science and technology policy in developing countries is the generation of new goods and services that can improve health in developing countries. Stimulating the biotechnology industry in developing countries is one way to achieve commercialization of R&D. Forward-looking economic policies have tended to improve conditions for private enterprise in general in recent years, allowing countries with large market potential like China and India to enjoy rapid growth in the private sector. These countries took steps to liberalize their economies and strengthen protection of intellectual property rights in order to create incentives for foreign direct investment. International collaboration between companies may also help foster private sector growth in developing countries (box 8.8).

Recently, Genematrix, an early-stage Korean biotechnology company, entered into a collaborative agreement with Variagenics, a U.S.–based pharmacogenetics company. Through this partnership, Genematrix hopes to gain expertise in applying pharmacogenomics to all phases of drug and diagnostic development. Variagenics will benefit from Genematrix's genomic data from targeted Asian populations.

Box 8.8

International research partnerships build capacity and direct funding toward neglected fields

Source: www.nitd.novartis.com/index.shtml.

International partnerships provide funding for research in neglected fields. One example is the partnership between the Novartis Institute for Tropical Diseases (NITD) and the Singapore Economic Development Board (SEDB), which seeks to make new drugs (initially for tuberculosis and dengue) available to poor people in developing countries at the lowest possible price. The partnership could use differential pricing strategies, financing the research by charging higher prices in developed country markets. It could create additional partnerships for developing, manufacturing, and distributing drugs. Novartis will patent novel compounds, but patents will not interfere with the goal of making drugs affordable for the poor.

The partnership represents a new business model for Novartis and a commitment to social responsibility. Novartis's interest is in broadening its research base in infectious diseases as well as helping find new treatments for diseases that are becoming major public health challenges. The effort is part of the company's effort to fulfill its role as a good corporate citizen through its commitment to the UN Global Compact. Its commercial interests are also clear: it strives to refinance the institute's activities and make it economically sustainable. Novartis retains marketing rights for compounds that have a significant commercial potential in developed markets.

SEDB seeks to strengthen Singapore's technology platform, develop its manpower capabilities, and commercialize technologies and products arising from the NITD. It expects the partnership will have positive spin-off effects, potentially leading to the proliferation of local biomedical start-ups. This example could be replicated, although persuading multinational corporations like Novartis to base a research institute in other developing countries will not be easy. Countries with strong research capabilities can influence the decisions of such firms to base their operations in their territories.

A mentoring scheme—in which an institution or firm in a developed country institution teams up with one in a developed—might be the answer. An institute based in Singapore could mentor one in Bangladesh, where there are opportunities for human resource development through farming out of projects, movement of scientists, and creation of technology incubators and spin-offs. This would encourage Bangladesh to devote more resources to R&D. Such involvement will not take place without a the help of an international agency, which could identify potential partners and promote their collaboration.

Initiatives to help small and medium-size enterprises in biotechnology are a recent and promising development in some countries

South-South collaboration between companies in developing countries can also create new opportunities for entrepreneurs. Cuba's Heber Biotech, a semi-private company, has helped commercialize Cuba's biotechnology products. By 1998 Heber Biotech was recording about $290 million annually in sales of hepatitis B vaccines and pharmaceuticals in 34 countries. Now the company is entering into partnerships with other developing countries. In 2001 it established a joint marketing venture with Kee Pharmaceuticals of India. The company's new division, Kee Biogenetics, has launched India's first recombinant DNA product, streptokinase, capable of dissolving coronary clots and preventing heart attacks. The resulting drug, Cardiostrep, is owned by Heber Biotech. The company aims to use special pricing to access the $11 million Indian market.

Specific initiatives to help small and medium-size enterprises in biotechnology are a recent and promising development in some countries. The eGoli BIO life sciences incubator, launched in 2003, is a business incubator that aims to nurture small, medium, and microsized biotechnology enterprises for commercialization. eGoli BIO seeks to act as a "development conduit for the commercialization of life sciences research, products, services and technology platforms" in South Africa. The company works closely with the Biotechnology Partnership for Development, itself charged with stimulating economic development, contributing to job creation, and building world-class skills and technology platforms to sustain and continue development.

Creating incentives for private enterprise is not likely to be sufficient for private sector growth without simultaneous growth in human capital. China has been trying to attract back its scientists trained overseas through various incentives (some of them, such as limiting the time spent abroad during post-doctoral training, controversial). Critical factors to consider for the growth of private firms in developing countries include the relatively small academic base, the lack of human capital and financial resources, the absence of a market-oriented research culture, the dearth of large national biotechnology companies, and inexperience by academic institutions in mechanisms to transfer research findings to companies.

The linkage between research activities and commercial enterprises continues to be weak in most developing countries. Strengthening this link could help provide fresh stimulus to academic research and re-energize universities. It could also be instrumental in translating basic research into important commercial products, such as molecular diagnostic tools, for local use.

Numerous efforts have been made, especially through the United Nations, to promote South-South cooperation (box 8.9). In additional to regional cooperation arrangements, opportunities for cooperation exist with Brazil, China, India, Malaysia, and Mexico, which could play important roles as technology mentors from other developing countries. Voluntary governmental science and technology agreements are becoming a common feature. The Ministry of Science and Technology in China, for example, has signed such agreements with

Box 8.9

Brazil, India, and South Africa are working together on nanotechnology and efforts to prevent and treat HIV/AIDS

Science ministers from Brazil, India, and South Africa have been working together to identify areas for trilateral cooperation over nanotechnology and efforts to prevent and treat HIV/AIDS. Their first meeting was held in October 2004, as part of the India-Brazil-South Africa trilateral commission. The meeting followed a meeting of the three countries' foreign ministers in Brasilia in 2003. That session identified science, technology, and innovation as one of the key areas for trilateral cooperation.

The partnership was inspired by the low level of investment in research on tropical challenges. This is the first major effort to promote cooperation with a focus on emerging technologies. It is likely that the collaboration will inspire other countries to want to join the group or seek to benefit from the results of the alliance. It is possible that industrial countries will seek to be party to this important initiative, at least indirectly.

96 countries—66 percent of them developing nations (G. Xu, Ministry of Science and Technology of China, personal communication, 2004).

The role of the diaspora in a global economy

Globalizing forces such as connectivity, mobility, and interdependence have made it possible for diaspora communities to strengthen their research and business connections to their countries of origin. The most notable case is the Taiwanese diaspora, which played a crucial role in developing the country's electronics industry (Saxenian 2001). To date this subject has been addressed largely in the context of remittances and other material flows. Attention is turning to possible opportunities that would enable developing countries to build international partnerships with the diaspora (box 8.10).

A number of countries have adopted policy measures aimed at attracting expatriates to participate in the economies of their countries of origin. These measures include investment conferences, the creation of rosters of experts, and direct appeals by national leaders. Efforts to encourage expatriates to return home often occur after countries emerge from periods of civil unrest or economic decline. Like other professionals, expatriates respond to incentives and a sense of purpose. The most important starting point is therefore to establish a clear mission around which the diaspora can rally. The onus is on developing country governments to design programs and offer incentives that enable expatriates to contribute to national efforts.

New barriers to technological learning

The Agreement on Trade-Related Investment Measures (TRIMs) is one of the Multilateral Agreements on Trade in Goods of the WTO. The objectives of the Agreement include "the expansion and progressive liberalization of world trade and [the facilitation of] investment across international frontiers so as to increase the economic growth of all trading partners, particularly developing country members, while ensuring free competition." The TRIMs Agreement

Box 8.10

Switzerland and Singapore are staying in touch with their high-tech expatriates

A number of significant experiments are underway around the world to make effective use of diasporas. The Swiss government has created a consulate (the Swiss House) in Cambridge, Massachusetts, to promote interactions between the Swiss in the Boston area and their counterparts at home. Swiss House was created in recognition of the importance of the area as the world's leading knowledge center, especially in the life sciences. (In addition to Harvard University and MIT, the Boston area is home to more than 50 colleges and universities and a cluster of biotechnology firms.)

In 2002 the National University of Singapore established a college at the University of Pennsylvania to focus on biotechnology and entrepreneurship. The arrangement is similar to its arrangement with Stanford University. It also established the Singapore-Philadelphia Innovators' Network (SPIN), to serve as a channel and link for entrepreneurs, investors, and advisors in the Greater Philadelphia region and Singapore. SPIN seeks to create opportunities for collaboration and partnerships in the area.

India is introducing a number of policy measures—including granting dual citizenship to Indians in countries of strategic interest—aimed at strengthening the role of diaspora in national development. This is a major change of policy, based on the study of how other countries have benefited from their diasporas. These approaches can be adopted by other developing countries, where the need to forge international technology partnerships may be even higher.

Guyana has a population of about 700,000. But nearly 250,000 Guyanans are estimated to live in the diaspora, most of them in New York and Toronto. They contribute significantly to the economy through remittances, but their impact could be even higher if there were a strategic approach to linking them into the economy through technology partnerships.

aims to prevent the adoption and utilization of legislative and other investment-related measures that may cause "trade restrictive and distortive effects" (A. Ratanawaraha, MIT, personal communication, 2004).

The Agreement prohibits trade-related investment measures that are inconsistent with the basic provisions of the 1994 General Agreement on Tariffs and Trade. These measures include local content requirements, which require firms to use at least a specified amount of local inputs; trade-balancing requirements, which limit the purchase or use of imported products by firms to an amount related to the volume or value of local products they export; foreign-exchange balancing requirements, which limit imports by restricting access to foreign exchange; and restrictions on enterprise exports, either by volume or value.

Many governments of newly industrializing countries have expressed concerns that implementation of TRIMs could potentially affect their industrialization and technological development. They fear losing the mechanisms that encourage multinational firms to transfer technology to local firms.

In the process of industrializing, many countries have used innovative mechanisms that promote technology transfers and local learning processes. Several of the development tools that they used were expected to foster technology transfer that came with foreign direct investment. For example, trade-

The priority for most developing countries is technology prospecting, identifying useful technologies and markets for the resulting products

balancing requirements tie the value of foreign investors' imports of raw materials and components to the value of their exports of the finished commodity. Local content requirements mandate that a certain percentage of the components that go into the making of a product be sourced locally. Many countries have used these policy tools to help domestic firms make the transition from low-technology to mid-technology industries.

The TRIMs Agreement prohibited most developing countries from using these measures, beginning in January 2000. The new rules prevented them from maintaining policies that had promoted local firms, enabled greater linkages to the domestic economy, and protected the balance of payments.

Several developing countries, including Brazil, Egypt, India, Indonesia, Malaysia, Pakistan, and Uganda, have requested that TRIMs be amended to provide developing countries the flexibility to continue to use such investment measures to meet their development goals (A. Ratanawaraha, MIT, personal communication, 2004). They argue that these policies are necessary because of the low level of development of the local sector, which would not be able to withstand free competition at this stage. As a result of TRIMs, developing countries may have lost some important policy options for technological learning to pursue their industrialization (A. Ratanawaraha, MIT, personal communication, 2004).

By banning some of the measures developing countries used to foster technological transfer and allow their infant industries to develop, the TRIMs Agreement has forced the governments of these countries to learn how to adapt and to find new policy tools (A. Ratanawaraha, MIT, personal communication, 2004). The question is whether these governments are capable of finding new ways of doing things.

Conclusion

Technological change has become intricately linked to the globalization of the world economy (Lundvall 1999). Traditional technology policy approaches designed in the 1960s and 1970s need to be revised to take into account the globalization of technology. Technology policies need to be rethought in order to exploit existing technologies, generate new ones, and engage in global technological collaborations. Much of the technology needed to advance the Goals is already available. The priority for most developing countries is technology prospecting, which involves identifying useful technologies and markets for the resulting products.

Chapter 9

Advising governments on science, technology, and innovation

Government policies play a critical role in creating a suitable environment for the application of science, technology, and innovation to development. But the existence of government policies is not sufficient. Leaders who understand the importance of science, technology, and innovation in development and who are open to advice on the matter are needed. Executive leadership, especially at the level of the president or prime minister, is a critical element in the ability of a country to benefit from the world's fund of scientific and technological knowledge.

Executive commitment is best articulated through the realignment of government functions with a strategic vision for development that emphasizes the role of technological innovation in development. In the absence of such a vision, leaders are unlikely to pay much attention to the role of science and technology. Indeed, countries and agencies that do not have such a vision often consider investment in technological innovation as a questionable expenditure. Improving the policy environment therefore entails adopting a broad policy framework that places science, technology, and innovation at the center of the development process.

Institutional adjustments are needed in the way governments receive advice on issues about the role of science, technology, and innovation in development. Advice needs to reach policymakers. For it to do so, an institutional framework needs to exist, and decisionmakers must commit to support such a framework.

The functions of scientific advisory groups

The growing recognition of the role of knowledge in economic transformation has resulted in a diversity of efforts aimed at strengthening advisory systems for science, technology, and innovation at all levels of government. The increased

Advisory groups should create a coordination function across government

emphasis on science, technology, and innovation has been accompanied by an increased awareness of the scientific and socioeconomic risks associated with technological transformation. In some cases, concerns over technological risks have resulted in delays in adopting new technologies that could help solve local problems. The paralysis in policy and decisionmaking continues to raise concern about the place of science, technology, and innovation in governance systems.

Countries and regional integration bodies are responding to the challenge by reviewing their advisory mechanisms to bring them in line with the demands of the knowledge economy. The links between science and democracy are becoming more apparent, requiring a more explicit approach to the subject.

Advisory functions differ widely across countries and include activities such as coordination, consensus building, adjudication, assessment of effectiveness of measures, and development of progress indicators. In carrying out these functions, advisory agencies are guided by a set of principles that include trust, credibility, and accountability. They also focus on inclusiveness.

Advising takes place at all government levels, and advice can be sought in a variety of ways. It differs in the level at which scientific input is received, how formal or flexible the advisory process is, the relative use of science advice in different branches of government (executive or legislative), and the degree of decisionmaking involvement by advisors.

Advisory groups should seek to create a coordination function across government, one that takes the different needs and missions of various agencies into account. Where possible, these needs should be addressed in an interdisciplinary fashion. Efforts should be made to seek consensus or to deliberate over views on investments and applications of science and technology. This process can involve representatives from government, business, and the public.

It is essential that adjudication mechanisms be explored to determine how to discuss and make decisions on highly contentious issues. The process should be as transparent as possible, making both the decisions and the decisionmaking procedures open to scrutiny by the public and the scientific community. A process of identifying emerging issues should be put in place, so that contentious issues can be anticipated and possibly mitigated by open discussion and research.

The advisor should work with experts to determine how to measure the effectiveness of public investments in science, technology, and innovation. It is common for advisors to collect internationally recognized indicators of science, technology, and innovation operations.

The structure of scientific advisory bodies

The structure of advising may follow a number of models, including the corporate nonprofit model, the independent advisory model, and the embedded advisory model. In each case, certain elements increase effectiveness.

The science advisor should work with those in power to establish a national vision

First, the advising function should have some statutory, legislative, or jurisdictional mandate to provide advice to the highest levels of government. This protects the advisor from being unduly influenced by political pressures, and it provides credibility and regularity to interactions between the advising and the decisionmaking roles of government. The advisor should have a trusted and regular link to those making decisions at the highest levels. This trusted link should have some privilege attached to it, so that the science advisor can offer frank advice without fear of being penalized by interest groups. However, the science advisor needs to strike a delicate balance between advice given in confidence to policymakers and some accountability to the public sector, lest the science advisor be seen as a "mouthpiece" for those in power and lose the ability to interact with the science, technology, and innovation community and the public at large.

Second, the structure should have its own operating budget and a budget to fund policy research. This helps the advising structure create an institutional memory of how decisions are made effectively and how they can be improved in the future. It also helps coordinate decisionmaking across government agencies and with outside groups.

Third, the science advisor should have access to good scientific or technical information, from within the government; from the science, technology, and innovation community; from national academies; or from international networks. This network of advice should be readily available, so that when decisions need to be made, technical advice is immediately at hand.

Finally, the advisory processes should have some accountability to the public and some method of obtaining public opinion. This may involve some outreach, through tools such as foresight exercises or regular interaction with legislative bodies.

The science advisor should work with those in power to establish a national vision, one that encompasses specific missions and targets for the sustainable use and enhancement of national capabilities. These types of mission statements exist in many countries. They offer guidelines that can be used by countries seeking to implement this type of strategic planning.

The establishment and maintenance of science, technology, and innovation advisory institutions in developing countries is an essential component of development planning. These activities are considered expensive, and their cost-effectiveness is often questioned. Several countries have found ways to both increase their effectiveness and reduce their costs. Malaysia, for example, has used members of national academies as volunteers.

Cross-country experience with national science advisors
Advising structures differ across countries, depending on their governance structures. The taxonomy of advising bodies and the circumstances under which they are established are also complex. Some committees are ad hoc and

**Funding
issues are
at the heart
of debates
over how to
establish
advice
mechanisms**

flexible, others are more permanent. In many countries, including the United Kingdom and the United States, a single person serves as chief scientific advisor to the head of state and chairs a panel of prominent scientists advising the executive branch.

In the United States input into the executive's decisionmaking is limited to an intimate circle of task forces and councils. In contrast, government ministries and departments in many countries are offered more opportunity for participation. In France, for example, responsibility for much of the advising process has been tasked to issue-specific agencies.

In France and the United Kingdom, issue-specific agencies have responsibility for implementing legislation. Some Swedish policy-oriented agencies also implement government policies, relying on researchers to provide scientific expertise for their decisions.

Sectoral agencies also rely on a mix of sources for advice. In Sweden sectoral agencies rely on internal experts that often overlap with executive science advisors. In France, Italy, and the United Kingdom, sectoral ministries and departments rely on a variety of committees for their information. Policymakers in the United Kingdom are informed by a variety of sources, including the Royal Society, the Royal Academy of Engineering, the Council for Science and Technology, the Office of Science and Technology, the prime minister's science advisors, individual departmental science advisors, a Parliamentary Committee on Science and Technology, and an Association for the Advancement of Science.

In both Germany and the United Kingdom, ministries have their own permanent science, technology, and innovation committees. In contrast, in Italy emerging problems are handled by ad hoc issues-based committees. In the Newly Independent States, sources of science, technology, and innovation advice to sectoral agencies have included national scientific, technical, and engineering academies; autonomous research councils and organizations; NGOs; and agencies of other governments.

Looking at the different science advisory mechanisms for legislatures, in the United States every Congressional office and committee has staff experts. In the United Kingdom science advisors provide expert oversight only for the executive branch. The China People's Political Consultative Conference (CPPCC) functions as an in-house advisory group of policy experts who serve the National People's Congress (NPC) and State Council, China's two primary legislative bodies. It is fully funded by the Chinese central government.

Funding issues are at the heart of debates over how to establish advice mechanisms. The robustness of China's science advisory mechanisms and their span across organizations seems due in large part to the funding they receive from the government. Government support and how it shapes (or does not shape) the nature of a science advisory institution, institutional procedures, and institutional capacity are recurring themes for budding science, technology, and innovation advisory groups in developing countries.

In 2003 the Canadian government took the bold step of creating the office of the National Science Advisor to the Prime Minister

The growing interest in strengthening science and technology advice is illustrated by recent efforts in various countries to establish new advisory structures.

Canada. In 2003 the Canadian government took the bold step of creating the office of the National Science Advisor to the Prime Minister. The position, the first of its kind in Canada since the late 1960s, reflected the desire of the newly elected Prime Minister to signal his commitment to receiving science advice at the highest level. Line responsibilities and operations functions of the government in science, technology, and innovation reside largely with the Minister for Industry and other science-based government departments. The National Science Advisor coordinates priority setting through the central bureaucratic arm of the government within the Privy Council Office. The National Science Advisor is the principal conduit through which science advice reaches the Prime Minister.

The National Science Advisor was tasked with a number of key public policy challenges, including developing a framework for strengthening the commercialization of research in partnership with the private sector, exploring priority setting within government research, developing a framework for decision-making on major science investments, and mobilizing Canadian R&D assets toward helping solve the needs of developing countries. The Prime Minister indicated that he hopes that at least 5 percent of the Canadian R&D envelope is committed to addressing developing country needs in the coming years.

The National Science Advisor is also Canada's representative to the G-8 Science Advisers and Science Ministers Forum, which meets twice a year. In this capacity, the advisor helps shape the design of global responses through effective science advice and provides a strong voice for Canadian science in the global arena.

Although the office of the National Science Advisor is relatively small, its ability to marshal support for key cross-cutting issues is unparalleled. It is currently working closely with the government and research community in shaping the establishment of an independent arm's length academy of sciences that will bring together the various research disciplines to tackle policy issues that have a strong science base.

The National Science Advisor is also exploring the development of a foresight capability able to anticipate and tackle medium- and long-term challenges. Working with the other elements of the national science advisory apparatus, the National Science Advisor will help shape an architecture that will be able to respond more effectively to new science and public policy demands from the government and the Canadian public. The transparency of advice needs to increase and the cross-cutting coordination of advisory structures needs to be properly managed to ensure that Canada will be able to meet the expectations of its domestic and global responsibilities in the rapidly emerging frontiers of knowledge.

The evolution of Malaysia's advisory system is linked to national decisions that have transformed the country's economy

Ireland. In 1997 Ireland made a strategic decision to undertake major investment in R&D in order to support wider economic and social development. It created a variety of research funding instruments, administered by different government agencies and departments. These instruments have different objectives and missions, including supporting the research strategies of individual or collaborating higher education institutions, conducting mission-oriented strategic basic research on ICT and biotechnology and mission-oriented functional research (on health and the environment, for example), and supporting individual researchers.

The rapid growth in the scale of research funding in Ireland (from very low levels in 1997 to €2.5 billion over 2000–06) and the number of research instruments has created a pressing need for coordination and oversight of overall national R&D policy and investment. Previous structures created were largely ineffective. A key deficiency was that these structures tended to be located in a single government department, which had a particular sectoral mission in research. These problems pointed to the need for research policy and research oversight to be located at the center of government.

In June 2004 the government appointed a Chief Science Adviser, the first ever appointed, to provide independent expert advice on science, technology and innovation. The government has decided to establish a Cabinet Committee, to be chaired by the Prime Minister, to address and coordinate science, technology, and innovation issues. The Cabinet Committee will be supported by an interdepartmental committee of senior officials with responsibility for science, technology, and innovation in their respective government departments. The initiative will ensure a "whole of government" approach to science, technology and innovation.

Malaysia. The evolution of Malaysia's advisory system is linked to national decisions that have transformed the country's economy (Lee 2002). Once a producer of raw materials, Malaysia now has a diversified economy that exports electronic products and associated information technology services. This transformation was guided by a set of advisory institutions that includes the Science Advisor's Office to the Prime Minister, established in 1984. The Office, headed by the President of the Academy of Science, Malaysia (ASM), incorporates the Malaysia Industry-Government Partnership for High Technology (MIGHT). Other relevant organs include the National Council of Scientific Research and Development (MPKSN), chaired by the Chief Secretary to the Government; the MPKSN Secretariat, consisting of the Ministry of Science and Technology and Innovation and top civil servants from most ministries, universities, industries, and professional organizations; and two standing committees, one for policy formulation, headed by the Science Advisor of the Prime Minister's Department, and the other for policy implementation, headed by Secretary General, Ministry of Science, Technology, and Innovation.

Providing advice is among the most important functions of professional academies

The Science Advisor's Office was in the vanguard of those recommending the creation of a new, independent academy-based advice mechanism (see next section). Other executive efforts include the advising of Malaysia's Ministry of Education on improving science, technology, and innovation literacy. These efforts are guided by Malaysia's strategic Vision 2020.

The Philippines. The executive branch of the Philippines relies on two main bodies, the Department of Science and Technology, a government body, and the National Academy of Science and Technology, a nongovernmental entity. The National Academy of Science and Technology was established in 1976 to serve as a reservoir of scientific and technological manpower for the country. It now it serves as an advisory body to the Department of Science and Technology, which advises the President and the cabinet on science and technology.

The Republic of Korea. The Korean Science and Technology Policy Institute (STEPI), a nonprofit organization, serves as an important source of policy advice to the Office of the Prime Minister. As a research institute and major science, technology, and innovation player in Korea, STEPI conducts research on social and economic issues that relate to national science, technology, and innovation policy. It maintains a stable network that promotes interaction and communication among key actors and serves as a national basis for the exchange of interdisciplinary ideas.

Taiwan (China). Taiwan (China) has a long tradition of relying on science, technology, and innovation advice to guide its development strategies (Lin 1998). In 1959 it established the National Science Council as an internal government body of the executive branch for the promotion of development in science and technology. The government also relied on the input of the Scientific and Technical Advisory Group (STAG), made up of members from Taiwan and elsewhere. STAG's efforts are complemented by those of the Academia Sinica (see next section).

Cross-country experience with academies

In many countries academies also provide advice (box 9.1). Providing such advice is among the most important functions of professional academies, and most academies function in an advisory capacity. Some have grown from the science, technology, and innovation community, independently of the government; others have been formed by government ministers.

The InterAcademy Council (IAC), headquartered at the Royal Netherlands Academy of Arts and Sciences, in Amsterdam, was established in 2000. It mobilizes the world's best scientists and engineers to provide expert knowledge and high-quality advice to international bodies, such as the United Nations, the World Bank, and other institutions.

Box 9.1

**The government
of Malaysia relies
on its Academy
of Sciences for
scientific advice**

An example of a highly successful science advisory system that has not adhered strictly to "established" principles is the Academy of Sciences Malaysia (ASM). ASM founders realized that developed countries lauded independence from government as an important principle of science advice, but they recognized that the financial wherewithal of the academy depended on significant support from the Malaysian government.

A decision was made early on that ASM should first and foremost serve national development objectives. ASM works closely with the Science Advisor's Office in providing advice to the Office of the Prime Minister. The Ministry of Science and Technology and Innovation and other ministries seek ASM's advice regularly, mostly in fields related to policy review.

ASM integrates not only national science and engineering experts but also the institutions that support scientific, technological, and engineering enterprises. It has sustained its financial well-being through an initial grant from the government, which underwrites a substantial part of its annual operating and maintenance cost. This funding has enabled ASM to retain a competent full-time staff.

Another important element of the success of ASM is its vigorous cultivation of international scientific, technological, and engineering linkages through regional and international organizations. This has enabled ASM to freely tap into the vast pool of international scientific, technological, and engineering knowledge, experience, and expertise.

ASM has been much less successful in providing scientific, technological, and engineering advice to industry. A characteristic of developing countries is the isolation of scientific, technological, and engineering academic organizations from the industrial community. The forms of certification and validation of merit are also different. There is a need to construct means by which the applied and engineering sciences are brought closer to academia. One way to do this is to encourage scientific, technological, and engineering academies and associations to take on more functional activities, such as training and certification of professionals and paraprofessionals working in industry. Member institutions of the World Federation of Engineering Organizations (WFEO) are already doing this.

The ASM financial model of a substantial launching grant from the government of $5 million that assures its financial wellbeing has served as a model for academies in Africa. Nigeria and South Africa have adopted the ASM financial model, while Zimbabwe and Tunisia intend to integrate scientists and engineers into their proposed academies.

National academies vary greatly in their degree of financial reliance on government. The Science Council of Japan is an organ of the Prime Minister's Department, while the Engineering Academy of Japan accepts no government funding, relying entirely on membership fees. The Chinese Academy of Sciences is fully funded by the government.

Financial jumpstarts and even ongoing support from government can be vital for young academies in developing countries with small scientific, technical, and engineering communities. This support is vital where neither the private sector nor prospective members can provide sufficient funds to initiate and run a successful academy.

Scientific and technical academies of all types (including science, technology, engineering, medicine, and agriculture) can play an important role in

The role of national academies in decision-making in developing countries is starting to generate interest among donors and international partners

providing advice to government. Where they do not exist, efforts should be made to create them.

Scientific and technical academies need to cooperate with other academies whose work affects scientific and technological development. Judicial systems around the world are increasingly dealing with scientific issues. The Philippine Judicial Academy is engaged in educating its members on the linkages between law and science.

In Taiwan (China) the Academia Sinica complements the National Science Council as the most visible nonstate advisor to the President on science, technology, and innovation policy. Academia Sinica reports directly to the presidency, pursuing the dual mission of conducting scientific research at its own institutes and providing guidance, channels of communication, and encouragement on raising academic standards in Taiwan (China). Its members provide advice to the government's executive branch upon request.

The role of national academies in decisionmaking in developing countries is starting to generate interest among donors and international partners. The African Science Academy Development Initiative is a new activity undertaken by the U.S. National Academies to help African academies of science build their capacity to provide independent, evidence-based advice to governments on health-related issues. Using a 10-year $20-million grant from the Bill & Melinda Gates Foundation, the National Academies will collaborate with African science academies to support a variety of activities at the national and regional levels. Three African science academies will receive support in advisory activities. The aim is to strengthen each academy's capacity in infrastructure, experience, and personnel and to develop and sustain a relationship between the academy and its government and nation. The goal will be to develop a trusted source of excellent scientific advice.

Volunteers from the U.S. scientific community and staff from the U.S. National Academies will work closely with their African counterparts to develop and test models of advisory interactions with the host government and other institutions of society. Activities may include bringing together members of academia, government, industry, and civil society for ongoing discussions to illuminate critical health-related issues and potential solutions consistent with the society's priorities, values, and resources. Other envisaged efforts include policy studies or other formal advisory activities to explore in depth an issue of national importance. In addition to the intensive partnerships, the project will involve the broader community of science academies from across Africa in a range of activities that will evolve over the life of the project. These will include annual symposia, collaborative workshops, and information resources generated through the program.

This initiative is expected to enhance communication between African decisionmakers and the scientific, engineering, and medical communities and to generate an increased appreciation of the benefits of objective, evidence-based

Recognition and appropriate treatment of scientific uncertainty and risk are important elements of science advice

advice in decisionmaking. African academy staff will strengthen their skills in setting up relationships with government and other organizations, planning and implementing projects, managing finances, writing reports and proposals, and raising funds.

Other advisory bodies

Other examples of creative institutional responses to these challenges are sprouting up around the world, due in large part to individual "connectors" who work to plug home organizations into the growing constellation of international alliances. Innovative relationship building is occurring in groups such as the Global Science Forum of the OECD, UNESCO, the International Council for Science (ICSU), and academy groups, such as the Council of Academies of Engineering and Technological Sciences (CEATS), and the World Federation of Engineering Organisations (WFEO), and the InterAcademy Panel (IAP) and its offshoot, the InterAcademy Council (IAC).

Ensuring good-quality advice

Maintaining the quality of expert advice depends on a variety of conditions, including early and appropriate identification of issues, recognition and appropriate treatment of scientific uncertainty and risk, and diversity of opinion and cross-disciplinary approaches. Academies in developed countries generally strive for independence and disinterestedness in outcomes. In contrast, academies in developing countries increasingly work toward improving engagement with government.[1] All academies aim for accountability to the public.

Early and appropriate identification of issues is a primary factor in the quality of science advice at high levels of government. Anticipation of hazards and salient issues for policy has become increasingly important. Responsiveness of science advisory mechanisms to emerging issues has proven to be particularly important in building and maintaining trust between science advisors and the public, politicians, and the wider scientific community. Proactive, rather than reactive, science advice has been invaluable in past experiences with crises, as reflected in how different national governments coped—or failed to cope—with the spread of the Severe Acute Respiratory Syndrome (SARS) epidemic.

Recognition and appropriate treatment of scientific uncertainty and risk are important elements of science advice. In environmental policymaking based on scientific analysis, the "precautionary principle" has been advocated. This principle states that reasonable concern should override some scientific uncertainty when policymakers are considering steps to prevent environmental destruction or environmental risks to public health. Science advisors and policymakers in the European Commission apply the precautionary principle when assessing risks associated with products such as genetically modified organisms. This approach differs from the regulatory approaches used in the United States.

Increasing the inclusiveness and openness of advice processes can strengthen public trust and improve the robustness of advice

Diversity of opinion and cross-disciplinary approaches in response to scientific questions are also essential. Soliciting a variety of perspectives improves the accuracy of scientific evidence, analysis, and conclusions, and it can boost public faith in the science advisory system. Developing countries with small technological bases may find it difficult to find a diversity of qualified advisors, particularly across disciplines. They therefore need to create a critical mass of experts in one multidisciplinary academy. In Malaysia, for example, ASM was first mooted as an academy of engineering. Its founders then had the wisdom to engage the entire Malaysian scientific and technological community, so that ASM now covers the entire range of sciences, engineering, and technology in government, academia, and industry.

Independence and disinterestedness in outcomes on the part of science advisors are also key principles governing many science advisory processes. Public trust in the advice and resulting policies depends to a great extent on whether or not the advice mechanism relies on information that comes from outside government and industry. Major factors in public perceptions of disinterestedness include organizational separation between advisors and advice recipients in government, freedom from political influence, and financial independence from the government.

Accountability to the public is crucial. This typically requires gauging public opinion, through tools such as foresight activities or legislative processes. Accountability should be promoted in ways that reduce transaction costs while enhancing the quality of advice. Subjecting every stage of the advisory process to public scrutiny, for example, may increase the level of oversight but not necessarily the quality of advice.

Making advisory bodies inclusive and open

Increasing the inclusiveness and openness of advice processes can strengthen public trust and improve the robustness of advice. In some countries, however, inclusiveness and openness are controversial. While they have taken quick root in the open climate of the advisory process in the United States and have recently become more prevalent in scientific advisory systems in other countries, such democratically influenced guidelines may not be appropriate for traditionally closed political systems. Science advisory mechanisms should still be informed by domestic political traditions, financial circumstances, and organizational history.

National responses to recent public health crises provide a good illustration of this reality. Damaged public trust and growing concern about the failure of governments to account for scientific analyses have increased expectations that science advisory processes should be inclusive and transparent. In established democracies these sentiments have been the primary force for changes in advice mechanisms: in the United Kingdom leaders acquire a breadth of advice, especially in cases of scientific uncertainty, and openly publish advice and related documents.

Academies and science advisory organizations in developing countries face tradeoffs between the need for openness and their traditions of control

Scandals in Europe over contaminated blood and mad cow disease have spurred efforts toward even greater transparency and interactivity in science advice. More meetings of the British science advisory committees are open to the public, and in France all science advice related to food and drug safety is now published online.

The international media put pressure on China to open up its public health advice system during the initial stage of the SARS epidemic. Although it failed to be candid with the public at the beginning of the crisis, China later demonstrated openness about SARS. China has also opened up rule-making on environmental policy to some public input, and it has modified both national and local laws to accommodate WTO requirements. But China's tradition of government control over information is still strong, representing a political perspective on information access that is fundamentally different from that of the United Kingdom and France.

Academies and science advisory organizations in developing countries face tradeoffs between the need for openness and their traditions of control. Their experiences suggest that governments should select guidelines that are reasonable given their countries' own circumstances. This pattern of behavior is valid not only for organizing the way they receive advice on science, technology and innovation matters but also for harnessing knowledge to development purposes.

Creating review and feedback mechanisms

Governments use a range of methods to review decisions and obtain feedback from the system, in order to ensure that the advice they receive serves the interests of government and the public good. Most of these review mechanisms focus primarily on the robustness of the discussion process rather than on the value of the advice itself.

Three models—agency outreach, independent advice, and convened advice—help illustrate how such review and feedback can work. All three processes for review and feedback bring the views of scientists and stakeholders to bear on government decisionmaking about science. The tradeoffs associated with each model differ depending on country circumstances.

Agency outreach. In developed countries many research agencies seek input from the scientific establishment to assist in the priority-setting process. This priority-setting model involves establishing workshops that bring together leading scientists and technologists from government, industry, and academia. Discussions and debate identify common themes for research within each field of science, which then compete at the program and directorate levels as budget priorities are set. This framework works well in countries that have established advisory systems in which advice recipients are accustomed to inclusiveness and openness in their decisionmaking processes.

Citizen councils have been used effectively to involve the wider society in issues of science and technology

Because the primary goal of agency outreach is to allow decisionmakers to draw on a diversity of perspectives, the approach may work more effectively in large countries with established science, technology, and innovation communities. Agency outreach may require more human and financial wealth than developing countries with scarce finances or new science, technology, and innovation communities can afford.

Independent advice. An independent advisory model offers more maneuvering room for developing countries. In this model the science agency turns to an outside group for input. A science, technology, and innovation academy would be an ideal leader for this kind of group. The group may form a task group, which in turn could convene workshops and panels to provide themes for priority setting in particular areas. This board could concentrate on scientific objectives rather than the methods by which the objectives are implemented, prioritize scientific questions of significance, and account for costs and technical feasibility. This kind of independent advisory group would add credibility to the advisory process.

This independent advisory model is a more promising option than the agency outreach model for small countries with developing science, technology, and innovation communities, because it allows for success with a range of institutional variation and financial circumstances. As long as the public and concerned actors feel confident that the advisor can provide objective advice, it may not matter whether such an institution is supported by government funds.

Convened advice. A third model for input from experts is the convened science advisory board model. These advisory committees can have members who serve for several years. The committees can be convened to advise on particular scientific and technical issues. Convened science advisory boards offer external advice and have a greater stake in outcomes than workshop panels. This model provides more flexibility for small and developing countries to tailor their review and feedback systems.

Involving the wider society

Science and technology are applied to innovation within a social and economic context. Citizen councils have been used effectively in Europe to involve the wider society in issues of science and technology. "Consensus councils" have a long tradition of settling contentious matters in science and technology. In the late 1980s the Danish Board of Technology defined consensus councils as bodies of lay citizens that would be convened to consider the evidence on a particular science or technology issue, participate in public debate, and ultimately provide a consensus report of their findings and policy recommendations. The purpose of the process was not to dictate policy but to help the legislature understand where the public stood on an issue before considering specific policies. The success of the councils led to the engagement of similar processes in France, the Netherlands, and the United Kingdom.

To be effective, such councils need to be convened at the local and regional levels around specific issues (such as genetically modified foods). In addition, they need to play a role in recommending policy changes that stick.

Polling public opinion on science and technology issues has been done in Europe, Latin America, the United States, and through some grass-roots organizations in India. The results of such polls can provide policymakers with important insights (box 9.2).

Conducting foresight exercises

Foresight exercises obtain the views of different parties, identify trends, create networks, and inform decisionmakers and the public about developments in science and technology. When well designed, these exercises can be an important source of advice to the science, technology, and innovation decisionmaking process (box 9.3).

Foresight studies and exercises have been conducted in many countries since the 1960s, to analyze defense planning, prioritization, subsidization, and other issues. Originally viewed as simply a tool for identifying new technologies,

---

Box 9.2

Better-educated people are more likely to understand the connection between R&D and development

Source: Arocena 1997.

A poll conducted in Uruguay in the late 1990s revealed that 57 percent of the population believed that conducting R&D with government resources would enhance the country's development prospects. Better-educated people indicated that science, technology, and innovation would reduce Uruguay's dependency on other countries, while people with less education believed that science, technology, and innovation would increase the country's dependency. These results may indicate that people with less formal education may have been less aware than better-educated people of Uruguay's capabilities in science and technology. A media effort highlighting the relevance of science and technology for enhancing development might have changed their views.

Box 9.3

Foresight exercises can be useful, but macroeconomic shocks can make their findings moot

Source: Watanabe 2000.

Through a participatory process of establishing "Visions" for science, technology, and innovation progress in Japan, representatives from government and the science, technology, and innovation community collaborated on ways to stimulate industry R&D and socio-economic development. The recent decline of the Japanese economy has demonstrated the limitations of "Visions" and similar foresight approaches. Science, technology, and innovation foresight is neither a failsafe predictor of future issues nor a cure-all for economic woes. In times of economic difficulty, finding the resources to maintain programs that were once high priorities becomes difficult. As the Japanese example suggests, while foresight can be important for strategizing how to use science, technology, and innovation for future growth, dire economic conditions can cut off the possibility of financial support for such activities. Developing countries often face this circumstance.

A major factor in determining whether to conduct foresight activities is the cost

foresight is now viewed as a way to increase understanding of the full innovation system.

Although foresight methods were developed in industrial countries, they have been used extensively in developing countries. Foresight activities can help developing countries apply science, technology, and innovation to meet the Goals.

Foresight can be used to establish priorities in science, technology, and innovation funding and craft policy based on analysis of current trends and expectations of future developments. It is particularly important for emerging fields, such as genomics, nanotechnology, and new materials.

The usefulness of foresight depends on identifying the key participants; delineating goals, especially the balance between desired process and product outcomes; defining how the foresight exercise will be used to stimulate innovation; and tying the foresight process into the national decisionmaking structure. A well-planned foresight process should consider governance, how the inherent uncertainty associated with all innovative processes and future projection will be addressed, and perhaps the means for evaluating the success of the foresight process as a whole.

Technology prospecting can provide the tools for developing countries to stay abreast of new developments. One way this could be done would be for researchers in developed countries to identify methods, sources, and assessment tools for understanding new scientific and technological developments and to provide these tools to researchers in developing countries. Another possibility would be to establish a global database of information provided by the world's top research centers. Countries, regions, and enterprises interested in tapping into and developing new technologies could learn about new developments from these databases. A third possibility would be to create public-private partnerships that track, transfer, and train developing country consortia in technology prospecting and the application of technology to business.

A major factor in the choice in determining whether or not to conduct foresight activities is the cost. Scenario planning across a range of technologies or national goals can be a lengthy and expensive effort, costing more than $500,000 (road-mapping efforts that focus on a single technology can cost less).

Foresight continues to consider traditional political borders and disciplinary structures as the parameters for discussion. This makes sense given the need to define and bound any problem for intelligent discussion. But trends toward the globalization of science, technology, and innovation mean that national foresight efforts may miss some of the very important global and cross-disciplinary trends that are emerging outside the bounds of their exercises.

Foresight exercises for developing countries should be tailored to each country's needs and capacities. Doing so will increase the chances that foresight will successfully provide more than mere advice to the decisionmaking process but have the greatest chance for successful development and commercialization.

Crafting of effective science, technology, and innovation policy requires civil servants able to conduct policy analysis

The experience of Malaysia provides an example of academy innovation that has transcended these constraints, an innovation driven by its founders' mantra of "the three M's": money, manpower, and mandate. Before ASM's inception, in 1995, the bodies positioned to provide advice through the Science Advisor's Office were government *cum* industry–funded research institutes. These institutes were focused primarily on major agricultural and plantation-based industries like natural rubber, palm oil, and forestry. They typically engaged in applied research and did not pursue holistic research in new technologies like ICT, biotechnology, nanotechnology, or space technology.

Since 1995 ASM has progressed a great deal in achieving its mission of national development. It has also expanded its advisory activities to include new and creative roles on the international scene. This has become an important element of academy innovation.

To be highly relevant to national development, ASM founders established ASM by act of parliament, emulating the U.S. National Academy of Sciences, which was established by act of congress and signed into law by President Abraham Lincoln. In other countries this strong connection to government might have led critics to challenge the academy's independence and disinterestedness. But ASM has risen above that issue, building its political credibility by participating in international partnerships and eliciting widespread participation from professionals in industry and from academic scientific community.

Building the capacity to provide advice

Crafting of effective science, technology, and innovation policy requires civil servants who are able to conduct policy analysis. Creating such capacity requires training facilities for policy analysis in local universities and research institutions. Training civil servants in technology management, science policy, and foresight techniques can aid the process of integrating science, technology, and innovation advice into decisionmaking (box 9.4). The Commonwealth Partnership for Technology Management has been successful in training civil servants from African countries toward this end.

In Singapore many civil servants have degrees in engineering. Inclusion of people with technical backgrounds in the decisionmaking process can be an effective way to integrate science, technology, and innovation into national strategies. In China almost all policymakers are engineers. Scientists and engineers are regularly invited to make presentations to high-level central government officials, including the prime minister and the president. These events take place several times a year, and government officials give them a high priority.

Establishing science and technology policy fellowships

Science and technology policy fellows attached to various branches of government improve the quality of decisionmaking by providing decisionmakers with the best available information on trends in science and technology (box 9.5).

Box 9.4

The Belfer Center's training program strengthens policymakers' capacity for policy analysis

Source: www.execprog.
org/programs.asp?
programid=144
&displaymode=view.

While science, technology, and innovation are increasingly recognized as important factors in the economic transformation of developing countries, their prominence in development policy is generally understated. To address this issue, the Belfer Center for Science and International Affairs at Harvard University's John F. Kennedy School of Government has launched a short-term training program on science, technology, and innovation policy. The program provides high-level leaders from government, academia, industry, and civil society with a unique opportunity to learn from others' experiences and strengthen their ability to integrate science, technology, and innovation into national development policy.

The program is designed for high-level decisionmakers (ministers, deputy ministers, senior civil servants, diplomats, development leaders, university presidents, and chief executive officers) from both developing and industrial countries. Participation is also open to senior advisors to heads of state and government. Participants are drawn from a variety of leadership positions, including finance, economic and development planning, industry, trade, science and technology, education, health, agriculture, energy, environment and natural resources, information and communications, and foreign affairs. Participants attend five days of classes, during which they develop collective approaches to problem-solving using case studies. Emphasis is placed on interactive learning involving participants from a diversity of backgrounds and interests.

These sessions assess developing countries' science, technology, and innovation policies. Attention is given to examining the emerging role of science, technology, and innovation in meeting basic human needs, strengthening the capacity of developing countries to participate in the global economy, and enhancing the ability of countries to make the transition toward sustainability. The sessions address specific policy themes related to biotechnology, ICT, and environmentally sound technologies. They explore issues such as science, technology, and innovation advice; human capacity; enterprise development; and investment in R&D. The curriculum covers innovation systems, international technology cooperation, technology and foreign direct investment, intellectual property rights, and managing new technologies.

Developing countries could develop a system of science, technology, and innovation fellows that could be attached to various branches of government.

Building science, technology, and innovation capacity among negotiators
Strengthening the capacity of negotiators to engage in technological issues is an essential aspect of international relations. The United Nations Conference on Trade and Development (UNCTAD) Science and Technology Initiative aims to equip diplomats from developing countries with the ability to address science, technology, and innovation issues related to trade, especially issues related to intellectual property, biodiversity, energy, and climate negotiations. The aim of the program is to spur collective learning from examples across the globe, while allowing diplomats to represent their countries through the analysis of complex issues. The WTO also seeks to build capacity by training trade negotiators from developing countries.

The term *science, technology, and innovation diplomacy* applies to activities of international cooperation and compromise on issues of science, technology, and

Box 9.5

Scientists are being posted as fellows at U.S. government agencies

Source: G. Atkinson, U.S. Department of State, personal communication, 2004.

The American Association for the Advancement of Science (AAAS) administers a science and diplomacy fellows program in which scientists work in various branches of government. The fellows help government officials gain access to timely and accurate scientific and technological information needed for decisionmaking.

To complement these efforts, in 2003 the U.S. Department of State created the Jefferson Science Fellows. Fellows are tenured scientists and engineers from U.S. institutions of higher learning. This program promotes closer engagement of the scientific, technological, and engineering community in the formulation and implementation of U.S. foreign policy. In 2004 the Department of State had 36 AAAS Science and Diplomacy fellows, 9 fellows from professional societies, and 5 Jefferson fellows working in 13 functional bureaus, regional bureaus, and other sections of the department.

innovation policy. The importance of this field has grown in recent years, in tandem with advances on issues ranging from infectious diseases and biotechnology to sustainability and information technology. In all of these areas international public servants and diplomats increasingly depend on expertise to make their policy decisions, although many currently do not receive systematic advice.

Most issues of science, technology, and innovation now cross lines of national sovereignty. Science and technology had already become a truly international activity in the twentieth century, with huge increase in transnational collaboration on science, technology, and innovation issues. In the past few decades, existing and new institutions have taken on the mantle of providing international science advice in innovative ways. International scientific assessments have contributed a great deal to both national and international policy formulation as well as private-sector decisionmaking on issues of stratospheric ozone depletion, biodiversity loss, and climate change. The communities of science, technology, and innovation and international relations have begun to recognize the urgency of improving their communications and collaboration. According to many experts, the input from this broad range of stakeholders and disciplines has been vital to progress on otherwise intractable transboundary conflicts.

The activities of and networks created by science, technology, and innovation diplomacy offer excellent opportunities for: exchanging lessons from past experiences, opening countries up to better funding opportunities from international sources, and sharing organizational capacity and science, technology, and innovation expertise. Participation in international networks can also help build the domestic political and scientific credibility of academies and science advisory institutions, especially in developing countries.

Science, technology, and innovation diplomacy still presents challenges, particularly due to the lack of formal procedures and systematization. The right people to "cross over" and serve in science advisory roles need to be identified. Relationship brokering at both formal and informal levels is needed

Policymakers need to tailor their systems to their countries' needs and available resources

to improve institutional coordination. More coordination along these lines is needed to improve decisionmaking on controversial issues. Both the science and the policymaking communities need to work to forge better channels and methods for formal and informal communication. Discussion of foreign policy issues need to be infused with solid scientific and technical knowledge. Scientists need to understand the global governance structures that may impinge on the conduct or reporting of their research.[2]

Conclusion

The diversity of political experience, resources, and constraints in both developed and developing countries means that the creation of advisory mechanisms cannot be guided by a one-size-fits-all mentality. To create and implement successful science advisory policies and mechanisms, policymakers need to tailor their systems to their countries' needs and available resources.

Chapter 10

Governing global technology

International organizations can play a critical role in promoting the application of science, technology, and innovation to the Millennium Development Goals. These organizations—especially the organs of the United Nations and allied intergovernmental bodies—have extensive influence on the development agenda. Deploying these organizations' efforts to meeting the Goals will require them to focus on their functions and competencies rather than jurisdictional mandates.

International norm setting

One area in which international organizations play a crucial role is in providing guidance and coordination, setting norms and standards, and providing scientific and technical advice.

Guidance, advocacy, and coordination

The five-year review of the implementation of the Goals to be held in 2005 should be used to generate fresh guidance and advocacy based on a deeper understanding of the role of technological innovation in economic growth. Policy guidance and advocacy are central functions of many international organizations. Guidance and advocacy are provided through universal bodies, such as the UN General Assembly, or through the decisions of the conferences of parties to various international agreements.

The Millennium Declaration is an example of a guidance and advocacy statement. The effectiveness of the declaration will depend largely on the extent to which its elements are translated into governmental and nongovernmental programs. The importance governments place on technology for development can be discerned from such guidance and advocacy documents.

Several international agencies are skeptical about—or even hostile to—technology, partly because it challenges traditional views about human progress

International rule-making and standards-setting institutions set a wide range of rules that affect the capacity of developing countries to build domestic scientific and technological capabilities

and partly because of their perceptions that its effects on culture and the environment are negative. Through its guidance bodies, the United Nations will need to take a more active role in articulating the importance of technology in economic transformation.

In December 2002 the Executive Committee for Economic and Social Affairs designated the United Nations Conference on Trade and Development (UNCTAD) as the lead entity for science, technology, and innovation within the UN system. UNCTAD provides intellectual support to the United Nations Commission on Science and Technology for Development (UNCSTD). The commission is one of the few organs of the United Nations Economic and Social Council with specific advisory responsibilities on science and technology.

The commission has the potential to play a key role in strengthening science and technology advice in the United Nations system. The first step would be to appoint an assistant Secretary-General to serve as the executive secretary to the commission and as the science and technology advisor to the Economic and Social Council and other organs of the United Nations as deemed appropriate. The Economic and Social Council would then adopt appropriate procedures for the work of the commission and its relationships with its other functional commissions. The commission could also forge close working relations with other research-related entities such as the United Nations University and its constituent institutes and programs (National Research Council 2002).

Rule making and standards setting

International rule-making and standards-setting institutions, such as the World Trade Organization (WTO), the International Organization for Standardization (ISO), and the Bretton Woods institutions, set a wide range of rules that affect the capacity of developing countries to build domestic scientific and technological capabilities. Many observers believe that the WTO Agreement on Trade-Related Aspects of Intellectual Property Rights (TRIPS) is the most important international treaty affecting technological innovation in developing countries. In fact, other agreements, such as the trade-related investment measures agreement under WTO, may have even more serious implications for technological innovation in developing countries. Equally important are standards relating to environmental management and other economic activities.

Scientific and technical advice

The UN system should strengthen its capacity to advise countries on the linkages between technological innovation and development. Doing so would entail building competence in science, technology, and innovation advice in the executive offices of the United Nations.

In his 2000 report to the Millennium General Assembly, entitled *We the Peoples* (UN 2000, pp. 5–6) UN Secretary-General Kofi Annan noted that that the United Nations "is the only body of its kind with universal membership and

UN governing bodies should create an Office of the Science Advisor or equivalent facility appropriate to their mandates

comprehensive scope, and encompassing so many areas of human endeavor. These features make it a uniquely useful forum—for sharing information, conducting negotiations, elaborating norms and voicing expectations, coordinating the behavior of states and other actors, and pursuing common plans of action."

The United Nations, especially those organs that address international peace and security issues, such as the Office of the Secretary-General and the Security Council, will increasingly address technological issues associated with development. It is therefore imperative that they equip themselves with the capacity to address technological issues. The United Nations Secretary-General could provide leadership in this area by strengthening the United Nations' capacity for science, technology, and innovation advice and by encouraging the creation of such facilities in other UN agencies, beginning with his own office (National Research Council 2002).

UN governing bodies that have substantial responsibilities for technology and development should each create an Office of the Science Advisor or equivalent facility appropriate to their mandates. Such bodies include the General Assembly, the governing bodies of specialized agencies, and the governing bodies of specially convened intergovernmental conferences, summits, and meetings. The Office of the Science Advisor should be located within the office of the Secretary General, the Director General, or the Executive Secretary of the organ or conference and should serve the governing body of the organization through the Secretariat. The function of this office would be to help the governing body and the Secretariat recognize policy issues that require or would benefit from science advice, help the governing body and the Secretariat formulate the scientific questions to be asked, carry out or commission from an external organization the science advice process to respond to the questions, help the governing body and the executive interpret the meaning and degree of uncertainty in the resulting report, and help the governing body and the Secretariat understand the possible policy implications of the science advice.

The Science Advisor who heads the office should be chosen based on his or her capacity to implement these guidelines. It is important to ensure that the work of science advisory offices is carried out in conformity with the highest standards of the scientific community.

Management of data and information requires a well-trained staff to serve the study committees. Staff can carry out extensive reviews of the literature, commission analytical papers, arrange expert testimony to the committee, and convene workshops at which a variety of experts present data and express their views to members of the committee. It is important to ensure the competence and independence of the staff and adherence to clear principles of science advice.

The experience of scientific academies and other organizations has led to the development and evolution of a set of procedures that characterize good science advice. These include careful attention to statement of the task, recruitment of a broadly based expert study committee with a balance of disciplines

**Each science
advisory
facility should
adopt an
appropriate
set of general
procedures
adapted
to special
circum-
stances
of the
organization**

and views, management of external inputs, production of a public report, and independent peer review. Processes associated with these elements are accepted by the scientific community as indicators of objective science advice. They can be carried out by a unit within an organization or commissioned from an outside entity. Each science advisory facility should adopt an appropriate set of general procedures based on those described in this report, adapted to special circumstances of the organization. These procedures should be widely publicized within the diplomatic and scientific communities

Operational activities

In the operational arena, international institutions can advance science, technology and innovation in developing countries by strengthening institutions and supporting R&D and capacity-building activities. Much of the work at the local level will be carried out by private enterprises (including multinational corporations) as well as NGOs that play an important role in community development. Indeed, the main challenge facing international organizations is figuring out how to engage effectively with the private sector and strengthening the technical capacity of NGOs.

The role of multilateral and bilateral institutions

Multilateral financial institutions led by the World Bank and the regional development banks should play a leading role in promoting technological innovation in developing countries. Bilateral institutions should place science, technology, and innovation at the core of their development assistance programs. This process will involve creating and strengthening institutions of science, technology, and innovation advice in multilateral and bilateral agencies.

The lending and operational activities of the multilateral financial institutions are already having a significant impact on technological innovation in developing countries (Watson, Crawford, and Farley 2003). Multilateral financial institutions can also play an important leadership role. The leadership task is particularly important because the World Bank has engaged in only modest activities on the role of technological innovation in development.

A number of international instruments adopted by the United Nations, the International Monetary Fund (IMF), and the World Bank, such as Common Country Assessments, UN Development Assistance Frameworks (UNDAFs), and Poverty Reduction Strategy Papers (PRSPs) could play an important role as mechanisms for advancing the role of technological innovation in development. All of the instruments are prepared under the leadership of developing country governments, with the participation of national interest groups, UN country teams, and other foreign donors. The official guidelines for preparing these documents do not include science, technology, and innovation for development. Modules need to be included in the guidelines on how to integrate science, technology, and innovation to solve development problems. Doing so

Developing countries could fully integrate technological consider- ations into the PRSPs and other planning tools

would open the doors to include science, technology, and innovation in the development work of the UN system in a more systematic and effective way.

The Common Country Assessment and UNDAF are the United Nations' strategic planning tools for field operations. The Common Country Assessment analyzes the national development situation and identifies key development issues. It takes into account national priorities, with a focus on the Goals and the other commitments, goals, and targets of the Millennium Declaration and international conferences, summits, and conventions. The statistical section includes indicators to measure, among other things, progress toward achieving the Goals.

As the common strategic framework for the operational activities of the UN system at the country level, the UNDAF provides a collective, coherent, and integrated UN system response to national priorities and needs within the framework of the Goals and the other commitments, goals, and targets of the Millennium Declaration, as well as the declarations and programs of action adopted at international conferences and summits and through major UN conventions. The UNDAF emerges from the analytical and collaborative effort of the Common Country Assessment. It is the foundation for UN programs of cooperation.

PRSPs provide the basis for assistance from the World Bank and the IMF as well as for debt relief under the Heavily Indebted Poor Countries (HIPC) initiative. Written every three years, PRSPs describe a country's macroeconomic, structural, and social policies and programs for promoting growth and reducing poverty. They also document associated external financing needs. PRSPs are prepared by governments through a participatory process involving civil society and development partners.

Developing countries, in close cooperation with the World Bank, the IMF, and other development agencies, could fully integrate technological considerations into the PRSPs and other planning tools. Their support to infrastructure could be pursued as standard lending projects, but the same activities could be structured as a foundation for technological innovation and linked to domestic research and entrepreneurial activities. Such leadership would not necessarily require additional funding, but it would require these institutions to upgrade their internal capacity to address technological issues. Both institutions need to create technology-related performance standards for their investment activities and demand that their partners use complementary standards.

Other development assistance measures, such as the Millennium Challenge Account recently launched by the United States, represent another opportunity to address the role of science, technology, and innovation in development. The Millennium Challenge Account uses a set of selection criteria that can easily include technological issues. For example, funding could be used to establish institutions designed to promote the creation of business enterprises using imported technology adapted to local conditions. The account could also serve as a source of incentives to encourage countries to make changes to their institutions of higher learning to bring them in line with development goals.

Providing such leadership may also entail strengthening the internal advisory capabilities of these institutions. Offices of chief scientists in these institutions may need to be strengthened to take on additional technological advisory functions to ensure that advice is provided to the leadership of these institutions and complementary technological issues are integrated into their operational programs. The United Kingdom is providing leadership in integrating science and technology into its international development assistance programs (box 10.1). Recognizing the importance of science and technology

Box 10.1

How important are science and technology to development assistance?

Source: United Kingdom, House of Commons, Science and Technology Committee 2004.

In July 2003 the Science and Technology Committee of the British House of Commons began an inquiry into how science and technology are informing spending decisions on the aid budget, how research is being used to support policymaking in international development, and how the United Kingdom is promoting science and technology in developing countries. The work focused on the Department of International Development (DFID), which is responsible for £3.8 billion (92 percent) of the 2004–05 aid budget.

The committee received more than 100 written submissions and held seven evidence sessions. These sessions involved officials from DFID; representatives of organizations involved in capacity building, in agricultural, forestry, and environmental R&D, and in engineering and health R&D; the Government's Chief Scientific Adviser; officials from the Foreign and Commonwealth Offices, the Trade and Investment Office, and the British Council; and the Secretary of State for International Development. The committee also visited several development institutes in the United Kingdom and traveled to Malawi, where it learned about agricultural and health projects and met with the President of Malawi, members of Parliament, and senior officials.

The committee stressed the importance of strengthening the role of science and technology in international development cooperation. Its findings will help support similar enquiries underway elsewhere. Only time will tell whether the recommendation will lead to a major reorientation in the operations of DFID.

The success of these efforts will depend largely on the ability of the United Kingdom to align its various governmental and nongovernmental institutions to help build scientific and technological capacity in developing nations as part of its foreign policy objectives. The government could benefit from working closely with institutions such as the Royal Society (the United Kingdom's national academy of science), which has strong connections with national academies, universities, and other scientific bodies around the world. To achieve tangible results, these efforts will have to go beyond the customary practice of convening meetings and short-term courses to focus on serious efforts in building human and institutional capacities. The United Kingdom is strategically positioned to make a major difference in bringing scientific research and technological innovation to bear on development. In 2005 the Commission for Africa, launched by Prime Minister Tony Blair, will release its findings, and it is hoped that the report will focus on strengthening the role of technological innovation in development cooperation and provide much-needed intellectual leadership for donor agencies. In 2005 the United Kingdom will also hold the presidencies of the G8 and the European Union. It should use the opportunity to promote the role of technological innovation in development cooperation.

Reforms to promote partnerships would be best served by creating internal offices that provide guidance on the role of science, technology, and innovation in international development

for development, it recently appointed a Chief Scientific Advisor in the Department for International Development. The decision was adopted partly as a result of advocacy by the Royal Society, the United Kingdom's national science academy (Royal Society 2004). It is hoped that such initiatives will lead to corresponding reforms by recipient countries to put science and technology at the center of their development cooperation programs (Juma 2002).

Additional funding may also have to be provided, or existing financial support may have to be retargeted. Multilateral financial institutions have a wide range of facilities that can be deployed to provide additional financial support that can provide incentives for innovation. The lessons learned from the Global Environment Facility, which provides incremental funding to investment projects to ensure that they provide global environmental goods, could be applied to technological innovation. The challenge would be to create mechanisms that leverage additional investment to innovation activities in lending projects. This funding does not need to be provided through a new fund; these institutions could commit to devote a certain share of investment funding to support innovation-related activities.

Bilateral assistance institutions play a critical role in promoting cooperation between industrial and developing countries. These agencies have made significant contributions in fields such as capacity building (with a focus on human resources and to some degree institutional development). They are also engaged in a wide range of specific projects around the world. Much of the work of these agencies is guided by changes in host countries and often reflects foreign policy objectives. Indeed, development assistance is more of an exercise in "development diplomacy" than economic transformation. Many of these agencies distinguish between programs for "poverty eradication" and programs for "economic growth." The scope of the projects tends to be limited and often delinked from long-term economic activities that involve private sector activities, which is where the impetus for growth actually lies.

A few bilateral development agencies have a strong focus on science and technology. But even where such programs exist, they lack strong links with domestic scientific institutions in donor countries. Improving this situation will require a review of the purpose of development assistance in light of the Goals. Aid programs need to reflect the view that the best way to address poverty is to stimulate economic growth. This will require a focus on science, technology, and innovation. This approach would create new opportunities for establishing and strengthening international partnerships involving government, universities, civil society, and the private sector. It would also provide opportunities for shifting from the current focus on development advocacy toward more practical programs that involve developing technical competence in poor countries.

Reforms will be needed in bilateral development agencies to promote such partnerships. They would be best served by creating internal offices that provide guidance on the role of science, technology, and innovation in international

Most UN agencies focus their science and technology–related activities on human and institutional capacity building, education, and training

development. This approach would deepen international cooperation by creating close linkages between economic institutions in donor and recipient countries.

R&D and capacity-building activities conducted or sponsored by the United Nations

The UN system undertakes a wide range of research activities, including basic, applied, and policy research. The diversity of these activities is a reflection of the complex nature of the global system (National Research Council 2002).

Most UN agencies focus their science and technology–related activities on human and institutional capacity building, education, and training. Much of this research addresses developing country challenges. UN agencies—such as UNESCO, the International Atomic Energy Agency (IAEA), the World Meteorological Organization (WMO), the World Health Organization (WHO), the Food and Agriculture Organization (FAO), and the United Nations Industrial Development Organization (UNIDO)—are engaged in a variety of scientific research activities. Much of this work—and the work of the United Nations itself and its regional economic commissions—is carried out through partnerships and alliances with other research institutions around the world.

Examples of research include the activities of the International Centre for Genetic Engineering and Biotechnology (ICGEB), located in Trieste, Italy, and New Delhi. ICGEB conducts research, provides services to member states, and leads training activities. The center's research includes both basic and applied research and emphasizes developing country problems. More than 300 people from 30 countries work in its laboratories.

The United Nations system also supports the Consultative Group on International Agricultural Research (CGIAR) (box 10.2). The CGIAR aims to contribute to food security and reduce poverty, improve nutrition, and improve natural resource management in developing countries through research, partnerships, capacity building, and policy support.

Box 10.2

The Consultative Group on International Agricultural Research (CGIAR) is a successful example of international scientific collaboration

Largely a consortium of public (and a few private) donor members, the CGIAR supports a network of 15 centers with activities in more than 100 countries. It operates on an annual budget of $350 million of voluntary funding provided by the development assistance agencies of developed countries, ministries of agriculture in developing countries, international and regional development organizations, and foundations. The CGIAR employs about 1,000 scientists and a larger number of support staff.

The CGIAR manages one of the world's largest *ex situ* collections of plant genetic resources in trust for the world community. It holds more than 500,000 accessions of more than 3,000 crop, forage, and agroforestry species. The collection includes farmers' varieties, improved varieties, and the wild species from which those varieties were initially derived. These collections have been placed under FAO administration.

The United Nations often lacks the requisite institutional arrangements that would help translate research knowledge into goods and services

Much of the United Nations' research is devoted to social issues. Agencies such as the United Nations University, the United Nations Research Institute for Social Development (UNRISD), and the United Nations Institute for Training and Research (UNITAR) have been at the forefront of such work.

Some UN organs have made important contributions to the understanding of the role of technology in development over the years. UNCTAD has been a leading supporter of policy research on the role of technology in development. The United Nations University, through its research centers, has also been a major player in policy research.

Many of the R&D activities of the UN system address the needs of the poor. But the United Nations often lacks the requisite institutional arrangements that would help translate research knowledge into goods and services. Links with other institutions, particularly those in the private sector, are generally weak. The CGIAR, for example, has not been able to establish effective and durable links with the parts of the private sector that hold the key technologies needed to advance agricultural production. Much of the challenge lies in differences in research cultures and the character of public sector funding upon which the system relies. Meeting these challenges will require more emphasis on designing institutional arrangements that allow for greater linkages between UN research and private sector activities.

UNESCO is the technical agency of the UN with a mandate for science and technology. It is active in the basic and applied sciences in such areas as mathematics, physics, chemistry, life sciences, applied sciences (such as water and earth sciences), engineering and technology, and science analysis and policy. UNESCO is host to four of the five intergovernmental programs in science: the Intergovernmental Oceanographic Commission, the Intergovernmental Geological Correlation Programme, the Intergovernmental Hydrological Programme, Man and the Biosphere Programme, and the Management of Social Transformations Programme. It is also working on the ethics of science and technology, hosting the Commission on the Ethics of Scientific Knowledge and Technology and the Universal Declaration on the Human Genome and Human Rights.

In the basic sciences UNESCO has proposed an international program that would foster networking and support centers of excellence. The focus in the basic and engineering sciences is on capacity building. Activities in the engineering and technology program include engineering education, accreditation, standards, and a specific program on engineering, technology and poverty eradication. UNESCO works closely with the International Council for Science and the World Federation of Engineering Organisations. Its Water Sciences division hosts the Intergovernmental Hydrological Programme. In the earth sciences the focus is on geoscience, space science, and disasters. Science analysis and policy focus on innovation, university-industry cooperation, the commercialization of R&D, and the role of innovation in development (Carayannis, Alexander, and Ioannidis 2000; Looy, Debackere, and Andries 2003).

The United Nations could contribute to capacity building in developing countries in the engineering sciences and technical education. UNESCO, in cooperation with other agencies such as the United Nations Industrial Development Organization (UNIDO), could create an interagency consortium (in partnership with universities, the private sector, and professional associations) to strengthen scientific, engineering and technical institutions in developing countries.

Open access to scientific and technical information

Despite the potential for cost-effective and virtually instantaneous dissemination of new research over the Internet, global access to scientific and medical literature has yet to be realized. "Open access" publishing is an exciting departure from the traditional subscription-based model of scientific publishing, a system that often frustrates the attempts of scientists, clinicians, and other interested users to search, read about, and share important scientific discoveries (box 10.3). While the prospect of free, comprehensive Internet archives of scientific literature is compelling, the logistics of open access remain a source of uncertainty for some stakeholders in scientific publishing. The United

Box 10.3

Unrestricted free access to scientific and medical literature to accelerate development

Source: www.plos.org/index.html.

The Public Library of Science (PLoS) is a nonprofit organization of scientists and physicians committed to making the world's scientific and medical literature a freely available public resource. The venture is led by Harold Varmus, former director of the National Institutes of Health and co-recipient of the Nobel Prize in medicine. Dr. Varmus currently serves as the president and chief executive officer of the Memorial Sloan-Kettering Cancer Center in New York.

Open access to scientific and medical literature allows anyone anywhere with a connection to the Internet to find and read published research articles online. Published material is archived in a public digital repository, which enhances the utility of all deposited papers by allowing sophisticated searching, manipulation, and mining of the literature using existing and emerging tools. Storing works in a public repository ensures the long-term preservation of the literature as a freely accessible resource, regardless of the fate of the depositing entity or of any change in its policies regarding open access. Immediately upon initial publication, a complete version of the work and all supplemental materials is deposited in at least one online repository supported by an academic institution, scholarly society, government agency, or other well-established organization that seeks to facilitate open access, unrestricted distribution, interoperability, and long-term archiving.

Immediate unrestricted access to scientific ideas, methods, results, and conclusions will speed the progress of science and medicine, and it will bring the benefits of research to the public more directly. To realize this potential, a new business model for scientific publishing is required that treats the costs of publication as the final integral step of the funding of a research project. To demonstrate that this publishing model will be successful for the publication of the very best research, PLoS is publishing its own journals. The first issue of *PLoS Biology* appeared, in print and online, October 13, 2003. *PLoS Medicine* began publication in 2004.

"Open access" publishing is an exciting departure from the traditional subscription-based model of scientific publishing

Nations has championed the need to promote open access to information and technology. It can play a critical role in promoting the concept of open access.

The dissemination of scientific discoveries and ideas provides the foundation for progress in science and medicine. The more widely and freely accessible information is, the greater is the value of peer-reviewed research. For authors open-access literature maximizes the potential impact of their work. Anyone can access their manuscripts, increasing the likelihood that their works will be read, cited, and used as the basis for future discoveries.

For the scientific community, open access unleashes full-text literature into a single information space. Unrestricted access to scientific data, such as genetic and molecular information, has revolutionized life science research in recent years; open access to the treasury of scientific and medical literature will have equally profound benefits for research. For research libraries open access will help contain the spiraling costs of subscriptions to scientific journals. Mergers and market concentration within the publishing industry are placing increasing pressures on the budgets of university libraries and other research archives. Open access to peer-reviewed journals is a long-term solution to the problem. Beyond the research community, open access will make scientific knowledge available to people who cannot afford to subscribe to journals, including clinicians and other health professionals, educators, students, and the general public.

Open access requires a systemic change in the way scientific publishing is funded. Scientists have historically relied on print as the most effective medium for sharing and promoting their work. Traditionally, the costs of printing and distribution accounted for a large share of publishing costs, and each additional copy entailed an expense for the publisher. In contrast, almost all of the cost of online publishing is in putting a document into electronic form; the marginal costs of producing and distributing additional copies are essentially zero. If revenue can be generated to fully cover the costs of producing the electronic version of a document, the document can then be made freely available to anyone with an Internet connection.

Open access is intended to increase the amount of information available, especially to researchers who cannot afford to purchase the information or who work in parts of the world where the journals may not be available. In acknowledgment of the fact that some authors may not be able to afford the cost of producing an electronic version of their document, the Public Library of Science and BioMed Central, the UK–based open access publisher, offer fee waivers or discounts for authors who cannot pay in full. BioMed Central has received support from the Open Society Institute through its Budapest Open Access Initiative to offset publication charges for authors from transition economies. Grants from other donors could support publications in particular disciplines or publications with urgent policy implications.

Extending the open access model to technological information would be a natural extension of current efforts

In the long run the open access model will thrive when there is a redistribution of funding in the scholarly publication system. Costly individual and institutional subscriptions can be eliminated, freeing up funds from libraries, universities, and ultimately research grants—funds that could then be used to pay for publication charges. Many research-funding agencies—particularly those that invest in health, the environment, and other areas of concern to developing countries—already acknowledge that the dissemination and sharing of information and data are crucial to the advancement of their goals. These agencies can do more to assert that open access publishing is an important mechanism to facilitate this global sharing of knowledge.

Advocates of open-access publishing recognize that not everyone has affordable, reliable, or uninhibited access to the Internet. The digital divide between the developed and developing world is a problem that must be addressed (Quibra and others 2003). But the digital divide should not prevent the international community from finding creative ways to promote access to knowledge. In fact, the existence of open access facilities such as the Public Library of Science should serve as a signal of the urgency of providing the infrastructure needed to link the developing world to the global fund of knowledge.

Open-access publishing is already addressing the knowledge divide, with support from publishers, funders, and other stakeholders. For the full participation of all researchers in the publishing enterprise, the international community can ensure that the divide is replaced by a multidirectional global flow of information and knowledge. The leadership of the United Nations can play a critical role in promoting measures that allow for the full use of facilities like the Pubic Library of Science by developing countries.

The emergence of an open access regime for academic journals raises interesting possibilities for extending the concept to technological fields. Every year thousands of patents expire, bringing into the public domain new knowledge that had been available only upon royalty payment. This knowledge represents an important reservoir of ideas that can be used to meet development needs. Little attention has been paid to this fund of knowledge. Inventors are increasingly interested in making their ideas available free of royalty for use in meeting the needs of poor countries. Only a handful of mechanisms are designed to promote such activities. Extending the open access model to technological information would be a natural extension of current efforts to broaden the space for human creativity.

The Internet has created an infrastructure for disseminating scientific and technological information free of charge. Indeed, many international organizations are distributing their research results over the Internet. The information is not readily accessible, however, so new networks are being created to serve as hubs for accessing information on the latest developments in science and technology of relevance to development. The most comprehensive of these efforts is the Science and Development Network (box 10.4).

Box 10.4

SciDev.Net provides free Web access to science- and technology-related information for developing countries

Source: www.scidev.net.

The aim of the Science and Development Network (SciDev.Net) is to enhance the availability of reliable and authoritative information on science- and technology-related issues that affect the economic and social development of developing countries. It seeks to ensure that people and organizations in developing countries have ready access to information needed for decisionmaking.

SciDev.Net pursues this goals though a free-access Web site. It has created regional networks of individuals and institutions that share the same goals and held capacity-building workshops and other events in developing countries. The Web site provides news, views, and information on science, technology and the developing world. The site provides information on key policy issues, including regional news and perspectives on these issues.

The venture is supported by the scientific journals *Nature* and *Science*, which provide free access to selected articles every week. It is backed by the Third World Academy of Sciences, based in Trieste (Italy), and funded by the U.K. Department for International Development, the Swedish International Development Co-operation Agency, the Canadian International Development Research Centre, and the Rockefeller Foundation.

Launching innovation-focused missions

Applying science, technology, and innovation to development involves operational activities that are implemented at the community, farm, and enterprise level. An approach that focuses on specific local problems could serve as an organizing framework from which to rally specific knowledge and other resources. This approach would not only require the clear identification of the problem to address, it would outline the options available for solving the problem and identify a choice of delivery mechanisms.

Mayors of cities could work with government, academia, industry, and civil society to design missions aimed at improving the lives of slum dwellers. Universities located in such cities could play key roles as loci of expertise, incubators of businesses, and overall sources of operational outreach to support private and public sector activities. Similar missions could be established in the natural resource and water resources fields. The missions would become the organizing framework for fostering institutional interactions.

This approach can help the international community isolate some critical elements that are necessary when dealing with a diverse set of problems such as conservation of forests, provision of clean drinking water, and improvement of the conditions of slum dwellers. In all these cases the first step is the integration of environmental considerations into development activities. This goal, however, is meaningless unless addressed within the framework of an entity that has jurisdiction over the development activities that may have a direct impact of natural resources, safe drinking water, and slum dwellers.

One of the main features of development experiments is the inadequate diffusion of promising innovations. In many cases the problem is lack of funding to scale up pilot projects. Most pilot projects are abandoned after their experimental

An approach that focuses on local problems could serve as an organizing framework from which to rally specific knowledge and other resources

phase ends, and the lessons learned from them are neither applied to subsequent phases nor integrated into policy learning. As a result, a large of part of development assistance efforts is devoted to dead-end projects that add little to learning about development. This challenge is complicated by the rapid rate at which donor agencies and their government partners change their thematic foci.

The lack of financing for technological innovation is a real challenge that confronts developing countries. A large part of the problem is the absence of convincing innovation policies that can be used to leverage donor assistance. But even where such policies exist—faulty though they may be—donors have generally paid little attention to the role of technological innovation in development. Developing countries have had to accept questionable approaches, such as "appropriate technology," that have tended to focus more on the scale of the technology and less on the dynamics of the challenges developing countries face.

The issue of financing technological innovation needs to be addressed at three levels. Developing country governments need to design innovation policies that link technological innovation directly to development challenges. This process would involve the convergence of R&D, education, and business policies, which tend to focus largely on funding for local R&D activities regardless of the impact of the results on the economy, and industrial policy, which emphasizes the building of technological capabilities. Although this approach has long been discredited, it continues to garner support from the scientific community. While scientific inquiry is an important aspect of human endeavor in its own right, it is difficult to justify research in developing countries that is not linked to productive activities. The fact that the Goals are silent on higher education should serve as an important warning for researchers in developing countries to relate their activities to practical realities.

This convergence can best be achieved through a coherent government policy or strategy that focuses on specific science, technology, and innovation missions that can serve as a basis for rallying both local and international resources. For example, East African countries have created the Lake Victoria Basin Commission, which seeks to serve as a coordinating mechanism for the management of the resources of Lake Victoria. Such a commission, if appropriately located in a research institution or university, could serve as an important organ for leveraging domestic and international resources. Similar research missions could include efforts to combat specific infectious diseases through the development of new products. Such an approach would differ from the conventional methods of seeking to allocate a certain proportion of the national budget to R&D without specifying the challenges that such funding must meet.

Most developing countries constitute small knowledge markets that do not offer incentives for the consolidation of domestic resources. Regional integration organizations could create potentially large markets, which could lead to the consolidation of financial resources to scales that could have significant

Finding novel combinations that link higher education to the productive sector is likely to increase the funding available for supporting technological innovation

economic impacts. In some areas of technological endeavor—such as infrastructure and manufacturing—the size of the market is a major investment incentive. Efforts to create regional integration organizations are therefore an important vehicle for generating additional financial resources.

Other forms of policy alignment could play an equally important role in generating funding for technological innovation. Most developing countries have separate ministries for higher education, R&D, economic planning, and industrial development. Finding novel combinations that link higher education to the productive sector through research and innovation is likely to increase the funding available for supporting technological innovation. One way to do so is to formulate a technology-led development strategy and to allocate part of the higher education budget specifically to technology missions and linkages with the private sector. This approach demands considerable political tact, but it could redirect existing government budgets to technological innovation.

Such realignments in government policy will need to be accompanied by corresponding changes in donor partners. Reforms in donor agencies to redirect some of the existing resources to technological innovation would go a long way toward helping developing countries support their own realignment efforts.

Technology-based approaches to development will need to delegate considerable authority to local communities. In many countries this would involve not only legislative reform but also incentives that promote experimentation. These incentives, ranging from tax exceptions to flexibility in the management of national standards, would help leverage local capital needed for technological innovation. A good example of this is the use of local materials in civil engineering projects.

Scaling up particular technological systems or rolling out certain applications involves changes in management systems. Scaling up or rolling out means more than simply providing more funding and manpower. The most critical element may be the design of management models suited to the new operational levels. A large number of technology-based projects fail to graduate from pilot phases to wider application because of management failure.

The issue of scaling up is tied with technological learning, which is in turn linked to intergenerational change in society. The long-term nature of social learning and its inherently experimental nature require innovation in funding strategies. Funding for drug development needs to reflect the timeframes associated with these activities. Ecosystem rehabilitation is usually a long-term process whose outcomes are uncertain. Less funding over a longer period may be more effective than more funding over the short run. Private foundations may be more receptive to such thinking than international organizations; results-oriented governmental agencies may need to adopt it as well.

A longer term perspective also allows for critical path analysis approaches in project planning. Donors have tended to vary in their strategic approaches to project design and implementation. Most have focused on specific outputs,

Scaling up or rolling out means more than simply providing more funding and manpower

ignoring the importance of institutional arrangements and infrastructure requirements. For example, plans to introduce computers in African schools have often been undermined by poor infrastructure, including the lack of electrical supply in most rural areas. A longer term approach would involve upgrading the physical infrastructure and providing initial training. This approach would result in donors undertaking fewer but more effective longer term projects or allowing for more systematic coordination of project activities with the appropriate sequencing.

Managing technological risks

Technological risks are becoming part of the public discourse worldwide, as reflected in regulatory approaches in fields such as agricultural biotechnology (Juma forthcoming). Managing these risks and responding to public perceptions of them are necessary if science and technology are to be effectively deployed to meet the Goals.

Perceptions of risks associated with new technologies

New technologies have been credited with creating new industrial opportunities but also with destroying the status quo. While investors focus on the benefits of new technologies, some people worry about their risks. Concerns range from the perceived risks of new technologies such as transgenic foods and mobile phones on human health to wider fears about the impact of technology on society.

In the past, technological risks were confined to countries in which new technologies emerged or even to the sectors in which they were applied. Concerns two decades ago over the use of microprocessors in industry were restricted to their possible impact on employment displacement in the manufacturing sector. Workers and labor organizations around the world protested the use of this emerging technology. Today echoes of these debates are still heard in discussions of the "deskilling" of the labor force.

Although interest in the impact of microelectronics on employment was expressed in many parts of the world, it did not become a mass movement involving a wide range of social groups, for at least two reasons. First, the possibility of job displacement was weighed against the benefits of raising industrial productivity. Second, the global economy was not as integrated as it is today, and many debates were localized. Globalization gives technological risk a wider meaning and turns local debates over certain products into mass movements. This is itself a source of new risks.

Risk perceptions vary considerably across technologies, and this defines the scale of social mobilization. Attempts in the 1980s to promote the adoption of renewable energy technologies were bedeviled with concerns about risks. Sporadic opposition was recorded in many parts of the world, but it did not translate into mass movements. Risk perceptions of pharmaceutical products

A focus on technological risks can overshadow the possible benefits of an emerging technology, which are often difficult to predict

are not a major challenge to the use of new medicines, partly because of the limited range of options available to consumers in life-threatening situations.

Fear of biotechnology stems from scientific, technical, economic, cultural, and ethical concerns. Opposition is differentiated along product lines (transgenic crops, fish, trees, cattle). Many people oppose biotechnology because of corporate control of the industry, which they perceive as a social risk.

A focus on technological risks can overshadow the possible benefits of an emerging technology, which are often difficult to predict (box 10.5). At the time of their invention, computers were envisioned as able to perform nothing more than rapid calculation in scientific research and data processing. The rise of the Internet as a global phenomenon could not have been predicted based on the early uses of information technology.

Technological risks have to be weighed against the risks of existing technologies as well as the risks of not having access to new technologies. The risks of not having access to the Internet may outweigh the risks of employment displacement that shaped many of the attitudes toward information technology in its earlier years. The concerns over employment displacement were genuine, but the risks were often projected to whole industries or sectors. The debate was then dominated by concerns over job displacement rather than the potential contributions of the new technologies to economic productivity.

There are also numerous cases in which society has underestimated the risks posed by new technologies or adopted them without adequate knowledge about their dangers. A family of chemicals that now fall under the umbrella of "persistent organic pollutants" has been widely used in agriculture and industry.

Managing global technological risks

Managing technological uncertainty will require greater investment in innovative activities at the scientific and institutional levels. At the technical level, technological diversity is essential to ensuring that society is able to respond to

Box 10.5

Even great inventors have failed to grasp the importance of their inventions

Source: Rosenberg 1996.

History is full of examples in which inventors have failed to foresee the impact of the technologies they invented. Mass communication would be inconceivable without the radio. But the inventor of the radio, Guglielmo Marconi, conceived his invention as a medium for private communication, not broadcasting. The radio was seen as a substitute for the telephone (hence the name "wireless"). Even when broadcasting was considered a use for the new technology, the options initially considered were limited to use in church sermons.

Patent lawyers at Bell Labs did not consider the laser worth patenting, because they could not foresee its relevance to the telephone industry. Laser technology has found wide application in communication, medicine, entertainment, printing, and a wide range of other industries.

The transistor is today heralded as one of the most significant inventions of all times. But at the time of its invention, no one thought of uses other than developing better hearing aids.

Trends in industry suggest that a combination of incentives and regulations can shift technological change to meet environmental goals

emerging challenges with the knowledge at its disposal. Technological diversity demands greater investment in scientific enterprises as well as the creation of measures to facilitate access to available technical options.

It also requires flexibility in institutional arrangements, to enable society to respond swiftly to technological failure. Such flexibility can be built into the design of technological systems themselves. Diversification of energy sources, for example, is an institutional response to the risks posed by dependence on centralized fossil fuel power plants. Similar diversification principles apply to information storage, especially as the world community moves into the information age.

Depletion of the ozone layer offers interesting lessons for environmental management. It was possible to ban ozone-depleting substances partly because of the promise of ozone-friendly alternative substances. This subregime was a direct result of public policy interventions that created incentives for developing environmentally sound products. An innovation-based strategy for environmental management would also need to take into account the need for the wider application of new technologies.

Trends in industry suggest that a combination of incentives and regulations can shift technological change to meet environmental goals. Already enterprises are responding to the growing environmental consciousness among consumers and starting to use new environmental standards. This work is being promoted through the International Organization for Standardization (ISO), whose ISO 14000 series is being used to set voluntary environmental standards.

Conclusion

International institutions urgently need to realign their activities to reflect the technological requirements for implementing the Goals. This effort will not only help deploy available financial and other resources to meet the Goals, it will also help identify gaps in available resources. These efforts need to be undertaken in the context of a better understanding of the sources of economic growth. The five-year review of the implementation of the Goals in 2005 offers a unique opportunity to start this reconceptualization process.

Chapter 11

Conclusions and outlook

Meeting the Goals will require a substantial reorientation toward development policies that focus on key sources of economic growth, including those associated with new and established scientific and technological knowledge and related institutional adjustments. To promote the use of science, technology, and innovation for development, countries need to adopt strategies for technological learning at the local, national, regional, and international levels. These strategies will involve continuous interactions between government, industry, academia, and civil society.

The focus on learning has far-reaching implications for international relations and demands the creation of partnerships that foster openness and the exchange of ideas. This new spirit needs to replace the distrust and concomitant use of extensive accountability mechanisms, which hinder the very learning processes that cooperation seeks to foster.

There are three primary sources of technological and scientific innovation. The first is government, which can act as a facilitator and promoter of technological learning. The second is institutions of higher learning, which create indigenous capacity in relevant fields. The third is enterprises, the engines of economic change, where technological capabilities of economic importance accumulate.

Several groups of stakeholders have a role in developing new science and technology—and thus in driving economic growth and human development. National policies, however, must fill an especially important role in facilitating the generation, use, and diffusion of knowledge and, in conjunction with other sectors of society, building up the requisite scientific and technical skills within the population.

Strategic outlook

The task force recommends a strategic approach that starts with improving the policy environment, redesigning infrastructure investment, fostering enterprise

The first step in improving the application of science, technology, and innovation to development is to align governance structures with technological missions or programs

development, reforming higher education, supporting inventive activity, and managing technological innovation. This strategy will allow countries to create the policies and institutions needed to address the longer term challenges associated with infrastructure, business, education, and research.

Improve the policy environment and enhance global technology governance

The first step in improving the application of science, technology, and innovation to development is to align governance structures with technological missions or programs. This cannot be done without articulating development visions and strategies that focus on the role of technological innovation in development. These strategies should seek to facilitate the transition to knowledge-based economies that are guided by sustainability principles.

Governments can improve the policy environment at the national level by promoting institutions such as an Office of Science Advisor to provide science and technology advice to top political leaders. Advice should be delivered through transparent and systematic processes that combine technical knowledge provided by institutions such as scientific and engineering academies with wider consultations based on democratic practices. International organizations, including the Office of the Secretary-General of the United Nations, need to create similar offices. Creating these posts would help international organizations and development agencies develop the science culture they need to effectively execute their mandates.

International organizations such as the United Nations and the international financial institutions should expand the application of science and technology, promote technological innovation in developing countries, and adjust rule-making and standard-setting activities to better meet the interests of developing countries. Poverty Reduction Strategy Papers should be used as vehicle for advancing the role of technological innovation in development. Bilateral programs, such as the United States' Millennium Challenge Account, should focus on science, technology, and innovation as a foundation for development cooperation.

International organizations should also help build and expand the open access regime for scientific publishing and technology development and expand its scope to cover technological innovation. Other critical research data, such as human genome sequences, should be made available free of charge and used as platforms for international research cooperation.

Redefine infrastructure development as a foundation for technological innovation

Governments seldom consider infrastructure projects as part of a technological learning process. But infrastructure development represents an opportunity to start integrating technological considerations into development goals.

Countries should devote resources to helping more young people— especially women— receive higher education

Countries should recognize the dynamic role infrastructure development can play in economic growth. Where feasible, they should acquire some of the technical knowledge available from foreign construction and engineering firms. In addition, governments should focus on developing adequate infrastructure—electric power, transportation networks, and communications infrastructure—without which further applications of technology to development will not be possible.

Build human capabilities, particularly in science, technology, and engineering

Building human capacity, especially in scientific and technical fields, is a long-term process that involves extensive political consideration. The first step in moving in this direction is for countries to review their educational systems and identify opportunities for aligning the mandates of existing institutions with development goals and technology missions.

Countries should devote resources to helping more young people—especially women—receive higher education, paying special attention to the barriers that appear at the level of secondary education. Countries should offer incentives to private enterprises, particularly small and medium-size firms, to hire young university graduates, in order to start a virtuous circle of technological upgrading. Although the education Goal is limited to achieving universal primary education, science education at the primary, secondary, and tertiary levels is also important for creating an innovative society.

Support entrepreneurship by creating and expanding links between technology and enterprise

Creating links between knowledge generation and enterprise development is one of the most important challenges developing countries face. A range of structures can be used to create and sustain enterprises, from taxation regimes and market-based instruments to consumption policies and changes within the national system of innovation.

Manage technological innovation by using existing technologies, investing in global technology generation, and forging international technology alliances

Countries should combine efforts to build manufacturing capabilities with strategies for advancing research and development. To do so, they need to expand access to and use of existing technologies, especially generic technologies that have broad applications or impacts on the economy.

Investments need to be targeted to underfunded research areas of relevance to developing countries, in fields such as agricultural production, environmental management, and public health. Research and development through international technology alliances can help developing countries take advantage of the growing globalization of research.

The World Summit on Sustainable Development provides one of the most elaborate articulations of the role of technological innovation in promoting sustainable development

Create mechanisms to manage the benefits and risks of new and existing technologies

The level of trust in technology and its advocates influences much of the debate over the impact of new technologies and existing technologies as well those who promote them. Efforts should therefore be made to find ways that enhance public trust in new and existing technologies. This can be done through broad consultations, appropriate technology management institutions, and deliberate efforts aimed at ensuring that the benefits of new technologies are shared widely. Technological diversity is key to ensuring that society is able to respond to emerging challenges with the knowledge at its disposal. Such diversity demands greater investment in scientific enterprises as well as the creation of measures to promote access to available technical options.

Looking ahead

The way ahead will be driven largely by the need to make the transition to knowledge-based economies guided by sustainability principles. Policymakers will need to take a critical look at the interactions between knowledge creation (in the form of scientific research and its technological embodiments) and institutional adjustment or innovation. Agenda 21, the comprehensive global plan of action agreed upon in 1992, identified technology as a critical means of implementing sustainable development goals. It also endorsed the use of environmentally sound technologies. The Rio conventions include a wide range of provisions on the role of science, technology, and innovation in meeting sustainable development goals.

The World Summit on Sustainable Development provides one of the most elaborate articulations of the role of technological innovation in promoting sustainable development. It calls for the promotion of "technology development, transfer and diffusion to Africa and further [development] technology and knowledge available in African centres of excellence" and calls for support to "African countries to develop effective science and technology institutions and research activities capable of developing and adapting to world class technologies."

Sustainable development agreements have also paid attention to the role of institutional change. The World Summit on Sustainable Development stressed that an "effective institutional framework for sustainable development at all levels is key to the full implementation of Agenda 21, the follow-up to the outcomes of the [World Summit on Sustainable Development] and meeting emerging sustainable development challenges." That summit outlined the measures needed at the international level and proposed institutional strategies that can be adopted at the national level. It also called upon countries "to make progress in the formulation and elaboration of national strategies for sustainable development and begin their implementation by 2005."

The five-year review of the implementation of the Millennium Declaration provides the international community with a unique opportunity to apply technological innovation to meet development needs in a sustainable way. This review should become a critical turning point in our understanding and application of science, technology, and innovation to human welfare.

Notes

Chapter 1

1. *Science, technology, and innovation* include all forms of useful knowledge (codified and tacit) derived from diverse branches of learning and practice, ranging from basic scientific research to engineering to traditional knowledge. It also includes the policies used to promote scientific advance, technology development, and the commercialization of products, as well as the associated institutional innovations. This report focuses on how a diversity of sources can be brought together—especially through institutional organizations—to solve practical problems associated with the Goals. *Science* refers to both basic and applied sciences. *Technology* refers to the application of science, engineering, and other fields, such as medicine. Innovation includes all of the processes, including business activities, that bring a technology to market. This report thus deals with the generation, use, and diffusion of all forms of useful scientific and technological knowledge as well as the evolution of associated institutional arrangements (Nelson 1994). The term *knowledge* encompasses codified, craft, and tacit knowledge. The main concern is "useful knowledge," as defined by Mokyr (2002).

2. For such capabilities to generate the necessary economic dynamism, certain complementary inputs are needed. These inputs include organizational flexibility, finance, human resources, support services, information management, and coordination competence.

Chapter 2

1. The rapid economic transformation of China offers some of the most contemporary lessons that show the close interactions between education, technological innovation, and business (Chen and Feng 2000; Wang and Yao 2003).

2. The role of science and technology in environmental management is being increasingly recognized as outlined in *Environment and Human Well-Being: A Practical Strategy* (UN Millennium Project 2005b) and *A Home in the City* (UN Millennium Project 2005c).

3. Strategies for promoting primary education and institutional innovations needed to empower women are outlined in *Toward Universal Primary Education: Investments, Incentives, and Institutions* (UN Millennium Project 2005d) and *Taking Action: Achieving Gender Equality and Empowering Women* (UN Millennium Project 2005e).

4. For strategic approaches to solve some of these challenges, see *Halving Hunger: It Can Be Done* (UN Millennium Project 2005f).

5. More an elaboration of strategies to address these health-related issues, please see: *Who's Got the Power? Transforming Health Systems for Women and Children* (UN Millennium Project 2005g), *Combating AIDS in the Developing World* (UN Millennium Project 2005h), *Coming to Grips with Malaria in the New Millennium* (UN Millennium Project 2005i), *Investing in Strategies to Reverse the Global Incidence of TB* (UN Millennium Project 2005j), and *Prescription for Healthy Development: Increase Access to Medicines* (UN Millennium Project 2005k).

6. Detailed approaches to addressing these challenges are outlined in *Health, Dignity and Development: What Will It Take?* (UN Millennium Project 2005l).

7. These innovations can also threaten global security. But improvements in social monitoring and dialogue have reduced the chances that science and technology will be used for nefarious purposes. Well-organized dialogue at senior levels and informed public opinion can help foster positive outcomes from the spread of science and technology.

8. For a detailed account of the role of international trade in development, see *Trade for Development* (UN Millennium Project 2005m).

9. In December 2004, Egypt, Israel and the United States signed a trade protocol that could change the economic and political map of the Middle East. The protocol creates Qualified Industrial Zones in parts of Cairo, Alexandria and Port Said. Goods from these zones will enjoy duty free access to U.S. markets, provided that 35 percent of their input is derived from Israeli-Egyptian cooperation. Some 11.7 percent of the input must come from Israel. The deal could create 250,000 jobs in Egypt in 2005, mostly in the clothing and textile industry, which is the country's main export field. The protocol will raise the annual trade volume between the two countries from $44 million to $70 million. Similar arrangements could be used to promote peace and prosperity in Sub-Saharan Africa, which is currently bedeviled with armed conflicts. Most conflicts in Africa arise from disputes over land, commodities, and natural resources. Conflict diamonds have fueled conflict in Angola and Sierra Leone while oil has been at the center of violence in Sudan and Chad. The scramble for columbite-tantalite (coltran) has helped to fuel the war in the Democratic Republic of the Congo. Promoting peace and prosperity in this region will require increased integration into the global economy through technology-based trade agreements.

Chapter 3

1. In vast regions of the developing world, however, particularly Latin America, universities are responsible for more than 75 percent of all R&D activities (Arocena and Sutz 2001).

2. A classic example is the competition between Betamax and VHS. Although Betamax may have had superior technological advantages, VHS eventually won. In the developing world, more serious implications arise when the technologies and their applications affect food, health, or education. The inability of science, technology, and innovation policy to promote wider diffusion of oral rehydration therapy or the Internet in the developing world is cause for concern. Commercialization and distribution of these technologies may require country-by-country analysis and policy support.

3. Biotechnology is the other major new technological area, but it is not prone to production fragmentation and has very stringent technological needs.

Chapter 4

1. Much of the debate over biotechnology focuses largely on genetically modified crops and ignores other fields that involve industrial and environmental applications. A review of these applications shows that biotechnology could be used to design more environmentally-sound industrial processes as well as use microbes to clean up the environment through phytoremediation techniques (Juma 2001). In addition, advances in genomics are also poised to revolutionize the energy sector by making biomass energy extraction economically competitive with fossil fuels. These developments should receive the support of those interested in environmental management.

2. These 10 biotechnologies were identified in a technology foresight study conducted by the University of Toronto in partnership with scientists with expertise in health and biotechnology and in-depth knowledge about public health problems of developing countries.

3. A PCR test for three complexes of New World Leishmania (*Leishmania braziliensis, L. mexicana,* and *L. donovani*), which cause a spectrum of diseases, was developed in Nicaragua. It uses a technique known as multiplexing to test for more than one disease at a time, saving both time and resources (Harris and others 1998).

4. The Population Council's Carraguard™ is a gel derived from seaweed that blocks attachment of pathogens to target cells. It is effective against HIV, HSV-2, and gonorrhea. Another gel, PRO-2000, developed by Interneuron Pharmaceutical, is a naphthalene sulfonate polymer that blocks attachment of HIV-1 and HSV-2 to target cells.

5. The AmA1 gene was obtained from the amaranth plant, which grows in South America.

6. One nanometer equals 1×10^{-9} of a meter. Nanotechnology deals with particles that measure 1–100 nanometers.

Chapter 5

1. The term *infrastructure* is defined here as the facilities, structures, and associated equipment and services that facilitate the flows of goods and services between individuals, firms, and governments. It includes public utilities (electric power, telecommunications, water supply, sanitation and sewerage, and waste disposal); public works (irrigation systems, schools, housing, and hospitals); transport services (roads, railways, ports, waterways, and airports); and R&D facilities.

2. Investment banks can play an important role in using performance criteria to incorporate technological dynamism into infrastructure projects. Multilateral institutions such as the European Investment Bank (EIB) could play a leading role in this respect in African countries where it provided loans and risk capital amounting to €2.4 billion over the last five years. The EIB, an arm of the European Union, has recently opened a branch in Nairobi in addition to its presence in Dakar and Pretoria. In recent years the bank has been focusing on support for the private sector and the improvement of infrastructure services such as energy, water, and communications. EIB leadership could also influence EU aid, but it could also promote similar approaches in other financial institutions such as the African Development Bank.

3. Programs designed to promote the spread of infrastructure in rural areas, for example, may have far-reaching implications for human welfare. Since 1998, for example, China has been promoting the "village to village initiative" to ensure access to eletricity, telephone, and television. Of the villages earmarked in the program, nearly 98 percent now have access to electricity and television, and over 90 percent to telephone service (Lu, Chinese Academy of Sciences, personal communication, 2004).

Chapter 6

1. Taiwan (China) invites expatriate scientists and engineers home to participate in key R&D projects for national development.

2. An example of a university deeply involved with commercial business is the Massachusetts Institute of Technology (MIT), which has been conceptualized as an "entrepreneurial" university (Etzkowitz 2003).

3. This interdependence was first observed in Latin America, during the 1970s.

Chapter 7

1. The distinction between technology and business incubators may be misleading, because many business incubators use new technologies, and technology incubators use the same instruments applied to promote business development.

2. Angel investors provide a large portion of funding for new technology ventures in industrial countries. Their contributions, however, remain poorly documented, mainly because private equity securities are not subject to strict disclosure requirements. In addition, no institutional mechanism supports this market, which is fragmented and highly localized.

3. On technology support in Sub-Saharan Africa, see Lall and Pietrobelli (2002).

4. The Berne Convention for the Protection of Literary and Artistic Works was substantially revised in 1971 to include an annex on "Special Provisions Regarding Developing Countries." The annex allows a country to "grant nonexclusive, nontransferable licenses to its nationals for the reproduction or translation of foreign-owned copyright work for educational or research purposes." These revisions were partly justified on the basis of national public interest. Similar revisions were attempted in other intellectual property regimes but were stalled by the Uruguay Round of negotiations. There have been no major efforts by developing countries to invoke the special provisions of the Berne Convention to grant copyright works to their citizens, mainly because of the difficulties associated with the use of compulsory licensing as a development policy instrument. Another source of justification for the revision was to allow copyright owners to more readily grant translation licenses. While compulsory licenses may be a problematic development tool, they can be an extremely useful tool for securing technology that developed countries would not otherwise provide. Simplified procedures may be needed for securing compulsory licenses or creating model compulsory licensing documents so that developing countries can more adequately use this potential innovation tool (Long 2004).

5. Inventions are protected under TRIPS only if they have been registered in the domestic patent office of the country in question.

6. A mutual recognition agreement is a document signed by national governments acknowledging that certificates issued by the certification bodies of one country are valid in the other signatory countries. The number of mutual recognition agreements is growing, but most of them have been signed by developed countries.

7. Given that the relative value attached by consumers to quality and health standards and technical regulations is a function of income levels, developing countries' optimal levels of investment in standards and technical regulations may be lower than those of richer countries. Governments in many industrial countries, including Australia, Canada, the United Kingdom, and the United States, make decisions on investments in hazard analysis and critical control points to mitigate health risks associated with contaminated foods based on cost of illness estimates. Because of income differentials, these costs are higher in industrial countries, which justifies a higher level of investment in hazard analysis and critical control points (Unnevehr and Hirschhorn 2000). Given the rapidly narrowing scope for quality differentiation between products aimed at export markets and those

aimed at domestic markets in developing countries, there is increasing pressure to increase in investment in skills and technological upgrading.

8. An illustrative example is the standard for toxic contaminants, such as aflatoxins or pesticide residues, applied by the European Union on imported foodstuffs. Imposition of the standard on aflatoxin reduced African exports of nuts, cereals, and dried fruits to the European Union by an estimated 64 percent, or $670 million (Otsuki, Wilson, and Sewadehc 2000). The standard is estimated to reduce the number of deaths in the European Union by about 1.4 per billion per year. To help developing countries comply with the food health and safety standards, the European Union has provided training for exporters and technicians. But this initiative is funded with just €30 million, spread across 77 African, Caribbean, and Pacific countries. Furthermore, it provides no support to meet the infrastructure costs of compliance. Being able to access EU supermarkets might add as much as 60 percent to fruit producers' overheads in countries such as Kenya.

Chapter 8

1. www.fundacionchile.cl/inicio_i/index_i.cfm.

2. Some of this is already being done by the CGIAR and its partners through an adjunct challenge program covering biofortification, genomics, and water.

3. The concept of charitable trusts can be traced to the 1601 Statute of Charitable Uses in England (popularly known as the "Statute of Elizabeth"). The preamble to the law laid out a guide to the kinds of activities that could be eligible for charitable contributions. In *Commissioners for Special Purposes of the Income Tax v. Pemsel* (1891) AC 531, the British judge noted, "Charity in its legal sense comprises four principal divisions: trusts for the relief of poverty, trust for the advancement of education, trusts for the advancement of religion, and trusts for other purposes beneficial to the community, not falling under any of the preceding heads." Developing countries have created space for the emergence of charities in these and other fields of social welfare. They have done less to create incentives that allow charitable trusts devoted to science, technology, and innovation to flourish.

Chapter 9

1. Science advisors in developing countries believe that disinterestedness and independence from government are feasible only in developed countries. They believe that engagement should be the ideal to which academies in developing countries strive. They believe that an academy in a developing country cannot afford to be financially disengaged from government.

2. One example of this phenomenon is the recent debate about whether scientific journals should withhold publication of articles that editors judge to have national security implications.

References

Acharya, T., A.S. Daar, and P. Singer. 2003. "Biotechnology and the U.N. Millennium Development Goals." *Nature Biotechnology* 21(12):1434–36.

Aghion, P., and P. Howitt. 1992. "A Model of Growth through Creative Destruction." *Econometrica* 60(2):323–51.

Amsden, A. 2001. *The Rise of 'the Rest': Challenges to the West from Late-Industrializing Economies.* New York: Oxford University Press.

Amsden, A., and W. Chu. 2003. *Beyond Late Development: Taiwan's Upgrading Policy.* Cambridge, Mass.: MIT Press.

Andreassi, T. 2003. "Innovation in Small and Medium Sized Enterprises." *International Journal of Entrepreneurship and Innovation Management* 3(1/2):99–106.

Archibugi, D., and C. Pietrobelli. 2003. "The Globalisation of Technology and Its Implications for Developing Countries—Windows of Opportunities or Further Burden?" *Technological Forecasting and Social Change* 70(9):861–83.

Arocena, R. 1997. *Qué piensa la gente de la innovación, la competitividad, la ciencia y el futuro.* Montevideo: Trilce.

Arocena, R., and J. Sutz. 2001. "Changing Knowledge Production and Latin American Universities." *Research Policy* 30(8):1221–34.

———. 2003. "Inequality as Seen from the South." *Technology in Society* 25(2):171–82.

Avalos, I. and Rengifo, R. 2003. "From Sector to Networks: The Venezuelan CONICIT Research Agendas." *Technology in Society* 25(2):183–92.

Branscomb, L., and P. Auerswald. 2001. *Taking Technical Risks: How Innovators, Executives, and Investors Manage High-Tech Risks.* Cambridge, Mass.: MIT Press.

Bruton, G., D. Ahlstrom, and K. Yeh. 2004. "Understanding Venture Capital in East Asia: The Impact of Institutions on the Industry Today and Tomorrow." *Journal of World Business* 39(1):72–88.

Cantner, U., and A. Pyka. 2001. "Classifying Technology Policy from an Evolutionary Perspective." *Research Policy* 30(5):759–74.

Carayannis, E.G., J. Alexander, and A. Ioannidis. 2000. "Leveraging Knowledge, Learning, and Innovation in Forming Strategic Government-University-Industry (GUI) Partnerships in the US, Germany, and France." *Technovation* 20(9):477–88.

Cassiolato, J.E., M.H.S. Szapiro, and H.M.M. Lastres. 2002. "Local System of Innovation under Strain: The Impacts of Structural Change in the Telecommunications Cluster of Campinas, Brazil." *International Journal of Technology Management* 24(7/8):680–704.

Chakraborty S, N. Chakraborty, and A. Datta. 2000. "Increased Nutritive Value of Transgenic Potato by Expressing a Nonallergenic Seed of Albumin Gene from *Amaranthus Hypochodriaccus*." *Proceedings of the National Academy of Sciences of the United States of America* 97(7):3724–29.

Chen, B., and Y. Feng. 2000. "Determinants of Economic Growth in China: Private Enterprise, Education, and Openness." *China Economic Review* 11(1):1–15.

Chen, S.H., M.C. Liu, and H.T. Shih. 2003. "R&D Services and Global Production Networks: A Taiwanese Perspective." East-West Center Working Papers, Economics Series 52. Honolulu, Hawaii.

Chocce, G.R. 2003. "Necessary Conditions for Venture Capital Development in Latin America: The Chilean Case." *International Journal of Entrepreneurship and Innovation Management* 3(1/2):139–50.

Clark, N., and C. Juma. 1992. *Long-Run Economic Growth: An Evolutionary Approach to Economic Growth*. London: Pinter Publishers.

Commission on Human Security. 2003. *Human Security Now*. New York.

Committee on the Geographic Foundation for Agenda 21. 2002. *Down to Earth: Geographic Information for Sustainable Development in Africa*. Washington, D.C.: National Academies Press.

Conceição, P., M.V. Heitor, and F. Veloso. 2003. "Infrastructures, Incentives, and Institutions: Fostering Distributed Knowledge Bases for the Learning Society." *Technological Forecasting and Social Change* 70(7):583–617.

Daar, A.S., H. Thorsteinsdóttir, D.K. Martin, A.C. Smith, S. Nast, and P.A. Singer. 2002. "Top 10 Biotechnologies for Improving Health in Developing Countries." Joint Centre for Bioethics, University of Toronto, Canada.

Dalrymple, D.G. 2004. "International Agricultural Research as a Global Public Good: A Review of Concepts, Experience, and Policy Issues." U.S. Agency for International Development,, Bureau for Economic Growth, Agricultural Development and Trade, Office of Environment and Science Policy, Washington, D.C.

David, P. 2004. "Understanding the Emergence of 'Open Science' Institutions: Functionalist Economics in Historical Context." *Industrial and Corporate Change* 13(4):571–89.

de Ferranti, D., G.E. Perry, I. Gill, J.L. Guasch, W.F. Maloney, C. Sanchez-Paramo, and N. Schady. 2003. *Closing the Gap in Education and Technology*. Washington, D.C.: World Bank.

DFID (U.K. Department for International Development). 2002. *Making Connections: Infrastructure for Poverty Reduction*. London.

Dolan, C., and K. Sorby. 2003. "Gender and Employment in High Value Agriculture Industries." Agriculture and Rural Development Working Paper 7. World Bank, Washington, D.C.

Dollar, D., and P. Collier. 2001. *Globalization, Growth, and Poverty: Building an Inclusive World Economy*. New York: Oxford University Press.

Dossani, R. 2003. "Reforming Venture Capital in India: Creating the Enabling Environment for Information Technology." *International Journal of Technology Management* 25(1/2):151–64.

Dutfield, G. 2004. *Intellectual Property, Biogenetic Resources and Traditional Knowledge*. London: Earthscan.

Edquist, C. 1997. "Systems of Innovation Approaches—Their Emergence and Characteristics." In *Systems of Innovation: Technologies, Institutions, and Organizations*. London: Pinter Publishers.

Ernst, D. 2003. "Pathways to Innovation in Asia's Leading Electronics Exporting Countries: Drivers and Policy Implications." East-West Center Working Papers, Economics Series 62. Honolulu, Hawaii.

Etzkowitz, H. 2003. "Research Groups as 'Quasi-Firms': The Invention of the Entrepreneurial University." *Research Policy* 32(1):109–21.

Everts, S. 1998. *Gender and Technology: Empowering Women, Engendering Development*. London: Zed Books.

Fan, S., and X. Zhang. 2004. "Infrastructure and Regional Economic Development in Rural China." *China Economic Review* 15(2):203–14.

FAO (Food and Agriculture Organization). 2004. *The State of Food and Agriculture 2003–2004*. Rome.

Finger, J.M., and P. Schuler. 2000. "Implementation of Uruguay Round Commitments: The Development Challenge." *World Economy* 23(4):511–25.

Freeman, C. 2002. "Continental, National and Sub-National Innovation Systems—Complementarity and Economic Growth." *Research Policy* 31(2):191–211.

Gallagher, K.S. Forthcoming. "Limits to Leapfrogging in Energy Technologies? Evidence from the Chinese Automobile Industry." *Energy Policy*.

Gibb, A., and J. Li. 2003. "Organizing for Enterprise in China: What Can We Learn from the Chinese Micro, Small, and Medium Enterprise Development Experience." *Futures* 35(4):403–21.

Grandi, G. 2001. "Antibacterial Vaccine Design Using Genomics and Proteomics." *Trends Biotech* 19(5):181–88.

Grimaldi, R., and A. Grandi. Forthcoming. "Business Incubators and New Venture Creation: An Assessment of Incubation Models." *Technovation*.

Harris, E, G. Kropp, A. Belli, B. Rodriguez, and N. Agabian. 1998. "Single-Step Multiplex PCR Assay for Characterization of New World *Leishmania* Complexes." *Journal of Clinical Microbiology* 36(7):1989–95.

Hobday, M. 1995. *Innovation in East Asia: The Challenge to Japan*. Brookfield, Vt.: Edward Elgar Publishing Limited.

Hsu, P.O., J.Z. Shyu, H.C. Yu, C.C. You, and T.C. Lo. 2003. "Exploring the Interactions between Incubators and Industrial Clusters: The Case of ITRI Incubator in Taiwan." *R&D Management* 33(1):79–90.

Hu W., Q. Yan, D.K. Shen, F. Liu, Z.D. Zhu, H.D. Song, X.R. Xu, Z.J. Wang, Y.P. Rong, L.C. Zeng, J. Wu, X. Zhang, J.J. Wang, X.N. Xu, S.Y. Wang, G. Fu, X.L. Zhang, Z.Q. Wang, P.J. Brindley, D.P. McManus, C.L. Xue, Z. Feng, Z. Chen, and Z.G. Han. 2003. "Evolutionary and Biomedical Implications of a Schistosoma Japonicum Complementary DNA Resource." *Nature Genetics* 35(2):139–47.

IADB (Inter-American Development Bank). 2001. *IPES 2001: Competitiveness: The Business of Growth*. Washington, D.C.

InterAcademy Council. 2003. *Inventing a Better Future: A Strategy for Building Worldwide Capacities in Science and Technology*. Executive Summary. Amsterdam.

ITU (International Telecommunication Union). 2003. *World Telecommunication Development Report 2003: Access Indicators for the Information Society*. Geneva.

Jomaa H, J. Wiesner, S. Sanderbrand, B. Altincicek, C. Weidemeyer, M. Hintz, I. Turbachova, M. Eberl, J. Zeidler, H.K. Lichtenthaler, D. Soldati, and E. Beck. 1999. "Inhibitors of the Nonmavalonate Pathway of Isoprenoid Biosynthesis as Antimalarial Drugs." *Science* 285(5433):1573–76.

Juma, C. 2001. *The New Bioeconomy: Industrial and Environmental Biotechnology in Developing Countries*. Geneva: United Nations Conference on Trade and Development.

———. Forthcoming. "The New Age of Biodiplomacy." *Georgetown Journal of International Affairs*.

Juma, C., K. Fang, D. Honca, J. Huete-Perez, V. Konde, S.H. Lee, J. Arenas, A. Ivinson, H. Robinson, and S. Singh. 2001. "Global Governance of Technology: Meeting the Needs of Developing Countries." *International Journal of Technology Management* 22(7/8):629–55.

Jun, Z. 2003. "Investment, Investment Efficiency, and Economic Growth in China." *Journal of Asian Economics* 14(5):713–34.

Kane A, J. Lloyd, M. Zaffran, L. Simonsen, M. Kane. 1999. "Transmission of Hepatitis B, Hepatitis C and Human Immunodeficiency Viruses through Unsafe Injections in the Developing World: Model-Based Regional Estimates." *Bulletin of the World Health Organization* 77(10):801–07.

Kim, L. 1995. "Absorptive Capacity and Industrial Growth: A Conceptual Framework and Korea's Experience." In B.H. Koo and D. Perkins, eds., *Social Capability and Long-Term Economic Growth*. New York: St. Martins.

———. 1997. *Imitation to Innovation: The Dynamics of Korea's Technological Learning*. Boston, Mass.: Harvard Business School Press.

Kim, L., and R.R. Nelson., eds. 2000. *Technology, Learning, and Innovation, Experiences of Newly Industrializing Economies*. New York: Cambridge University Press.

KRI International Corporation. 2004. "The Study on Strengthening Capacity of SME Clusters in Indonesia." Final report. Japan International Cooperation Agency, Tokyo.

Lalkaka, R. 2003. "Business Incubators in Developing Countries: Characteristics and Performance." *International Journal of Entrepreneurship and Innovation Management* 3(1/2):31–55.

Lall, S. 2000. "Technological Change and Industrialization in the Asian Newly Industrializing Economies: Achievements and Challenges." In L. Kim and R. Nelson, eds., *Technology, Learning, and Innovation, Experiences of Newly Industrializing Economies*. New York: Cambridge University Press.

Lall, S., and C. Pietrobelli. 2002. *Failing to Compete: Technology Systems and Technology Development in Africa*. Brookfield, Vt.: Edward Elgar Publishing Limited.

Lee, Y.C. 2002. "The Academy of Sciences Malaysia as a Role Model for Academies in Developing Countries." InterAcademy Panel Symposium, World Summit on Sustainable Development, August 26–September 4, Johannesburg.

Lin, O.C.C. 1998. "Science and Technology Policy and its Influence on Economic Development in Taiwan." In H.S. Rowen, ed., *Behind East Asian Growth: The Political and Social Foundations of Prosperity*. New York: Routledge.

Link, A.N., and J.T. Scott. 2003. "US Science Parks: The Diffusion of an Innovation and its Effects on the Academic Missions of Universities." *International Journal of Industrial Organization* 21(9):1323–56.

Liu, X., and C. Wang. 2003. "Does Foreign Direct Investment Facilitate Technological Progress? Evidence from Chinese Industries." *Research Policy* 32(6):945–53.

Looy, B.V., K. Debackere, and P. Andries. 2003. "Policies to Stimulate Regional Innovation Capabilities via University-Industry Collaboration." *R&D Management* 33(2):209–29.

Lowe, R.K. 2003. "Animation and Learning: Selective Processing of Information in Dynamic Graphics." *Learning and Instruction* 13(2):157–76.

Lucas, Robert E., Jr. 1988. "On the Mechanics of Economic Development." *Journal of Monetary Economics* 22(1):3–42.

Lundvall, B.Å. 1999. "Technology Policy in the Learning Economy." In D. Archibugi, J. Howells, and J. Michie, eds., *Innovation Policy in a Global Economy*. Cambridge, U.K.: Cambridge University Press.

Mokyr, J. 2002. *Gifts of Athena: Historical Origins of the Knowledge Economy*. Princeton, N.J.: Princeton University Press.

Mrazek, M.F., and E. Mossialos. 2003. "Stimulating Pharmaceutical Research and Development for Neglected Diseases." *Health Policy* 64(1):75–88.

Muchie, M., P. Gammeltoft, and B.A. Lundvåll, eds. 2003. *Putting Africa First: The Making of African Innovation Systems*. Aalborg, Denmark: Aalborg University Press.

National Research Council. 2002. *Knowledge and Diplomacy: Science Advice in the United Nations System*. Washington, D.C.: National Academies Press.

Nelson, R. 1994. "Economic Growth via the Coevolution of Technology and Institutions." In L. Leydesdorff and P. van den Besselaar, eds., *Evolutionary Economics and the Chaos Theory: New Directions in Technology Studies*. London: Pinter Publishers.

Nelson, R., A. Peterhansl, and B. Sampat. 2004. "Why and How Innovations Get Adopted: A Tale of Four Models." *Industrial and Corporate Change* 13(5):679–99.

Neto, I., M. Best, and S. Gillett. 2004. *License-Exempt Wireless Policy: Results of an African Survey, MIT Communications Futures Program*. Cambridge, Mass.: Massachusetts Institute of Technology.

Nightingale, P. 2004. "Technological Capabilities, Invisible Infrastructure and the Un-social Construction of Predictability: The Overlooked Fixed Costs of Useful Research." *Research Policy* 33(9):1259–84.

Nolan, A. 2003. *Entrepreneurship and Local Economic Development: Policy Innovations in Industrialized Countries*. Paris: Organisation for Economic Co-operation and Development.

OECD (Organisation for Economic Co-operation and Development). 1997. *Technology Incubator: Nurturing Small Firms*. Paris.

———. 2003. "Integrating Information and Communication Technologies in Development Programmes." Policy Brief. Paris.

———. 2004. *GrameenPhone Revisited: Investors Reaching Out to the Poor*. Paris: Organisation for Economic Co-operation and Development.

Okejiri, E. 2000. "Foreign Technology and Development of Indigenous Technological Capabilities in the Nigerian Manufacturing Industry." *Technology in Society* 22(2):189–99.

Otsuki, T., J. Wilson, and M. Sewadehc. 2000. "A Race to the Top? A Case Study of Food Safety Standards and African Exports." World Bank, Washington, D.C.

Peilei, E. Forthcoming. "Catching Up Through Developing Innovation Capability: Evidence from China's Telecom-equipment Industry." *Technovation*.

PLoS (Public Library of Science). 2003. *Open-Access Public of Medical and Scientific Research*. San Francisco, Calif.

Poon, T.S.C. 2002. *Competition and Cooperation in Taiwan's Information Technology Industry: Inter-Firm Networks and Industrial Upgrading*. Westport, Conn.: Quorum Books.

Putranto, K., D. Stewart, and G. Moore. 2003. "International Technology Transfer and Distribution of Technology Capabilities: The Case of Railway Development in Indonesia." *Technology in Society* 25(1):43–53.

Quibra, M.G., S.N. Ahmed, T. Tschang, and M.L. Reyes-Macasaquit. 2003. "Digital Divide: Determinants and Policies with Special Reference to Asia." *Journal of Asian Economics* 13(6):811–25.

Ramasamy, B., A. Chakrabarty, and M. Cheah. 2004. "Malaysia's Leap into the Future: An Evaluation of the Multimedia Super Corridor." *Technovation* 24: 871–83.

Romer, P.M. 1990. "Endogenous Technological Change." *Journal of Political Economy* 98(5):S71–S102.

Rosenberg, N. 1996. "Uncertainty and Technological Change." In T. Ralph Landau, and Gavin Wright, eds., *The Mosaic of Economic Growth*. Stanford: Stanford University Press.

Rosenberg, N., and L.E. Birdzell. 1986. *How the West Grew Rich: The Economic Transformation of the Western World*. New York: Basic Books.

Rothschild, L., and A. Darr. Forthcoming. "Technological Incubators and the Social Construction of Innovation Networks: An Israeli Case Study." *Technovation*.

Rouach, D., and D. Saperstein. 2004. "Alstom Technology Transfer Experience: The Case of the Korean Train Express (KTX)." *International Journal of Technology Transfer and Commercialisation* 3(3): 308–23.

Royal Society. 2004. "Royal Society Response to the House of Commons Science and Technology Committee Inquiry into the Use of Science in UK International Development Policy." Policy Document 02/04. London.

Sagasti, F. 2004. *Knowledge and Innovation for Development: The Sisyphus Challenge of the 21st Century*. Chiltenham, U.K.: Edward Elgar Publishers.

Santini, J.M., L.I. Sly, R.D. Schnagl, and J.M. Macy. 2000. "A New Chemolithoautotrophic Arsenite-Oxidizing Bacterium Isolated from a Gold Mine: Phylogenetic, Physiological and Preliminary Biochemical Studies." *Applied Environmental Microbiology* 66(1):92–97.

Saxenian, A. 2001. "The Silicon Valley-Hsinchu Connection: Technical Communities and Industrial Upgrading." *Industrial and Corporate Change* 10(4):893–920.

Scaramuzzi, E. 2002. "Incubators in Developing Countries: Status and Development Perspectives." World Bank, InfoDev Program, Washington, D.C.

Solow, R. 1956. "A Contribution to the Theory of Economic Growth." *Quarterly Journal of Economics* 70(1):65–94.

———. 1957. "Technical Change and the Aggregate Production Function." *Review of Economics and Statistics* 39(3):312–20.

Thirtle, C., L. Lin, and J. Piesse, 2003. "The Impact of Research-Led Agricultural Productivity Growth on Poverty Reduction in Africa, Asia, and Latin America." *World Development* 32(12):1959–75.

UN (United Nations). 2000. *We the Peoples: The Role of the United Nations in the 21st Century*. New York.

———. 2004. *A More Secure World: Our Shared Responsibility*. Report of the High-Level Panel on Threats, Challenges and Chance. New York.

UNCTAD (United Nations Conference on Trade and Development). 2004. "Investment Policy Review for Brazil." Geneva.

UNDP (United Nations Development Programme). 2001. *Human Development Report 2001: Making Technologies Work for Human Development*. New York: Oxford University Press.

———. 2004. "Unleashing Entrepreneurship: Making Business Work for the Poor." Report to the United Nations Secretary-General. New York.

UNIDO (United Nations Industrial Development Organization). 2003. "Trade Capacity Building: The Role of UNIDO and the Multilateral System." Background paper prepared for the Informal Consultative Group on Trade Capacity Building. Vienna.

———. 2004. *Industrial Development Report 2004: Industrialization, Environment and the Millennium Development Goals in Sub-Saharan Africa*. Vienna.

United Kingdom, House of Commons, Science and Technology Committee. 2004. *The Use of Science in UK International Development Policy*. Vol. I. London: The Stationery Office.

UN Millennium Project. 2005a. *Investing in Development: A Practical Plan to Achieve the Millennium Development Goals*. New York.

————. 2005b. *Environment and Human Well-Being: A Practical Strategy.* Report of the Task Force on Environmental Sustainability. New York.

————. 2005c. *A Home in the City.* Report of the Task Force on Improving the Lives of Slum Dwellers. New York.

————. 2005d. *Toward Universal Primary Education: Investments, Incentives, and Institutions.* Report on the Task Force on Education and Gender Equality. New York.

————. 2005e. *Taking Action: Achieving Gender Equality and Empowering Women.* Report of the Task Force on Education and Gender Equality. New York.

————. 2005f. *Halving Hunger: It Can Be Done.* Report of the Task Force on Hunger. New York.

————. 2005g. *Who's Got the Power? Transforming Health Systems for Women and Children.* Report of the Task Force on Child and Maternal Health. New York.

————. 2005h. *Combating AIDS in the Developing World.* Report of the Task Force on HIV/AIDS, Malaria, TB, and Access to Essential Medicines, Working Group on AIDS. New York.

————. 2005i. *Coming to Grips with Malaria in the New Millennium.* Report of the Task Force on HIV/AIDS, Malaria, TB, and Access to Essential Medicines, Working Group on Malaria. New York.

————. 2005j. *Investing in Strategies to Reverse the Global Incidence of TB.* Report of the Task Force on HIV/AIDS, Malaria, TB, and Access to Essential Medicines, Working Group on TB. New York.

————. 2005k. *Prescription for Healthy Development: Increase Access to Medicines.* Report of the Task Force on HIV/AIDS, Malaria, TB, and Access to Essential Medicines, Working Group on Access to Essential Medicines. New York.

————. 2005l. *Health, Dignity and Development: What Will It Take?* Report of the Task Force on Water and Sanitation. New York.

————. 2005m. *Trade for Development.* Report of the Task Force on Trade. New York.

Unnevehr, L., and N. Hirschhorn. 2000. "Food Safety Issues in the Developing World." Technical Paper 469. World Bank, Washington, D.C.

Varmus, H., R. Klausner, E. Zerhouni, T. Acharya, A.S. Daar, and P.A. Singer. 2003. "Grand Challenges in Global Health." *Science* 302(5644):398–99.

Vedovello, C., and M. Godinho. 2003. "Business Incubators as a Technological Infrastructure for Supporting Small Innovative Firms' Activities." *International Journal of Entrepreneurship and Innovation Management* 3(1/2):4–21.

Verez-Bencomo, V., V. Fernández-Santana, Eugenio Hardy, Maria E. Toledo, Maria C. Rodríguez, Lazaro Heynngnezz, Arlene Rodriguez, Alberto Baly, Luis Herrera, Mabel Izquierdo, Annette Villar, Yury Valdés, Karelia Cosme, Mercedes L. Deler, Manuel Montane, Ernesto Garcia, Alexis Ramos, Aristides Aguilar, Ernesto Medina, Gilda Toraño, Iván Sosa, Ibis Hernandez, Raydel Martínez, Alexis Muzachio, Ania Carmenates, Lourdes Costa, Félix Cardoso, Concepción Campa, Manuel Diaz, and René Roy. 2004. "A Synthetic Conjugate Polysaccharide Vaccine against *Haemophilus influenzae* Type B." *Science* 305(3683):522–25.

Verjovski-Almeida, S., R. DeMarco, E.A. Martins, P.E. Guimaraes, E.P. Ojopi, A.C. Paquola, J.P. Piazza, M.Y. Nishiyama Jr., J.P. Kitajima, R.E. Adamson, P.D. Ashton, M.F. Bonaldo, P.S. Coulson, G.P. Dillon, L.P. Farias, S.P. Gregorio, P.L. Ho, R.A. Leite, L.C. Malaquias, R.C. Marques, P.A. Miyasato, A.L. Nascimento, F.P. Ohlweiler, E.M. Reis, M.A. Ribeiro, R.G. Sa, G.C. Stukart, M.B. Soares, C. Gargioni, T. Kawano, V. Rodrigues, A.M. Madeira, R.A. Wilson, C.F. Menck, J.C. Setubal, L.C. Leite, and E. Dias-Neto. 2003. "Transcriptome Analysis of the Acoelomate Human Parasite Schistosoma Mansoni." *Nature Genetics* 35(2):148–57.

von Zedtwitz, M. 2003. "Classification and Management of Incubators: Aligning Strategic Objectives and Competitive Scope for New Business Facilitation." *International Journal of Entrepreneurship and Innovation Management* 3(1/2):176–96.

Wagner. C., I. Brahmakulam, B. Jackson, A. Wong, and T. Yoda. 2000. "Science & Technology Collaboration: Building Capacity in Developing Countries?" RAND MR-1357-WB. RAND, Santa Monica, Calif.

Wang, Y., and Y. Yao. 2003. "Sources of China's Economic Growth 1952–1999: Incorporating Human Capital Accumulation." *China Economic Review* 14(1):32–52.

Watson, R., M. Crawford, and S. Farley. 2003. "Strategic Approaches to Science and Technology in Development." World Bank Policy Research Working Paper 3026. Washington, D.C.: World Bank.

World Bank. 2002. *Constructing Knowledge Societies: New Challenges for Tertiary Education.* Washington, D.C.: World Bank.

———. 2003. "ICT and the MDGs: A World Bank Group Perspective." Washington, D.C.

———. 2004. World Development Indicators 2004. Washington, D.C.

WHO (World Health Organization). 2004. *World Health Report 2004: Changing History.* Geneva.

WTO (World Trade Organization). 2002. "Trade and Transfer of Technology." Working Group on Trade and Transfer of Technology. Geneva.

Xie, W., and S. White. 2004. "Sequential Learning in a Chinese Spin-off: The Case of Lenoro Group Limited." *R&D Management* 34(4):407–422.